Garden Cemeteries
of New England

Garden Cemeteries
of New England
1796–2019

Trudy Irene Scee

Down East Books

Down East Books

Published by Down East Books
An imprint of Globe Pequot
Trade division of The Rowman & Littlefield Publishing Group, Inc.
4501 Forbes Blvd., Ste. 200
Lanham, MD 20706
www.rowman.com
www.downeastbooks.com
Distributed by NATIONAL BOOK NETWORK

ISBN 978-1-60893-907-7 (hardcover)
ISBN 978-1-60893-908-4 (e-book)

∞™ The paper used in this publication meets the minimum requirements of American National Standard for Information Sciences—Permanence of Paper for Printed Library Materials, ANSI/ NISO Z39.48-1992.

Printed in the United States of America.

For Michelle Marie Galvin
And
Kathleen A. "Kate" Kelly

Who Died Much Too Young
And Made the Clouds Cry

And For Our Other Beloveds

Contents

Preface

I BEGAN THIS PROJECT WITH A SOLID KNOWLEDGE OF ONE OF THE CEM-eteries discussed herein—one that I can literally see from my backyard—and with fond memories of another garden cemetery—one that I would have chosen for a backyard as a child had I been given such a choice.

One of my earliest memories as a child was being pushed over a high iron fence by my big brother. He had taken my sisters and me to Brook-side Cemetery in Watertown, New York. I did not know it at the time, but it was a garden cemetery. What I did know was that it had ponds with islands and swans! We lived in a housing unit, and we did not have swans or ponds or islands at our house. I was totally captivated by the cemetery, and from it came my desire to have the title of this book be *The Swans' Islands: The Garden Cemeteries of New England.* However, I would find something else when I went out to the cemeteries as an adult, and the name would change, a little.

Although I do not remember climbing over the fence to get into the cemetery—maybe my brother took us in before the place closed, I'm not certain— I do remember my brother lifting me over it on the way out. I do recall swimming or wading in one of those ponds, which, as an adult, I would not deem the best idea, but maybe there were fewer waterfowl there then than there are now. I remember feeling that we were not sup-posed to get caught climbing the fence, or swimming, or even being in the cemetery. Moreover, in the interests of full disclosure, as well as something that will be of no surprise to anyone who knows my brother, my brother did a have a girlfriend nearby. Her name was Kay Clark. As a child, the name you learn is the name you remember. So my brother was going to see Kay Clark, who lived across the street from the cemetery. After we climbed over the fence, that is. That may have had something to do with *why* we had to climb the fence. I had no idea; I was too smit-ten with swans to worry about mere mortals. I do know that we did not climb the fence near the gate but rather near Kay's house. However, no matter; the garden cemeteries thereafter always beckoned. I was never afraid of cemeteries, and the beautiful ones were parks; to a child, they were parks. It is funny, or not so funny, what we carry with us throughout our lives. I carried cemetery memories, along with others.

Therefore, I wrote one history of a garden cemetery, Mount Hope Cemetery in Bangor, Maine, and then revised it, adding in an entire century, for a second edition. I wanted to write a book about garden cemeteries in general, and after some time, Michael Steere of Down East Books was able to accept the proposal on behalf of Rowman & Littlefield. And hooray! I was to be the official photographer, too, and the writing and photography have both been rewarding, surprising, and overall quite fun. There were a couple of hairy moments; sometimes the undead—the humans, I mean, and perhaps the more dangerous ones—haunt some of the cemeteries. And I am no big-city driver, and a few big cities in the seven states I covered were encountered along the way. Well, at least there were no car accidents!

Initially, I anticipated that the following chapters would be similar in content and scope, but then realized after going to another one or two locations that, in addition to the two referred to above, the coverage of each would vary considerably, although essential historical points and current attractions would be covered in each. What remains of the historical documents, indeed what remains of original cemetery structures and monuments, varies from one place to another. Points of interest, topography, and birds and wildlife vary with regard to their prevalence and type. Some cemeteries have more intriguing stories than do others. Some had more pressing needs for burial space than others did. In addition, as the decades passed, the field of landscape architecture became an art and science of its own in America, influencing some elements of cemetery design. With all these and other variables, it follows that to provide the best coverage of each cemetery and to provide a solid overview of garden or rural cemeteries as a group, the content of the following entries will vary to some degree.

With the first chapters, the reader will learn how the garden or rural cemetery movement began, as well as what it took to establish one in the first years of the movement. Fortunately, both Massachusetts's Mount Auburn and Maine's Mount Hope have sufficient records to make that possible, as does New Hampshire's Valley Cemetery, at least for some years. They are very different entities though, so the coverage varies. With some of the other, later cemeteries, the reader will learn more about unique opportunities and challenges faced by each, especially as the decades passed. With others, the monuments and people interred perhaps take a starring role in the coverage, although each chapter includes some of these. The final chapter introduces a few other cemeteries, as well as a transition one that closes the era.

By the end of this book, the reader will have a solid understanding of the way the cemeteries were created, the driving forces behind them—both generally and specifically—and the importance of the garden cemeteries in American history and culture, and he or she will have seen images of some simply fantastic monuments and structures as well as some of the more simple memorials and the natural landscapes of the cemeteries and their flora and fauna.

Some of the statues in the rural cemeteries have been described as "larger-than-life" or "life-size." I wondered about these phrases, especially when applied to angels, until I walked up to an angel standing on a short step at Cedar Hill Cemetery in Connecticut, an angel described as being life-size, and discovered that, yes, it was almost the same height as I was. In that sense, the descriptors "life-size" or "larger-than-life" might apply, and so they have been used here also, from time to time. With statues some fifty or sixty feet in the air, however, I have just had to trust cemetery sources that they are indeed life-size or larger than that. Moreover, I have tried to inform the reader of sources consulted as the chapters unfold, but in some instances, it is simply an on-the-ground observation that applies.

I have enjoyed this undertaking considerably, so thank you again, Michael for your support, and thank you, Bub for taking me to Brookside. And thank you to everyone who spoke with me at the cemeteries and over the telephone, and to Juanita, Peter, Ralph, and Val for visiting some of the cemeteries with me, watching, no doubt, with both exacerbation and amusement as I zigzagged back and forth on foot, examining and photographing memorials and buildings and birds and whatever else I found of interest, before going back to the exact spot two or three times more. I went to the various cemeteries in different seasons to observe the changes, often alone, but sometimes with different people, who humored me by driving about the various locations, while I repeated my zigzagging.

There is beauty on many levels in garden cemeteries. There is a beauty in the landscape, often a landscape with rolling hills and open water, be it a pond or a stream or a view of something larger. There is a beauty in the plantings—in the trees and flowers and shrubs so basic to a garden cemetery. Moreover, there is a beauty in the memorials, sometimes simple, sometimes ornate beyond—almost—belief. Graves vary from unmarked enclosures or grasses to rugged tombs and ornate mausoleums, to those with emotionally moving statues, sometimes of museum quality, from noted artists. The "residents" of the cemeteries varied in their wealth and influence and opulence; so, too, do those of their gravesites, monuments, and their "cities of the dead."

Some of the cemeteries include architectural structures and buildings that are themselves on the National Register of Historic Places for their beauty, their history, and their architects. Unlike in my other books, I do offer a few opinions here, but they are easy to discern as opinions. For example, I may say that the Sphinx at Mount Auburn is the cat's meow, but you can tell that that is an opinion; when I give you the date of its carving and the name of its designer, those are facts.

Coverage of the garden cemeteries—also known as rural and, less commonly, as pastoral or suburban cemeteries—discussed herein varies, but together, these chapters tell and illustrate what was a new chapter in American history, one that has undergone revision over the decades and centuries but that remains a popular and active part of our culture. The appeal of garden cemeteries continues.

And by the way, what I found out in the field was not swans—although I did see a couple of the beautiful creatures, but they were too far away for my camera to capture with justice—but herons, great blue herons, and perhaps a lone gray heron and a white one, too. I rescued a great blue heron at one of the cemeteries. I had wanted to see one up close, and I did. I helped one get out of a trap, and I touched it briefly. A friend who was nearby, but who was not at the water with me, said it would attack me, but it didn't. I freed the bird, and it was able to fly away. I had wanted to see one up close, but not like that. I think we were both in tears, but the bird made it. I think the title here now could well be *The Herons' Havens: Sculpture and Nature in the Garden Cemeteries of New England.* Look at the cover; did that title make it? The bird I freed did, as have many birds of many species over the years, finding sanctuary in the ponds and waters of the rural cemeteries and food and habitat in the horticultural landscapes—as have various species of animals—and that is the important thing.

The art survives, too. Acid rain and basic weathering have taken their toll on funerary art and buildings and other structures, but there is still great beauty out there. Go see it. Look at the trees, the birds, and the little creatures if you do not see the larger ones, and study the sculptures, the memorials, the flowers, and the stone steps. If you can't see, then listen, feel, and smell; there are wind and water and birds and animal calls and flower scents galore.

Introduction

By the 1820s, civic leaders throughout the American Northeast were searching for solutions to community burial needs. Church lots (and spaces underneath the churches), the common areas or "greens," and other burial spaces in many cities were becoming full and impractical. Relatively primitive burial lots located next to residences and businesses—and in certain cases, in spite of local laws, some people still buried their dead in backyards or wherever else they could squeeze them in—led to concerns about health and the spread of disease. It was not unknown for gases caused by decomposing bodies to escape into churches and along city streets as well as for bodies to protrude during interments or construction. Sometimes many layers of bodies were buried atop one another. People who wanted their families or loved ones buried together were generally out of luck. While some people may have had stone monuments or tombstones to honor their lives and their passing, many or most did not. The use of prime city space to serve as generally plain and depressing disposal lots for the dead also occupied the minds of many. One could take little comfort in the rituals and burials of death in urban America.

It was New England that first turned a novel idea into reality. That idea was to create a place that would serve not only as a resting place for the dead but also as a haven of beauty for the living. In the crowded cities of New England, green space was about to be introduced in a manner not seen before. It would be introduced first just outside the large city of Boston, on the borders of Cambridge and Watertown, Massachusetts, in a celebrated "garden of the dead" and next in the smaller but bustling city of Bangor, Maine. New England created and led the garden cemetery movement in America. Other smaller and less ornamental attempts to introduce something along these lines may have occurred earlier, but it was with Boston and Bangor that the garden or rural cemetery movement gained hold and led a nation to cemetery expansion and beautification. However, a little experiment in New Haven, Connecticut, preceded these cemeteries and, in a sense, ushered them in.

1

The Forerunner

The New Haven Burial Grounds, or Grove Street Cemetery, New Haven, Connecticut

Is the New Haven Burial Grounds a rural cemetery? It may not be, strictly speaking. Is it a garden with graves? Yes, absolutely. This is a cemetery hard to categorize, but it has elements of both the older-style graveyards—the overcrowded, unsightly urban cemeteries—and those that started the garden or rural cemetery movement in the 1830s. It is compelling, it is attractive, and it has stone and iron walls, an Egyptian entryway, and Victorian monuments and symbols mixed with older death-skull markers. It is, one might argue, transitional.

WHETHER OR NOT TO INCLUDE THE NEW HAVEN BURIAL GROUNDS was not a major question. Instead, the question was whether to consider it America's first garden or rural cemetery and exactly where to place it in the book—as a chapter on its own or as part of the introduction. Only after visiting several other cemeteries and then this one was that decision made, but it was not an easy one. The New Haven Burial Grounds, or Grove Street Cemetery as it became known, does have several elements of a garden cemetery, and its history is unique. For those reasons alone, it is worth including here.

Perhaps best classified as a transitional cemetery, much like Hope Cemetery in Barre, Vermont, which can be considered a transitional cemetery of the late 1800s, Grove Street was the first known cemetery to become fairly large scale and able to tackle some of the issues confronting burial practices and realities in the late 1700s and early 1800s.

Mount Auburn Cemetery in Watertown and Cambridge, Massachusetts, has long been recognized as America's first rural or garden cemetery. In its scale and magnitude, it certainly is, but it was not the first cemetery to try to escape some of the problems plaguing the day's overcrowded and unhealthy urban cemeteries; Grove Street was, and it did so three decades before Mount Auburn opened. Other, less successful attempts may also have occurred.

While a few Massachusetts residents worked out their plans to create a garden cemetery starting in the mid-1820s, thirty years earlier, a group of citizens in New Haven, Connecticut, were already trying to address the issue. They did so partly in response to a series of yellow fever outbreaks in 1794–1795, following on the heels of outbreaks of other contagious diseases, as well as the overcrowded and "unsightly" conditions at the city's major cemetery at what was then known as the "Green," and had open space that also served as churchyard space. That graveyard—established in 1639—purportedly held up to 5,000 remains at the time, in a space perhaps 70,000 square feet, or just over 1.6 acres. That was a tremendous number of interments for such a small space, although many of the remains would have greatly deteriorated, or almost disappeared, by the late 1790s. In many public burial grounds of the day, bodies were buried several deep or packed in any way that worked, and this would seem to have been the case here as well.

James Hillhouse, a US senator, was one of the New Haven residents seeking a solution. According to cemetery and Friends of the Cemetery records, Hillhouse initially considered establishing a cemetery just for his own family, but he soon realized that that would be impractical. Such a cemetery might pass from the possession of his family as the decades passed, and what would then happen to it might be in question. He decided the best solution would be to create a new city cemetery, but this one would be much different than the one then located on the Green.

Hillhouse had in mind a small parcel of property near the edge of New Haven he thought suited to the purposes he intended, and he was able—with the aid of thirty-two other residents—to purchase it along with a few other small parcels to make a cemetery there possible. The details of the negotiations are unknown, although the former owners are identified in extant records. The cemetery alliance—consisting of thirty-plus families and individuals—established a southeasterly boundary in 1796, according to a cemetery publication, although the cemetery's charter was not approved until the following year.

The cemetery received its charter in 1797 from the General Assembly of the State of Connecticut as the New Burying Ground of New Haven. It is recognized as one of the oldest corporations in the United States, and its charter specified near the outset that the cemetery would be "better arranged for the accommodation of families." This was something new, as an individual cemetery lot holder would have control over his or her own plot, while the cemetery as a whole was managed by a corporation, which was a nonprofit, a previously unheard-of entity in America and, seemingly, the Western world.

One of the earliest cemeteries to have a planned design or landscape, the cemetery founders laid out the grounds with a grid work of paths and avenues; this was unlike later garden cemeteries, which would favor winding paths and avenues, and was perhaps a design more practical for the more limited space available in New Haven at the time. Hillhouse was a great admirer of ornamental trees and helped the city establish elm trees along its streets, and he is also credited with persuading the cemetery to plant a large number of Lombardy poplars. As the decades passed, additional ornamental plantings—both trees and shrubs—would further soften the overall look of the grid-based cemetery layout. This feature would both precede and reflect the growing interest in landscaped garden cemeteries after the 1830s. At the same time, other aspects of Grove Street would be different.

However, this first corporate cemetery in America with its privately owned family lots, its planned avenues, its "permanent" memorials that recognized the sanctity of the human body—the need to treat the body with respect—as Peter Dobkin Hall observed this in a 2008 article, made New Haven's new cemetery "a whole redefinition of how people viewed death and dying." In 1797, the New Haven Burial Grounds set the stage for what would follow: planning plot spaces as opposed to burying people "every which way," which in itself was "a totally revolutionary thing."

Lots were offered for sale in 1796 and thereafter. A few were donated and designated for "People of Color," for the poor, for "strangers" (generally meaning indigent people who died in the city), for a few church societies who had had burials on the Green, and for Yale University, which already had a great presence in New Haven and near which the cemetery was located.

The first burial took place in November 1797—that of Martha Townsend—and lots on the eastern portion of the cemetery sold quickly. In 1814, therefore, Hillhouse and others purchased additional land, essentially doubling the size of the cemetery. A question soon arose about fencing in the new cemetery, but before then, focus shifted back to the old burial grounds.

After burials shifted to the new grounds—although a few burials continued at the Green, the last one taking place in 1812—some of the land on the New Haven Green was used to build or expand churches. The burial grounds on the Green continued to deteriorate, however, to the point that the community decided that instead of building a fence around the grounds to protect and perhaps hide the old burial sites, the most effective way to address the problem was to move the old tombstones to another location—ultimately meaning to Grove Street. This removal was completed by 1821. In some cases, bodies were moved to private lots at Grove Street; in other cases, they were not.

A number of bodies at the Green, however, were buried beneath new construction, with permission granted for the same with the understanding that the remains not be disturbed. At the Center Church, which had had a church on the Greens already but wanted a larger one, the new church was built right over, but not touching, burials on the oldest part of the burial grounds. In effect, the church created a crypt, one that is now open to the public. This did resolve part of the problem; although in-church burials were something many communities would try to end in the 1800s—but there were seemingly no new burials in what was essentially the church basement, now called the New Haven Crypt. Cement and then bricks, when cement proved problematic, covered the dirt while the stones remained as they were, complete with bodies underneath. Some 137 bodies have been identified in the crypt, but about 1,000 may be there.

Concerning removals to Grove Street Cemetery, human remains were generally not moved, but instead only the tombstones—for those people who had them—were moved to the New Haven Burial Grounds. Hundreds of them remain today, most lining the inside of the walls that were later constructed, although some can be found with family or other lots at the new cemetery. Although some of the old markers are almost illegible, other ones can be read, and their words and carvings may lead the viewer to reflect on an earlier time, of deaths that often came early, of love expressed for people long since gone.

In some cases, there do seem to have been reinterments at Grove Street, or at least space was left to mark the remains, if remains were there. This may be true for tombstones placed within a family plot, but they are more noticeable when older stones, it seems, are set aside on a plot of their own, or, in some cases, replaced by new ones. This is true for people who fought in the American Revolution.

Some of the older markers highlight history in a way seen in few other locations. Toward the far side of the cemetery, three stones commemorate three men who fought in the Revolutionary War. Although these stones postdate the lives of the men, they nevertheless give the names and years of life for the men whose remains were, seemingly, reinterred at Grove Street.

In front of these three are five stones for men who fought in the American Civil War. Civil War graves are found in most of the garden cemeteries, often with large memorials built and donated by the Grand Army of the Republic or other persons or organizations. In this transitional cemetery, more men than are represented by these few stones are buried, but this shows an early use of these types of small marble or other white stone slabs that became common markers for New England veterans.

As noted, the cemetery had donated land to the poor, creating its own "Potter's Field" or "Strangers Row," as plots for the indigent would be called, near what would later become the front of the cemetery and the location of the current chapel. However, during the early 1800s, much of that area was sold to individuals, and the poor were granted a new location near the northwestern corner—where many of the old tombstones would come to be located. The boundaries of the cemetery shifted somewhat during these years as the then northeastern corner of the grounds was lost to the construction of a canal, and the cemetery also deeded a small parcel to the city after some changes occurred in nearby roadways. It would deed over another small parcel in 1877 for the completion of Canal Street. The cemetery remains an irregular five-sided shape in the twenty-first century, containing roughly eighteen acres.

Well before the later parcels were purchased, however, word of the unique burial grounds—the term "cemetery" was not yet widely used—was spreading. By the close of the first decade of the 1800s, the president of Yale University was bringing foreign visitors to Grove Street. He said that people from throughout the eastern United States were admiring the dignity of the grounds, and he wanted to showcase the novel site. The ornate flora was an attraction in and of itself, and by the early 1800s, numerous markers that were more decorative than most of those of the 1700s were already in place. Within another decade or so, many family lots were being set off by enclosures, some by iron fences—often very ornate ones—several of which remain in place today.

A few families or individuals built vaults or tombs at the grounds in the first decades, ones that protruded only partially aboveground, whereas most of those seen in the garden cemeteries in following decades would have a front wall or face entirely aboveground with the rest of the structure built into a hillside. The New Haven Burial Grounds did not have hills, however, so a tomb necessarily would be largely underground. One example of such a vault is that of the Charles Nicholl, his vault dated 1835. Nearby, the Orcutt tomb of a similar age emerges from the ground.

Another monument for a death that occurred early in Grove Street's history was that of Yahudi Ashmun, who had served as an agent of the African Colonization Society. The society promoted the resettlement of America's black population in Liberia, Africa. Ashmun had a brownstone (generally meaning a dark sandstone) sarcophagus built for him after his

1828 death. As true elsewhere, such memorials in the United States generally did not hold bodies, although they were large enough to look as if they might.

As noted, the decision to move the older stones from the Green had been made by the early 1800s. By the time the project was finished, the question of how to best enclose the new burial grounds had become an important issue. The concern would also arise for the garden cemeteries proper.

The cemetery began raising funds while it considered its fencing options. The cemetery board initially considered installing new wooden fencing. A short wooden fence had been constructed earlier, but it was rotting, and instances of vandalism had occurred. However, after the board successfully raised some $14,000 in the 1830s and early 1840s and later reached $25,000, according to the Friends of the Cemetery, they decided to build a stone wall. Three sides of the cemetery were therefore enclosed, primarily with Portland stone or brownstone.

Then, after careful consideration and to provide some views into the grounds, the cemetery decided to use wrought iron fencing along the entrance sides of the five-sided cemetery and to build an impressive gateway. A dignified gate was needed to complement the grounds. The gate would be constructed of sandstone at the corner of what is now Grove and High Streets, along the boundary fronting Grove Street. Egyptian Revival was popular at the time, and it was thought an Egyptian design would not offend any particular religious denomination. Therefore, an archway in that style was chosen.

Henry Austin and Hezekiah Augur, local architects (both of whom would later be buried on the grounds), designed the massive gateway. In 1839, Austin began the design work, which featured thick, sloping walls or sides and an overhanging cornice, a unique design, yet one not dissimilar to a few to be seen elsewhere in following years. According to the Yale Peabody Museum, Austin designed only this one Egyptian-style edifice, and he unknowingly used "the very shape" in his pylon that was "a solar symbol used in an ancient Egyptian thought," and therefore, he "unknowingly used an architectural form that expressed eternal renewal and resurrection."

Austin used the temple of Esna North as one of his inspirations, and according to the museum, the depth of his gateway is much closer to the true Egyptian style than those seen in other Egyptian-revival gateways of the era, such as that at Mount Auburn Cemetery. Austin added a "square column behind each main column" such as those appearing in extant depictions of several Egyptian temple designs, even if the temples themselves no longer existed.

In July 1845, the community celebrated the dedication of the gateway with some fanfare. The gateway would remain the only cemetery entrance into the twenty-first century, although discussion did arise over the years about adding a new entrance along another wall, possibly a pedestrian one.

The City of New Haven assumed care of the cemetery in the 1840s, and in 1849, they made the official name of the site the New Haven City Burial Ground. This necessitated changing the cemetery's charter, which was changed again in the 1870s when the cemetery took on responsibility for perpetual care for the gravesites. The local population knew the burial grounds as the Grove Street Cemetery by the 1870s, however.

During the first half of the 1800s, much like the early garden cemeteries, the New Haven Burial Grounds undertook a "beautification," or "improvement" as it was more commonly called, of the grounds. Some of this may have happened earlier, but after the new walls were built, the process began in earnest, according to the Friends of the Cemetery. This involved removing some older wild cedars and planting numerous new evergreens, as well as planting shrubs. It may be at this point that the cemetery started naming its avenues and lanes—some of which are now paved, while others are not—after trees and other flora. This practice was common for garden cemeteries.

Other improvements followed. In 1872, the cemetery erected a stone chapel for funeral services. Located just in front of or behind the gateway, depending on one's perspective, the cemetery opens up behind and to either direction beside it. The chapel features a gilded bee (some people interpret it as a moth or butterfly), which symbolized the flight of the soul to the ancients, and again, such a feature was not likely to offend any local religious groups. The building now serves primarily as office space for the superintendent and staff.

During the 1880s, Grove Street began placing curbstones along the avenues and pathways. During those years, the cemetery also decided to remove the older stones from the Green from the previously established city plots. It was at that time stones were placed along the northern and western walls, in alphabetical order, of those that could be ascertained from the writing, where they remain today.

As with the rural or garden cemeteries established in the 1830s and beyond, many famous people and scholars were buried at the New Haven Burial Grounds. These include Lyman Beecher, the father of Harriet Beecher Stowe and a well-known abolitionist and clergyman in his own right. Beecher, born in 1775, died before the Civil War ended in 1863; hence he did not live quite long enough to see resolved the battle he had fought to end slavery, but he would have known that the battle was on and likely to be won. His is a sarcophagus-style marker.

Eli Whitney, the inventor credited with developing the cotton gin—although more recent research credits his landlady with that invention—is also buried on the grounds, essentially right next to Lyman Beecher, in an area that also includes Noah Webster, lexicographer of dictionary fame. They are buried along the unpaved Cedar Avenue. Statesman Roger Sherman, who signed the Articles of Association of the US Colonies, the Declaration of Independence, the Articles of Confederation, and the US Constitution—and was the only person to sign all four of these major documents establishing the United States—is also buried at the cemetery, but he is on the opposite side of the grounds, as is another Whitney, Eli Whitney Blake—Eli Whitney's nephew—an inventor, gun-maker, and businessman who has a large family lot with a central obelisk and various individual stones and granite curbing. Roger Baldwin Sherman, a US senator and the thirty-second governor of Connecticut, is also buried at Grove Street.

More than a dozen presidents of Yale University are buried on the grounds, as are several Yale professors, a variety of scientists of various specialties, and numerous professionals. Among these are Charles Goodyear, who invented vulcanized rubber, and Nathan Smith, MD, who founded the Yale School of Medicine. Located next to Dr. Smith's sarcophagus are a few now traditional forms of funerary, including a broken column that was often used to convey a life cut short, a life that ended too soon.

Besides the more noted individuals buried at Grove Street, as well as the older slate and other slab markers, the cemetery also came to hold the same types of monuments and markers that would be seen elsewhere in the rural cemeteries, with, as they have been interpreted, their Victorian motifs and symbolism, although they might not be as large, in some instances, or as numerous as in some of the larger or newer cemeteries.

The Marsden family, for example, erected one of the most noted memorials at Grove Street. Set near the southeastern or Prospect Street wall, it features a statue of an angel, classically robed with flowing hair and holding a "blooming branch" in her hands. Smaller stones set in front of her mark individual family members (two being noted on the high stone base of the memorial), an arrangement that would become popular in many of the garden cemeteries in the mid to late 1800s, when it seems this one was erected. The angel towers over the nearby wall. Behind her, tall city buildings remind one that they are indeed in the heart of a city; that is something sometimes forgotten when one wanders farther into the grounds.

Across the grounds, the Peck family erected another classic figure. This time, the female statue is a woman, not an angel, her hair covered and her hands joined in prayer. She presides over the family lot, which is surrounded by a stone and iron wall.

Some of the family lots would become rather complex and crowded with memorials, something the larger garden cemeteries would try to avoid, but space was limited at Grove Street, and it was decades older than its successors. Such lots might have a variety of memorials, such as an obelisk, a sarcophagus or two, a "cradle" marker for an infant or young person, a tablet set on the ground, a tabletop marker or two, an "animal" stone generally meant for a child, and so forth.

For example, the extended Trowbridge family would have a few lots at the cemetery, but one, in particular, stands out for its varied and generally ornate markers, which are crowded in quite close to one another. The Henry Trowbridge lot was named for a family patriarch who died in 1818, some thirteen years before Mount Auburn Cemetery opened. Eventually, the lot would hold an ornate sarcophagus and a temple- or canopy-style memorial as well as a large obelisk inscribed for Timothy Trowbridge, who was born in 1631 and died in 1734. Timothy Trowbridge had been a merchant as well as a soldier and politician. Jane Trowbridge, another lot "resident," had died in childbirth, preceded by her newborn son as well as twin daughters. Her stone marker features a bas-relief of an angel bearing a woman aloft to meet her three young children in heaven. A similar style marker at the Comstock lot shows another person borne aloft toward the skies.

The lot fittingly holds a cradle memorial, a style of marker used for children or young people with room left in the center of the "bed" for plantings or flowers. Sarah Bay Trowbridge died at eighteen years old, and hers is an ornate version of a crib memorial with flowers and leaves decorating the "headboard" and side panels.

In addition, two similar large markers with fine detailing are topped by urns, a classical symbol of mourning, and a flat "tablet" cross is laid on the ground near the foot of an upright cross set upon a rough-cut, stone-style base. Other upright markers also grace the family lot, and the entire lot is set off with decorative stone curbing. This blending of styles would be seen elsewhere.

A few rows over from this Trowbridge lot is another Trowbridge lot, one not quite as crowded but still containing a few monument styles, including "free-standing" decorated crosses—one featuring lilies, a popular choice in the Victorian era—plus flat ledger memorials and two or three sarcophagi of styles found throughout the garden cemeteries. One of the sarcophagi is for Henry Trowbridge and, it seems, his second wife. It was sculpted in an Egyptian style and features clawed feet and curved sides and top, and it rests upon a somewhat larger base. Near this is a sarcophagus memorial for another wife. A third sarcophagus memorial marks the life of Thomas Rutherford Trowbridge, who died in 1887, and his wife, Caroline Hoadly, who died in 1910. A fourth substantial marker carved with flowers and vines marks the life of the next generation of Trowbridges. A number of smaller stones also grace the lot, which has decorative curbing.

A third Trowbridge plot features a large, rough-hewn stone cross with an angel standing on steps leading up to the cross, with an urn provided for flowers. The angel-with-a-cross would be a popular type of memorial in garden cemeteries; some, in later years, were almost identical, perhaps because they were carved by the same stonecutter or at the same stonecutter's shop. Stonecutting became an important industry in the late 1800s, largely to meet the demands of America's new cemeteries. This angel, however, created for E. H. Trowbridge and Grace Allen Quincy Trowbridge, is unique.

The St. John family lot, located near the center of the cemetery, is interesting for several reasons. It takes an element of the Egyptian style seen at Henry Trowbridge's memorial and takes it much further. It contains an aboveground vault, a mausoleum in the most proper sense of the word. Moreover, the flat-roofed mausoleum, constructed of huge blocks of brownstone, is built in what is called the Egyptian revival style, as is the very detailed iron fencing surrounding the lot and its iron gate. The front of the mausoleum holds ornate symbolic carvings above the entrance as well as detailed ironwork covering the door. A paved walkway leads from the gate to the mausoleum. Two large ornate sarcophagi are located to either side of the mausoleum and diagonally from one another.

Carrying on the theme seen in its gateway, the St. John lot, as well as in a few other markers, Grove Street recently saw the addition of two small, female Greek sphinxes to mark a family lot. Although not exactly alike, the sphinxes are very similar, and being placed near one another, they add a striking accent to the cemetery.

The cemetery also includes stone benches or "seats" to memorialize the dead, as well as a small archway in the style of the Arc de Triomphe of Paris, inscribed for Jane Wakeman Dwight. Near it is another stone bench or seat, which is a simple one with carved feet. It could be interpreted as a raised sarcophagus-style marker, but it is actually rather small for that designation. Most sarcophagi in America, even though they generally do not hold bodies, are large enough that they could have done so. The arch and bench are older markers.

Flowers are spread throughout the cemetery, as are shrubbery and trees, and these attract numerous birds as well as smaller animals. The cemetery does not have the woods and water of some of the larger, rural cemeteries, and generally, it does not see the larger animals seen in those locations.

Zinc memorials, frequently called "zinkies," are also seen at Grove Street. Zinc memorials began to appear in the 1870s in American cemeteries, with a Connecticut company, the Memorial Bronze Company of Bridgeport, located not far from New Haven and with several subsidiaries elsewhere, leading the way. The next most influential companies, according to the Smithsonian Institute, were the J. L. Mott Irons Works and J. W. Fiske & Company of New York. The Memorial Bronze Company called its markers "white bronze" and offered hundreds of models to choose from, as well as custom-made memorials. Markers were cast of 99 percent pure zinc, in molds, and have generally held up well. Off-the-shelf statues included those known as *Hope, Charity*, and *Faith*. The company used a sandblasted finish to make its markers look similar to stone. Most companies developed a blue-green patina over time. The two New York companies painted their statues of soldiers and firemen to resemble bronze, and they created a bronzed *Stag*, marketed to the Benevolent Order of the Elks. A few other companies also marketed zinkies.

At Grove Street Cemetery, the Hill memorial represents a standard, yet individual, zinc memorial. Its base is architectural in style and is topped with a flaming urn, a symbol of everlasting life. Sheaves of wheat and other symbols are attached to the sides of the base, and individual nameplates are bolted into the memorial.

A second memorial of zinc at Grove Street uses symbolism common for children who died young. Eva M. has a wonderful figure of a young child with curly hair and draped robes for her memorial. The child statue holds a blanket as well as a tiny lamb. Another lamb, common on children's graves during the era, rests at her side. The statue could represent a boy or girl, but in this case, it was clearly meant to memorialize the family's beloved Eva.

Another lamb for a child can be found on a nearby lot. This one is carved of stone, and it sits close to the ground. The lamb rests on a small base and is inscribed for Lucy. Time has taken its toll on Lucy's lamb: her ears have been broken off and the body is showing signs of weather damage. Similar markers would be seen at various garden cemeteries.

A number of stones and materials can be found at Grove Street, from marble to sandstone to various types of granite. These have been formed into standard obelisks, crosses of varying types, and sarcophagi, as noted. Although there are numerous family lots at the cemetery, there are also smaller plots for one or two people, and these, in some cases in their groupings, show a great variety of styles, such as the James Babcock granite obelisk and surrounding markers.

The cemetery also boasts an early memorial topped by a uniformed police officer, which is on the Hemingway lot. The marker features an ornate architectural base, and the statue is as intricate as any at the cemetery.

In addition to the veterans discussed earlier, other military members were also buried at the cemetery, some with ornate memorials to mark their passage. For example, New Haven native Colonel Noah Lane Farnham, born in 1829, served as a fireman in New York City and then as an assistant engineer with the New York Fire Department. He entered the military with the 7th Regiment and early in the Civil War joined fellow New York firefighters and was promoted to lieutenant colonel of the 11th NY Infantry, the First Fire Zouaves, soon becoming its colonel after his predecessor's death. He, too, soon died; but first, in August 1861, following a head injury at Bull Run, he rose from his sickbed to march with, and lead, his men at Manassas. Farnham has an ornate draped column at the cemetery, one adorned with tassels, an eagle, military horns, and other symbols of his service.

In another example, Rear Admiral H. Gregory has a large marker topped by a bronze anchor marking his resting place. He died in 1866. Major General Alfred Rowe Terry, designated as a Civil War hero but who was also George Custer's commanding officer in the 1876 battle against the Sioux, has a large family lot, one that shows that other members of his family also served the nation in war and peace.

Each of these graves and others are honored at the cemetery. Moreover, every year, on the Fourth of July, the members of the Governor's Foot Guard march into the cemetery in their red jackets and continue onto the grave of David Humphreys, who served as an aide-de-camp to George Washington during the American Revolution.

During the twentieth century, Superintendent William Cameron Jr. worked to gain such recognition for the cemetery—not just military recognition but also historic recognition, according to his daughter—and he worked to increase the garden features of the cemetery, adding more trees (some of the older ones had died over time) and shrubbery and other ornamental flora. Cameron has a stone marker in the cemetery he so loved during his life, but he is not interred there. In an interview with the *New York Times*, he said that taking care of the cemetery was more than a full-time job, that he often worked seven days a week, and that his wife Jane did bookkeeping and other work but still sometimes had to help with burials, although there were fewer interments as time passed.

The New Haven Burial Grounds is recognized as the oldest planned cemetery in the United States, and it was added to the National Register of Historic Places in 1997. It became a National Historic Landmark in 2000, and it is now owned by Yale University. Other small municipal cemeteries on this same sort of design plan and scale did appear in a few American cities between about 1820 and 1840, but these generally failed to survive or simply did not progress in the same manner as Grove Street.

The next step forward, after the early decades of the New Haven Burial Grounds, was the garden cemetery movement proper, which included both private and municipal cemeteries, each seeking something better than what had gone before. The garden cemeteries proper would introduce an element of "landscape design" not seen at New Haven by way of creating or modifying ponds and waterways, designing winding avenues and paths, utilizing rolling hills when possible, and so forth. However, Grove Street was first with its deliberate design, its use of horticulture, and its private and public lots with enduring interments and a variety of memorial styles. Visit Grove Street, enter its massive Egyptian gateway, and explore its tree-lined avenues; you will be entranced.

An invaluable map and short history of the cemetery, published in 2005 by the Cemetery and Friends of the Cemetery, is available at Grove Street Cemetery and the Friends' online information is also well worth reading. "The

Grove Street Cemetery, A Paper Read Before the New Haven Colony Historical Society, October 27, 1947," is in the Society's collection. *Quotes from Peter Dobkin Hall are taken from an interview with him in Steve Grant's 2008 article, "History Disinterred." The quote on the entrance is taken from the online article "Entrance to the New Haven Cemetery" by the Yale Peabody Museum. An interview with the superintendent and an article on Grove Street also appeared in the* New York Times. *The article contains other information on the entrance that is well worth reading. Cameron's daughter, during an informal meeting at the cemetery, talked briefly about her father. Also see* The Grove Street Cemetery, New Haven *(Whaples–Bullis Company, 1947). And visit Grove Street Cemetery; it is fascinating and, like the others, it has information on its markers and other structures.*

2

America's First Recognized Garden Cemetery

Mount Auburn Cemetery, Watertown and Cambridge, Massachusetts

When you first go to Mount Auburn, before you reach its Egyptian Gateway, you may feel pressed in by the busy traffic on the nearby thoroughfares. When you first enter, you may think that this is a lovely place, an impressive place. But keep going in, go a bit farther, and you will find its secret: this is a phantastical place. Here you will find mythical creatures and a medieval tower, the graves of some of our most honored citizens, and trees of such stature you may wonder if they were born with the nation. Keep going, explore further. You will be pleased that you did.

OFFICIALLY THE FIRST GARDEN OR RURAL CEMETERY IN AMERICA, Mount Auburn, located within the cities of Cambridge and Watertown, Massachusetts, holds a special place in history. However, it is not only Mount Auburn's age but also its beauty and popularity that makes it a place well worth visiting and studying.

Faced with a lack of sanitary burying space, in the mid-1820s, a few residents of the Boston area started to plan for a new burial ground. Joseph Bigelow, a physician and Harvard professor, lead the call for a new cemetery, one to be located outside the settled areas of town, one to be different than any yet seen.

Bigelow wrote the following almost three decades later: "My attention was drawn to some abuses in the rites of sepulture as they then existed under churches and in other receptacles of the dead in the city of Boston." Simultaneously, he wrote, "A love of the country ... led me to desire the institution of a suburban cemetery, in which the beauties of nature should, as far as possible, relieve from their repulsive features the tenements of the deceased." Such a cemetery would also lend "some consolation to survivors ... in gratifying ... the last social and kindred instincts of our nature."

Bigelow led this movement in the Boston area, but he did not initiate it. As early as 1820, a Harvard graduate of the class of 1796 had proposed that Boston purchase land outside the city for use as a burial grounds, and the mayor of Boston, Josiah Quincy, had formed a committee to look into this idea, but nothing substantive had come of it.

According to Bigelow in his 1859 *History of the Cemetery at Mount Auburn*, as well as according to some of his biographers, Bigelow took the lead in Boston in 1825 by calling together an organizational meeting to implement the idea of a new burial spot. The organizers needed land, however, and purchasing suitable property would prove a problem for several years. Initial plans did not work out.

The Massachusetts Horticultural Society, incorporated in 1829, would prove instrumental in finding and purchasing the new cemetery grounds, and it would designate one part of the site as a horticultural garden. The society was a rapidly growing one with ambitious goals, including holding exhibitions, starting a library, and collecting seeds and plant species. It agreed to the idea proposed by Bigelow of combining its own goal of creating a large experimental garden with the idea of creating a resting place of beauty for the dead. George Watson Brimmer, a member of the horticultural group, owned the property recently proposed for a combined cemetery and garden, and he agreed to sell it at cost—at a personal and economic loss to himself.

Therefore, after some initial failures to purchase other properties by Bigelow and the society, the society purchased seventy-two acres in 1831; the land was known as Stone's Farm and, by some people, as "Sweet Auburn" after a 1770 poem. A subscription drive—a popular way to raise funds at the time—was used to acquire the $6,000 needed for the land purchase. The society agreed to purchase the land from Brimmer once one hundred lots had been sold. Initially, those subscribers who "paid a premium" above the basic subscription rate would be able to choose their lots; others would have their lots chosen for them, although this would prove to be more flexible than it might sound. The Massachusetts Legislature quickly approved the land being used as a cemetery of the new rural or garden type already seen in Europe.

General Henry A. S. Dearborn, president of the Massachusetts Horticultural Society, undertook the overall design of the new cemetery, with much input by members Bigelow and Alexander Wadsworth. Dearborn described the combined cemetery and garden as a "New Eden," a beautiful resting place for the dead just as the Garden of Eden had been "the first abode of the living." Dearborn clearly saw the new venture as a "garden cemetery," with the "garden" part stressed, whereas Bigelow tended to describe it as a "suburban cemetery." The cemetery association planned to erect a stone Egyptian-revival-style gate at the cost of $10,000 (initially a cheaper wooden gate in the same style would go up), and later, a granite tower on the highest hill, overlooking all of the countryside, would be added, clues perhaps that this was not to be an ordinary cemetery. Indeed, in its entirety, Mount Auburn was something new on the American landscape.

However, some attempts at creating a garden cemetery may have been made before Mount Auburn opened its gates. Mount Auburn's key founder, Joseph Bigelow, wrote that by 1829, "no ornamental cemetery *deserving of notice* [italics added]" existed of the "plan and magnitude" that Mount Auburn reached by 1859, which was when Bigelow published a short history of the cemetery. As discussed previously, one example of an early move to create something new and to move a cemetery outside of a congested setting was that of the New Haven Burial Grounds or Grove Street Cemetery, established in 1796. Although it was located fairly close to the community of the time and contiguous to Yale University, it would become a cemetery with some ornate markers, an Egyptian-revival-style gate, and attractive landscaping. A private corporate cemetery, it served as a bridge to the garden cemeteries, as no doubt did some other urban cemeteries. Grove Street did not address all the concerns the garden or rural cemeteries proper would address, however, nor was it as expansive as many of them would be, but it did set a precedent from which they could learn and develop.

The first president of the new Mount Auburn Association (as developed separately from the horticultural society), Supreme Court Justice and former congressman Joseph Story, delivered the dedication address at Mount Auburn on September 24, 1831. Story's dedication has been deemed influential in terms of American political orations for its style and content. Certainly, the *Boston Courier* lauded his speech, which was heard by 2,000 people seated in a temporary amphitheater fairly deep into the woods, one that was created for the consecration services in a natural dell. The Boston Band performed, hymns were sung, and local ministers participated.

Of death, Story asked, "What is the grave to us, but a thin barrier dividing time from eternity, and Earth from Heaven?" He shared a brief history of burial practices in his speech, evoking the Greek use of the word "cemeteries" as "places of repose," places separated from the cities and located instead in "shady groves, in the neighborhood of murmuring streams and mossy fountains," places where people studied "philosophy and nature." Mount Auburn was to be such a cemetery, not the "graveyard" of America to date. At Mount Auburn, Story said, "Let us erect the memorials of our love, and our gratitude, and our glory." And memorials would indeed be erected at Mount Auburn, memorials of such beauty and caliber that the cemetery, in the twenty-first century, would be designated as, essentially, a museum of funerary art.

Meanwhile, the more practical cemetery association established some key policies for its "garden of graves." With the cemetery's almost immediate popularity among the general public, the association determined that it should and would regulate essentially all aspects of the grounds, including reserving the right to remove any monuments it considered "offensive and improper." Only lot owners or "proprietors" could have vehicles on the grounds, and only they could visit the grounds on Sundays and holidays; this visitation policy was set after it had initially allowed "promiscuous admittance . . . to persons on foot, on horseback, and in carriages." Some people had driven carelessly (it is unknown if the walkers had walked carelessly or otherwise caused problems), and such instances had created difficulties with other visitors.

The first burials at Mount Auburn occurred in the middle of 1832. By then, some avenues suitable for carriages had been laid out and footpaths established, and other work was underway, including the construction of a holding tomb in which to keep bodies until they could be buried. A temporary wooden fence was built that year, too, along Mount Auburn Street. Early on, private lot fencing was popular and set an individual lot off from others, as well as from the grounds themselves, which were not yet far removed from their natural state.

Lots were originally set at 300 square feet, at a cost of $60, and lot owners were encouraged to erect stately and solemn monuments. According to the cemetery's "Master Plan," Dearborn had ordered numerous books, especially from France, for guidance as to types of monuments suitable for the new cemetery. Early monuments at Mount Auburn were typically constructed of granite or marble in a classical form. The use of one central monument per lot was urged, as was the building of such monuments before anyone was interred on a lot.

Another contiguous twenty-four acres of land were purchased in 1832, and they, too, saw "improvements" undertaken. Over the next couple of decades, some low areas would be filled in, including a few small ponds with stagnant water, and trees were planted, although some people, like Bigelow, warned against planting too many trees, as they would obstruct views. (The cemetery had come blessed with both evergreens and a selection of hardwoods, including mature elms, oaks, beeches, and walnuts.) Tombs were not originally encouraged, as the initial plan was to have just one or two people buried in a gravesite, but over the decades, numerous tombs and mausoleums would be constructed. Initially, there were problems with gases leaking out of tomb doors.

In 1835, with their goals and desires not always in unity, the Mount Auburn proprietors' association purchased the cemetery grounds from the Massachusetts Horticultural Association. Thereafter, Mount Auburn continued as a private, nonprofit cemetery. The proprietors were the members of the cemetery, and they paid the horticultural society a portion of revenues collected for decades to make up for the dissolution. The exchange was not made completely without rancor, and interestingly, Dearborn, who had done so much of the layout of the grounds at Mount Auburn and had emphasized its garden aspect, would later become involved in the establishment of nearby Forest Hills Cemetery, and he would do critical design work there also.

Within a few years of opening, the popularity of Mount Auburn was apparent. Late in the 1830s, an unofficial guide to the cemetery, *Picturesque Pocket Companion and Visitor's Guide*, was published. It contained descriptions of some of the more notable grave markers as well as prose and poetry related to death, with perhaps its most famous contributor being Nathaniel Hawthorne. Caroline Gilman, a travel writer, observed the following in 1838: "Daily, hourly, a line of carriages stands at its lofty gate" to await entry to see Mount Auburn's "unrivaled variety."

By the mid-1840s, with its twenty-five-foot-high by sixty-foot-long Egyptian gate now up, in its final granite version, as well as a Bigelow-designed iron fence installed in place of the earlier wooden one, and more than 1,000 trees planted—most of them saplings planted along the main street frontage—the cemetery had become even more of a tourist destination. The tide of visitors, Bigelow wrote, was the reason the cemetery began to require that everyone who wished to visit the cemetery secure a "ticket" to gain entrance.

During the next decade, while other improvements continued, the Washington Tower was built, a truly impressive structure that continues to hold great allure in the twenty-first century. Constructed of granite, with solid blocks smoothed to create both the inner and the outer walls, the tower and the steps leading up to it cost the cemetery about $22,000, which was a huge expense at the time. The tower rises above the summit of "Mount Auburn" by some sixty-two feet. (The cemetery has seven hills according to the official count, with Mount Auburn the tallest of them.) As Bigelow described it, and as the Tower remains today, "It is built on the general plan of the feudal ages, and contains a gallery, battlements, Gothic windows, and a spiral staircase of stone." He also noted that the tower rises above the highest trees in the area, and its gallery provides a panoramic view of the countryside below. One can see Boston, Cambridge, Watertown, and the Charles River from the tower. Even when the tower is closed, as it is in winter, the base of the tower offers exceptional views.

In the 1840s, while planning was underway for the tower, the cemetery built a magnificent chapel, the Bigelow Chapel. Jacob Bigelow himself designed the building in the Gothic revival style. Mount Auburn had held a design competition, but Bigelow won the contest. Construction started in 1844, and stained glass windows—a feature only Bigelow's design had included—were imported in 1845 from Scotland for the Quincy granite structure.

The chapel had some problems, however, and it was soon rebuilt, in the 1850s, to strengthen it. At the end of the century, Willard Sears, who would do other design work at the cemetery, renovated the interior. The redone chapel included a crematory. Additional reconstruction was undertaken in recent years. The chapel, with its many fantastic spires, is visible from the top of the tower as well as from elsewhere in the cemetery, especially when the leaves are off the trees.

In 1860, the cemetery established a formal garden near the front of the grounds, as envisioned by the original plan for the cemetery, but it was seemingly forgotten or pushed aside after the horticultural society exited the realm. Both the plants grown in the garden and its layout would evolve over the years. During the late 1800s, the garden, located near the main gate, took on a Victorian style, and in the 1930s, it became a formal rose garden. In the 1960s, it became a less formal flower garden, according to cemetery records, and in the late 2010s, it began another renovation, one aimed at making the garden reflect the work of botanist Asa Gray, for whom the garden was renamed in 1942 and who is buried at Mount Auburn.

The development of the garden near the main gate did not happen in a vacuum. According to the cemetery's "Master Plan," at mid-century, "descriptions in the guidebooks of the period stressed the monuments and individual lots . . . the emphasis was on the monuments and social and genealogical history rather than the natural landscape." However, during 1853 through the 1860s, Mount Auburn would undergo "the most dramatic transformation in its history with a major reshaping of its land and a remarkable shift in character." The rural cemetery would be truly transformed into "a garden cemetery dominated by marble and granite." Besides establishing the garden near the main gate, which was located in low-lying land and was "seasonally wet," which led to it being filled in to raise its ground level before plantings commenced, another spot, known as Hazel Dell, was also filled in, as well as a few other small wetland locations. Also, a few of the hillsides were leveled off.

During the era, the cemetery also added a few fountains to the ponds. Meadow Pond was dredged and greatly expanded in the late 1850s, and it was renamed Auburn Lake. A fountain capable of sending out hundred-foot jets of water was added, and smaller fountains were added at Hazel Dell and in the Lawn, according to cemetery records. Another fountain was soon added near an area undergoing development. The fountains, in ponds or built into lawns, added a new element of interest although they also suffered water supply issues.

It is important to remember, however, that by 1850 Mount Auburn was not the only garden cemetery in America, nor had it been so for some time. Mount Hope had opened in Bangor, Maine, in 1834. This was just a couple of years after Mount Auburn, and within the decade, several other garden cemeteries had opened in New England. Just as Mount Auburn no doubt influenced the earliest of these cemeteries, they, too, would influence developments at Mount Auburn. Indeed, Joseph Bigelow would tour some of them in 1854 and return to Mount Auburn reporting on how a more open vista was being kept at some of them, with trees "kept trimmed high" to keep views even more open.

Perhaps reflecting what Bigelow had seen at other garden cemeteries, Mount Auburn records noted the next year that "many of the superfluous trees have been removed." In 1860, by which time much of the formerly open vistas and spaces were being filled with graves, trees, memorials, fencing, and curbing, Bigelow further advocated that the number of trees at the cemetery be cut in half, and such a task was undertaken. The landscape changed greatly under this new policy, and many of the larger trees were cut down. During the same era, fencing was removed around many of the lots, and curbing was placed around many, as was being done elsewhere, especially in the 1860s. Curbing in later years would also lose its favor. Over the years, Mount Auburn tried to respond to the grounds being overcrowded with ornaments, fencing, curbing, and the like, and older fencing in the older sections was eventually removed from numerous lots. Lower-growing ornamental species were also planted in some locations during the era.

No matter the number of trees or the presence of fencing and curbing, people continued to flock to the cemetery and to request interment there. Mount Auburn and its proprietors had improved the surroundings and built some wonderful structures over the years, and they continued to do so in the following years.

After 1870, however, Bigelow was no longer around to guide the overall vision of the cemetery. Some new portions would be developed in a different style than earlier ones, lots were often measuring a hundred square feet instead of 300, generally without fences or curbs, and other changes were likewise introduced. The cemetery would adopt—amending it to its own situation—the landscaped lawn cemetery style developed by Adolph Strauch of Cincinnati, Ohio's, Spring Grove Cemetery. Strauch would otherwise influence the garden cemetery movement in New England.

The Story Chapel, built during 1896–1898 to provide an additional and "lighter" space for cemetery services and functions, memorializes one of the founders of the cemetery, Joseph Story. The cemetery held a competition for the chapel's design, and architect Willard Sears placed first. Constructed of Potsdam sandstone for its rich color variations, the design was selected in part to fit with the Egyptian-revival gateway. Yellow brick was used in the chapel's interior. In 1928, according to cemetery records, a local glass artist, Earl E. Sanborn, designed stained glass windows for the chapel. Sears also designed the administration building next to the chapel, the two almost flowing into one another. The chapel is still used for services, and it also holds the visitors center.

Mount Auburn had tried for a short time in the late 1800s to loosen the controls over who could enter, and then it tightened them again. After 1911, however, with automobiles arriving on the scene, people could enter without a pass if they behaved in a respectful and decorous manner.

Perhaps the cemetery's two most impressive "monuments" are the Washington Tower and the Sphinx. While the tower is easy to spot once you get to the center of the cemetery, the Sphinx—depending on one's approach—can appear quite suddenly on the landscape, a delightful mythical creature that towers above the surrounding shrubbery. The installation was built in 1872 to commemorate the soldiers who helped abolish slavery in the United States. Bigelow, who was the designer of the Sphinx as well as of the tower and main gate, made certain that his statue had a few distinct American touches. He included an American lily in one location along with a more traditional Egyptian lotus at another, and he had an American eagle headdress carved on the female Sphinx's forehead. Bigelow donated the Sphinx to Mount Auburn, after commissioning its sculptor, Martin Milmore, and having its granite—a block weighing nearly forty tons—brought in from Hallowell, Maine, via railroad.

According to some sources, Bigelow designed the Sphinx as he was losing his eyesight, and he would check on the work's progress as his eyes dimmed by running his hands over the surface. It was his great farewell gift to the cemetery he so loved. And it was a magnificent gift. The Sphinx measures fifteen feet in length by eight feet in height. The Sphinx was chosen to be a female one for its symbolization of "repose, strength, beauty, and duration," Bigelow stated. On the base of the statue, inscribed in both English and Latin, are the words Bigelow wrote:

American Union preserved,
African slavery destroyed,
By the uprising of a great people,
By the blood of fallen heroes.

Bigelow wanted his Sphinx, a symbol of antiquity, though looking like something from the far past, to now look forward "to illimitable progress." The Sphinx certainly causes one to stop and ponder.

Impressive as the Sphinx is, there is also the Washington Tower, located on the top of Mount Auburn, the highest point in the cemetery, with a stunning view of the grounds below. Although some people find the Bigelow and Story Chapels the cemetery's most notable edifices, for those who are a bit of a kid at heart there is no outdoing a feudal tower and a sphinx. The Bigelow Chapel, however, is a bit magical itself, especially its roofline, which one can see from many points in the cemetery. Moreover, the Sphinx is just behind it, a guardian of sorts even if not intended that way.

In spite of earlier concerns, Mount Auburn has come to hold many, many private tombs and mausoleums, a number of them situated on what is essentially prime real estate along a couple of the ponds and some in wooded vales. Some of the mausoleums and tombs are truly impressive edifices, designed by noted architects, while others are plainer structures built into various hillsides and slopes.

A few fine examples of mausoleums at the cemetery include the Ralph H. White mausoleum (erected in 1900 and designed by Willard T. Sears), the Lorenzo Maynard mausoleum (erected in 1904), and the Nathan Tufts Jr. tomb (d. 1887). These are built in various styles, but they still represent only a few of the many located at Mount Auburn.

The Hicks-Endicott tomb is an Egyptian-revival-style one, built into the hillside behind the Washington Tower. It features two columns flanking the doorway, above which is a symbol of an ancient orb with spread wings. In a quite different style, located well on the other side of the hill, is the W. Read tomb, which features a more classical front, complete with decorative carvings on the roof and a garland suspended from a sideways figure eight, a symbol of eternity, on its doorway.

One lovely structure might be mistaken for a small mausoleum or tomb but is actually not one. Built in 1834, the Appleton classical temple monument, built of Italian marble, has attracted visitors since its installation. The twelve-by-six-foot memorial features a number of adornments, including funeral lamps along the roof, and in the pediment section above the door, there is a complicated motif of a snake eating its tail, encircling an hourglass with spread wings. Although not common, the hourglass with spread wings is seen elsewhere, but adding the serpent circle to the symbol used to signify regeneration and eternity does make the design unique. On the door, which is decorative only, are small evergreen wreaths. The temple also has low relief pilasters—essentially columns attached or coming out from a wall such that they are not "free-standing" but rather offer decoration instead of weight-bearing support—with Corinthian capitals—ornate carvings on tops of columns, or in this case pilasters.

Samuel Appleton, the man who purchased the temple, had run a successful Boston import business. He traveled extensively in Europe, imported European goods for his business, and also devoted time to philanthropy. His memorial was said to have been one of the most expensive in the country at the time he had it shipped to America. He lived until 1853, and therefore had time to appreciate his temple marker prior to death.

A different sort of monument is situated on a pond known as Halcyon Lake; the 1917 Mary Baker Eddy memorial. Eddy founded Christian Science and published the *Christian Science Monitor*. After her death in 1910, her church commissioned her memorial, which was created in a classical or neoclassical temple design. Designed by Egerton Swartwout and made of Vermont Bethel white granite, according to Meg Winslow in her book on the cemetery's funeral art, thirty-four marble workers labored on the "open temple" with its fifteen-foot colonnade of eight columns on its tiered stone base. Curving steps flank each side leading down to the pond. The memorial features numerous inscriptions and carvings, and space is provided in the center of the colonnade for ornamental plantings.

Ornamental mausoleums, statuary, towers, and so forth are part of what the cemetery proudly maintains and has been cataloging as its "commemorative art." The art spans three centuries, and in its totality at this National Places cemetery, it reflects changes in American society and culture. This is true to a greater or lesser degree in the other garden cemeteries also, but it is perhaps most developed at Mount Auburn in terms of its curation, preservation, promotion, and so forth. The cemetery holds more than 60,000 memorials ranging from plain to spectacular— and the cemetery itself played a role in promoting funerary memorials as art at its inception. Preservation is a key component of current operations at the cemetery.

Mount Auburn holds a veritable gallery of statuary art. A few of the more spectacular monuments with two figures are the Whitney, Appleton, and Chickering ones. Each is well worth seeing.

The 1883 Charles and Sarah Whitney memorial, which features a gray granite base on which rests a white marble sculpture of a raised sarcophagus and two angels, is one of Mount Auburn's more spectacular markers. A short flight of steps leads from the base up to the sarcophagus, and on it rests a delightful carving of an infant angel or cherub, often referred to as Putto, holding two floral wreaths. On the sarcophagus above Putto stands a triumphant angel, with one hand raised to the heavens and the other holding a large shroud, which partially drapes the sarcophagus. Charles Whitney, a lumber manufacturing baron and an humanitarian, commissioned well-known Italian sculptor Nicola Cantalamessa Papotti to create his memorial in Italy.

Another memorial with two figures is that of the 1872 sculpture called *The Realization of Faith*. Sculpted by Thomas Bell, the marble monument features the "Angel of Death," as the artist that created it called the young male angel, who was "lifting the veil from the eyes of Faith." Before the unveiling, Faith could only see as "through a glass darkly." Faith kneels and holds a small cross to her chest while below her, in bas-relief marble, is carved the muse of music. The muse holds a lyre in one hand and a wreath in the other. Flower garlands and inscriptions also adorn the memorial. Jonas Chickering, a musician, noted piano maker, and philanthropist, commissioned the memorial of a relative, and it was sculpted in Italy.

Another celebrated memorial with two figures is that of Thatcher Magoun, created in 1851, again before the death of the man who commissioned it. Entitled *Grief*, the sculpture depicts a woman comforting a young girl. Both figures are in distress, and both are kneeling. According to Meg Winslow, the sculpture was a copy of a bas-relief carved by Irish-born John Henry Foley, but the sculptor of the actual memorial is unknown. A Boston stoneworker is credited with carving the marble base of the memorial, however. Magoun earned his fortune as a shipbuilder, a business his son would enter with him. A few relatives were reinterred at the site in 1850, with others interred there later. The family lot holds a variety of markers.

Memorials that have one figure instead of two or three depicted in statue form are more numerous at Mount Auburn, as they are elsewhere. Mount Auburn does, however, have an extensive and fantastic array of them, too large to enumerate here. Some favorites include the Olive Rich 1864 marble sculpture of a kneeling woman, the Maria Frances Copenhagen 1872 marble sculpture of an angel, and the 1859 larger-than-life marble statue of Reverend Hosea Ballou, erected by his Universalist congregation.

The 1847 bronze sculpture of Nathaniel Bowditch, cast in Boston from a portrait by Robert Ball Hughes, also warrants close attention. Author of an 1802 navigation manual deemed invaluable in his day and still consulted, the self-educated scientist, astronomer, and mathematician is seated high above the grounds on a granite pedestal. Bowditch's likeness holds a copy of a scientific book he translated, with an octant and globe at his feet. The figure was the first life-size, human bronze statue cast in the United States, according to cemetery records.

There are some statues at Mount Auburn that are simply striking and that speak to the heart without explanation, much like Magoun's *Grief*. These include the Holbrook angel, the Moses Hunt, the Wade, and the Benjamin Humphrey and Oriens Turner classical female figures holding large anchors—anchors often being symbols of hope, strength, and sometimes of early Christianity, or used to mark the graves of sailors and others who traveled the seas.

And then there is the Dutton figure, one arm broken off and the other crossed over her chest, her eyes cast upward and wearing an expression of expectation. There are others, so many others in this garden of death and life and art. Many statues speak to the age's Romantic belief in a better world to come and a faith in art to point the way.

However, there are the children's memorials, too: the cradle graves, the praying and sometimes laughing children, and the dogs faithfully waiting at their people's resting place. Mount Auburn has a wonderful 1881 cradle grave that looks remarkably like an actual cradle or bassinet, even with the "hood" part raised, carved to memorialize Mary Wigglesworth, who died of diphtheria before she reached her second birthday. Her marble cradle even has a marble pillow, one seeming to bear the imprint of a child's head.

Also, there is a child praying, seemingly a girl, one the author calls Florence, although that may not be her name. That is the name of a child angel seen elsewhere and of a child met long ago who hauntingly resembled the child model of the 1800s, who it seems may have been the model for a number of similar funeral statues.

Leopold Morse Jr. has such a "Florence" child on his grave. The child bends on one knee, her (or his) eyes cast upward, with her hands folded together and her hair loose and curly. Another "Florence" is found praying on the more ornate memorial for James Bartlett and his family. In this case, the girl sits atop a large ornate base, with a lamb on either side. It is possible that three children rest here, or perhaps three older people do. "James" is inscribed under the kneeling figure in the center, and the other two have lamb statues over theirs.

Some wonderful dogs are likewise part of some Mount Auburn memorials. Some are representations of animals owned by the deceased.

William Frederick Harnden founded what his memorial describes as the "Express Business in America," which was an express mail and package delivery company and a model for the later American Express and Wells Fargo. He died at age thirty-one, and the Express Companies of the United States, according to cemetery publications, raised the money to create an elaborate memorial at the cemetery for him. As constructed, the memorial is a four-pedestal canopy with "dormers" that create a hipped roof. A winged hourglass graces one of the panels. The other panels or tablets are carved with a globe and cross, a dove, and an eye encircled by a snake—each of them symbolic. Beneath these are carved, one on each side, the words "Hope," "Charity," "Justice," and "Faith"—the four cardinal virtues. Inside the canopy, a large draped urn rests on a base that features side panels of white marble with engravings. Also, at the foot of the memorial rests a life-size English mastiff, with the following words: "Because the King's business requires haste." The canopy structure and entire memorial rest on a tiered stone base.

Not too far away, a dog guards the tomb of his family. Born wealthy, Thomas H. Perkins started a large trading house in China in the early 1800s, was a patron of the arts, and started the Perkins School for the Blind, among other things. He was initially buried in a church tomb, but after his family built a tomb at Mount Auburn, they had his body reinterred there. The 1843 Newfoundland marble dog atop the family tomb was carved by Horatio Greenough, whose career Perkins had supported and who sculpted the statue of George Washington at the US Capitol. The dog was placed on the tomb, and the stone surrounding the Newfoundland is inscribed with family names.

Although not the only other canine in the cemetery, one of the most moving dog statues is found at the gravesite of Francis Calley Gray. The 1837 marble sculpture of an English setter rests atop a large marble plinth, his head down, as if weary and waiting. Gray, a politician, philanthropist, and art supporter, commissioned English sculptor Joseph Gott to make the statue for him, but later, Gray gave it to a dear friend. His friend saved the statue, intending to put it on Gray's grave someday. When Gray died in 1856 at age sixty-six, his dog statue soon went to his resting place, where he lays perpendicular to a flat ledger stone with Gray's name and dates.

There are other animals at Mount Auburn too, both live ones and statues. Birds appear on statuary art here and elsewhere, including the American eagle, a favorite on the monuments for veterans of American wars. The most noted one at Mount Auburn, perhaps, is that atop a memorial for the First Corps of Cadets of Massachusetts, established in 1741, when America was still a colony of England. Members of the First Corps served honorably, most notably in the French and Indian Wars, the Revolutionary War, the Civil War, and World Wars I and II.

After the death of fifteen members of the First Corps in one month during the Civil War, the corps purchased a lot at Mount Auburn and commissioned the twenty-two-foot high memorial. Made of white Concord granite, the obelisk on a pedestal is ornately carved and includes the names of the men who died in the "War of Rebellion." The iconic bald eagle stands proudly on the capstone. Located near the front of the cemetery, it is a memorial the visitor might quickly encounter and admire.

Some less than spectacular monuments grace the graves of some truly spectacular historical figures. For example, Dorothea Dix of Maine, a Civil War–era nurse and then hospital reformer, has a simple stone stating just her name and dates and is located inconspicuously along one of the lanes. Harriet Jacobs also has a fairly small marker at her gravesite, although that of her daughter Louisa, born to Jacobs in 1836, accompanies her stone. Harriet Jacobs, a slave who escaped her bondage and became a nurse and abolitionist, is best known for her autobiographical book *Incidents in the Life of a Slave Girl*. Louisa Jacobs, also born into slavery, would become an activist in her own right.

Some other abolitionists are buried at Mount Auburn Cemetery as well, as the Boston region was heavily involved in the abolitionist movement for decades before the Civil War actually started, such as Reverend Charles T. Torrey. His monument, a rather simple low obelisk or "pillar" memorial, seems rather plain at a distance until one looks more closely. And then one sees the bronze bas-relief portraits—one of Torrey and, on another side, one of a slave woman escaping her chains. Known as the *Slave Monument*, it was erected for Torrey, who had died in a Baltimore jail in 1846 of tuberculosis. He had been held there for helping slaves escape to freedom. The Boston Friends of the American Slave commissioned the memorial to the longtime member of the Underground Railroad. The marker is also heavily inscribed.

Numerous writers and artists, some of them very much political activists, are buried at Mount Auburn, perhaps the most famous of them being painter Winslow Homer and poet Henry Wadsworth Longfellow. Both have relatively simple graves, especially Homer. Longfellow has an established family lot, as well as his own sarcophagus-style marker, deemed a neoclassical one and made of Indiana limestone. Before his death in 1882, he rather famously stated, "I was at Mount Auburn, and saw my own grave dug. . . . I assure you I looked quietly down into it without one feeling of dread. It is a beautiful spot, this Mount Auburn." And so it is.

Many of those buried at Mount Auburn, like Longfellow, had family plots, but not all. Early on, Mount Auburn set out to accommodate those who could not afford to purchase a large family or other lot. According to its "Master Plan," the cemetery established public lots for those who wished for or could only purchase a single lot, and in some instances, a public lot could be purchased by a group of people to commemorate an individual or group, with a memorial also erected by the group. Some groups, such as the First Corps, did take advantage of this. However, there were still some people who could not purchase even one small plot for themselves or for a loved one.

There are graves of many people of whom history knows little at Mount Auburn, as at most of the garden cemeteries of New England. At Mount Auburn, in the Scot's Charitable Society lot, some 220 bodies of the poor are buried within a fenced-in area. There are no stones for these people. Their names are not listed. Sadly, this is not uncommon in either private or municipal cemeteries, although a few locations do have the names of the poor inscribed on individual or group markers. This is true at Mount Hope Cemetery in Maine for some benevolent organizations, although the pauper graves in Strangers Row in the city section are not marked by individual stones, as they are at another cemetery to be discussed, Lakeview Cemetery in Burlington, Vermont. The Scot Charitable Society is deemed the oldest, still-operating, benevolent organization in America, however.

An iron fence was added to the Scot lot in 1841. Moreover, a massive Japanese snowball tree near the gate appears to be standing guard, much as the dog and angel statues of the wealthy seem to guard their tombs and as the Sphinx and medieval Washington Tower seem to watch over everything and everyone at Mount Auburn.

With the purchase of additional property over the years, the cemetery, at 174 acres, would become Watertown's largest contiguous green space, and it ranks high on Cambridge's list, too, especially as it borders two other cemeteries: the Cambridge City Cemetery and Sand Banks Cemetery. The cemetery remains extremely popular, and it holds a plethora of activities each year, from regular tours to talks about associated writers and artists, to birding and botanical tours.

At the present time, the grounds contain four ponds as well as a major hill and a rolling landscape. Many of the cemetery's trees are labeled such that a visitor can walk up to a tree and determine its common and Latin names. As such, the cemetery is also an arboretum, and it is a delight to the dendrologist—a person who formally studies trees. As new trees are added as the years pass, younger ones can take the lead as the older ones fade away or become too damaged to salvage. This emphasis on trees is common to other garden cemeteries also, although some manage their silviculture better than do others. Horticulture, in general, is critical in maintaining a garden cemetery. At Mount Auburn, as true in other cemeteries, the tree species emphasized has changed over time.

Mount Auburn Cemetery is truly spectacular to behold in spring and summer when the bushes, trees, and flowers are in full bloom, and it is also beautiful when autumn has changed the colors of much of the foliage. The winter months offer something special as well, and as in the late autumn and early spring, that season allows for a more open view across the landscape, with monuments often easier to see from a distance. While this is true for other rural cemeteries with various hills and valleys and bodies of water, some of the monuments and structures at Mount Auburn are especially compelling.

Some other sources you might wish to consult about Mount Auburn Cemetery include: the Archival Holdings of Mount Auburn Cemetery, and its "Master Plan;" A History of the Cemetery at Mount Auburn, *Joseph Bigelow, 1859;* The Lively Place, *Stephen Kendrick, 2016;* Dead in Good Company, *John Harrison and Kim Nagy, eds; and* Silent City on a Hill, Picturesque Landscape and Memory of Boston's Mount Auburn Cemetery, *Blanche M. G. Linden, 1989 and 2007. The latter work and* The Art of Commemoration and America's First Rural Cemetery: Mount Auburn's Significant Monument Collection, *Melissa Banta with Meg L. Winslow, will provide you with greater detail about the monuments at Mount Auburn, including their artists. A few short articles are also available online. And, as for all the cemeteries covered, touring the grounds and reading the inscription adds an immeasurable amount of knowledge.*

3

America's Second Garden Cemetery

Mount Hope Cemetery, Bangor, Maine

If you are looking for an important garden cemetery in a smaller city, Mount Hope Cemetery is the place to go. Centrally located in Maine, Mount Hope provides an opportunity to see not only the tombs of the wealthy but also the graves of the indigent and, just as importantly, those of average citizens. Located on the Penobscot River, the river and the cemetery have always been linked. Moreover, when you finish your tour of Mount Hope, you are just an hour's drive down the road to Bar Harbor and the Maine coast, or two hours north to Baxter State Park. A beautiful cemetery in its own right, it also is located near some of the most stunning land in New England. Mount Hope's history, like its appeal, is rich. But its major attraction, perhaps, is its tranquility. Tranquility is a constant feature of Mount Hope, and locals and visitors alike enjoy it year-round. Even in the aftermath of a winter storm, people are out walking in Mount Hope. Mount Hope has all the beauty you might expect to find in a garden cemetery, and if you look a bit closer you may find some beauty you had not expected: climb Cemetery Hill, and you will see the Penobscot and the surrounding countryside spread out below you.

WHILE MOUNT AUBURN CEMETERY WAS OPENING ITS GATES IN MASsachusetts, farther north, in Bangor, Maine, a small group of citizens was planning their own garden cemetery, one that would come to hold the graves of both famous and infamous people. It, too, would attract the public over the decades and centuries to walk along its winding paths and roadways, picnic on its lawns, and watch its wildlife, especially its waterfowl.

Prominent memorials to the dead, notable mausoleums, a miniature fort complete with real cannons, a circular granite trolley-car waiting room, gazebos, and other structures would add their own beauty and interest to the nation's second oldest garden cemetery. The gravesites of Hannibal Hamlin, vice president under President Abraham Lincoln; Fan Jones, an infamous yet generally respected madam; and that of Alfred Brady, a gangster and public enemy number one, would all prove particularly popular to cemetery visitors. The author previously published histories of Mount Hope Cemetery, the Brady Gang, and Bangor, Maine; insights on these and other factors of the cemetery and its burials can be found in those books, and the research for these serve as sources for much of what follows.

True to its roots as a garden cemetery, Mount Hope Cemetery of Bangor was initially envisioned in 1833—if not earlier—by a horticultural society. The Bangor Horticultural Society sought to establish a safe and attractive place to bury the dead, as well as a beautiful place the living could enjoy. The group's goals were especially critical at the time, as, by 1830, Bangor had some 8,000 residents, and the town was quickly running out of burial space. The burial space that remained was generally unattractive, and in some instances was a public health hazard, lying as much of it did in the congested downtown area. Burying fresh bodies near the marketplace was not highly desirable, and in at least one instance, the bones of the dead surfaced during a neighborhood construction project.

Therefore, in early 1834, the newly incorporated Bangor Horticultural Society negotiated to buy land for a cemetery. The society raised the necessary funding through subscriptions, ultimately selling shares to thirty-five people. Their chosen property lay at the edge of town along the Penobscot River—a river that enjoyed the business provided by a booming lumber frontier. River drives down to Bangor were common, and Bangor was soon known as "The Lumber Capital of the World." The Penobscot, being navigable by ocean-going ships as far north as Bangor, served as a critical shipping route for all sorts of goods.

The Penobscot River provided a scenic background for the new cemetery, and it opened a vista out over the surrounding hills. The cemetery would, for a time, lease some of its shorefront property to a lumber boom company, one of several that helped manage the lumber driven down the river. The grounds of Mount Hope contained one major hill—Cemetery Hill—which overlooked a large turn in the Penobscot such that one could see the river and countryside from multiple directions, in addition to a number of smaller undulations on the landscape, each of which would contribute to the beauty of the cemetery.

Originally containing 50 acres, the cemetery would eventually encompass 264, even after selling 30 acres to the City of Bangor in the 1830s for the creation of a municipal cemetery. The private Mount Hope Cemetery established its boundary with the adjacent city property along a natural dividing line—a small valley—running partially beside a meandering stream—one that would see its course modified over subsequent years.

Even before the initial land purchase of fifty acres had gone through in 1834, however, the organizing body had reincorporated itself as the Mount Hope Cemetery Corporation, the name that it would retain to the present time. Each subscriber or shareholder was deemed a proprietor of Mount Hope. An executive committee would thereafter manage the cemetery, and it has successfully done so ever since, simply undergoing a name change to the board of trustees in the 2010s. Despite the reincorporation and name change, the 1830s group still sought to create an aesthetically pleasing cemetery. To this end, it designated one section of the grounds specifically as the "Garden Lot" and dedicated it to horticultural purposes. In essence, however, the entire cemetery would become a garden.

Local architect George G. Bryant designed Mount Hope's overall layout. As seen with Mount Auburn and as would be true for some years, there were not any "landscape architects" available for hire in the United States. However, Bryant had traveled to various locations in America and was cognizant of the emerging desire to create green spaces in urban landscapes, something to which the garden cemetery movement would contribute invaluably. Some of the committee's first tasks included laying out an access road into the cemetery (soon known as Western Avenue), deciding what species of trees and other flora to plant, and tackling the issue of fencing, some rudimentary portions of which would be built over the next few years. The committee did this within Bryant's organizational plan.

On July 21, 1836, Mount Hope Cemetery held a dedication ceremony. The public was invited, and the service or celebration took place near the brook, close to a location that would later house the cemetery's "Lodge" or administrative building. Local papers advertised the event, and the *Bangor Daily Whig & Courier* observed that on that day, "nature crowned every hill and shrub and tree with her most precious and delightful smiles, and every heart seemed to enter deeply into the feelings of [the] occasion." Every seat was filled, and the weather proved "delightful." Edward Kent, Bangor's mayor and later a state governor, presided over the event. His address stressed the beauty of the location and its ability to lead people's thoughts to "study nature in her works, and to God as the great author." Three ministers also spoke, and singing purportedly "echoed among the trees." The ceremony had a religious, Protestant tone, but the cemetery would be nonsectarian.

The cemetery officially consecrated, a small number of lots were put up for sale via a bidding process. Burials started soon thereafter. The Executive Committee set the original minimum bids at $25 a lot, with higher bids allowing a purchaser to secure a more choice location. For years to follow, the standard price would be $30 for a twenty-foot-square lot. By the late 1890s, a price of $285 per burial site was common.

The first interment at Mount Hope occurred in mid-1836; it was that of Samuel Call, on a Cemetery Hill lot purchased by his brother. By the time of Call's burial, however, General Samuel Veazie—a local businessman and later a railroad magnate for whom the town of Veazie was named—erected a tomb on the lower western slope of Cemetery Hill. His vault, with a flower and leaf decorative motif and an urn topping the marble upper portion of the tomb, remains a prominent feature of the cemetery's landscape. Before Veazie died, he allowed the cemetery to store bodies in his tomb over the winter months when the ground was frozen. At Mount Hope, even the poor might rest in a wealthy family vault for a time.

There was concern about allowing tombs at the cemetery, but a few were built. Another tomb, located around the hill from the Veazie one near the steps leading up from the Garden Lot, was the Blake tomb. Set high above the river on a very steep section, the tomb has a commanding view of the grounds below. Its lines are Egyptian revival style, and its iron door with flanking pilasters is fairly simple in design.

Numerous bodies were reinterred at Mount Hope after the cemetery opened, especially during the earlier years. Bangor's first known Caucasian murder victim, Frenchman Joseph Marie Junin (or possibly Junion), was laid to rest at Mount Hope just inside the border with the city property in 1836. He had been murdered in 1791, purportedly by his nephew. Junin had initially been buried in a downtown plot. A slate tombstone with a rather elaborate inscription accompanied his remains to the new burial site.

Not all interments and reinterments at Mount Hope proceeded smoothly or even officially. One problem the cemetery faced during its first decades was that of burials taking place without the approval of the cemetery board, or, in some cases, its knowledge. In addition, some lots had boundaries in dispute, and in other instances, people transferred lots to other individuals without notifying the cemetery. Moreover, some people "bought" lots, put them into use, and then failed to pay for them. Others claimed to have purchased lots but had no certificates or other proof to show that they had indeed purchased a burial site. A surveyor was brought in to try to address some of these problems while the board tried to tackle other ones through various means. In addition, whether aboveground tombs or mausoleums would be allowed in the future soon became an issue, as well as the question of exactly what else people might construct on cemetery lots.

Moreover, by 1844, the plan to have a separate plot of land set aside and leased specifically for horticultural purposes—the Garden Lot—and to fence it in from marauding bovines and other possible intruders, had become problematic. The original leesees had not fulfilled their duties satisfactorily, and after some debate, the board gave the current lessee a final chance to fulfill his obligations before they terminated his lease and reissued another lease for a smaller portion of the land to another person for horticultural and agricultural purposes. The new lessee was also to erect a couple of buildings and undertake the fencing.

In 1849, a cholera epidemic struck Bangor, causing more than 160 deaths that year alone and forcing the city and Mount Hope to examine various issues related to the increased fatalities and contemporary burial practices. Not only cholera but also chickenpox, measles, and tuberculosis erupted suddenly from time to time, keeping the cemetery uncertain when large numbers of burial lots might be needed. All sections of the cemetery had not yet been laid out for lots, and the cemetery had to try to plan for future needs. Of those lots already surveyed, some were given out as dividends to cemetery proprietors from the 1830s to the 1850s, and therefore, these could not be automatically requisitioned in an emergency situation.

Even after the cholera epidemic abated, how to best manage cemetery holdings continued to be problematic, and the 1850s saw a new challenge emerge: the coming of the railroad. The Old Town Railway Company requested an easement along the cemetery's highly valued riverfront. The board overall did not want the loud and highly visible steam engines of modernity encroaching upon their bucolic cemetery. They turned down the request, even though some members of the board were active railroad promoters. It soon became apparent that a railroad would indeed follow the Penobscot River in the Bangor-Veazie area, however, and in 1853, the board decided to settle. The railroad was built and rebuilt over the years and would be owned by several companies, transport both people and freight, and remain crucial to the regional economy into the twenty-first century. However, the cemetery retained its waterfront property.

Confronted by the railroad issue, outbreaks of infectious diseases, and other issues, Mount Hope considered all of its options, and the committee ultimately voted to have all future proceeds from lot sales go to the corporation instead of being used as shareholder dividends and to lay out portions of the Garden Lot for graves where possible. A few years later, in 1857, the committee also voted to pay no further monetary or land dividends to the proprietors. Instead, all proceeds would go to the corporation and having the shareholders convey "all real estate and personal property, and all right, title, and interest in, and to all, real estate" to the cemetery would make Mount Hope a nonprofit corporation. It reincorporated as such in 1858, and it remains so today. All lot owners became members of the new corporation.

Following its reincorporation, Mount Hope began a new program to beautify the cemetery and increase cemetery efficiency. The Executive Committee held a subscription drive to have iron fencing built along the increasingly popular public road at the front of the cemetery to make the cemetery's appearance more pleasing, to keep the cemetery proper separate from the roadway, and, most especially, to separate it from the railroad bed constructed along the riverfront. The committee also decided to build a new entrance to the cemetery and to purchase additional parcels of land along the public or county road, later known as State Street.

By 1850, Bangor had a population of 14,000 people, and city demographics were changing. An increasing number of Catholics lived in the city, and a new cemetery opened in Bangor in the 1850s—Mount Pleasant, a private Catholic cemetery. The city, meanwhile, continued to own smaller cemeteries as well as its public grounds at Mount Hope. However, the private Mount Hope Cemetery remained prominent on the urban landscape, and that preeminence would only increase in subsequent years as Bangor's population reached 22,000 residents in 1900 and 39,000 in 1960. Subsequently, population figures did not change dramatically, although other demographics did evolve.

Still needing a place to hold bodies over the winter, the city decided—after the cemetery considered undertaking such a project itself—to build a large receiving or holding tomb for that purpose. The receiving tomb was built on the border of the private and city sections of Mount Hope, and it was finished circa 1870. The large quarry-cut stone and brick-lined tomb was built into a hillside, fronting Western Avenue, with only its granite face visible. Roughly forty-nine feet square with a vaulted ceiling and doorway, the tomb had its face adorned with a Presbyterian-style cross at its peak. Large pillars (or, more accurately, pilasters) built into the wall and roofline grace either side of the entrance with smaller ones at the corners of the face. The tomb contained niches for sixty or more caskets. It was heavily utilized throughout the late 1800s into the late 1900s, primarily during winter and in other inclement weather. A few bodies were stored there in the early twenty-first century, but by then, the tomb proved as much a center of attraction for cemetery visitors as it did a working receiving tomb.

Over the next few years, Mount Hope purchased additional land and new cemetery plan. The board tackled the issue of fenc-wering a superintendent to have additional fencing con-1 the cemetery gates during the daytime and close them : any "stray cattle or horses" found on cemetery grounds 1 to be in charge of the general day-to-day care of the ally a temporary job, the superintendent's position soon 1tial full-time one, especially as more carriage roads were :r developments occurred. This would be true for other garden cemeteries also.

Livestock running free remained an issue in Bangor and elsewhere in the mid to late 1800s, with roaming pigs being a particular problem. As the grounds at Mount Hope were initially hayed, they proved especially attractive to stray livestock. Keeping the animals out was a challenge the cemetery faced for decades even after it hired a superintendent.

By the 1870s, the grounds were becoming increasingly dotted with gravestones and monuments, so cutting the grass uniformly—and keeping the grounds attractive—was also becoming an issue, marauding animals or not. Unoccupied gravesites could be easily cut for hay or for appearance's sake, but occupied lots were more difficult. Some people tended their burial lots or those of their deceased, while others did not. Thus the cemetery grounds, to some people, had "an uncouth and unpleasant appearance." In light of the situation, some lot owners decided to deposit funds with Mount Hope for the continued upkeep of their sites, a practice later known as "perpetual care." It would take Mount Hope decades to bring all of its sites under perpetual care provisions, however, as would be true in many places. Not until 1932 did almost all gravesites come under the policy. Meanwhile, other work on the grounds progressed.

Mount Hope built a substantial slate-roofed pavilion in the 1870s on the southern part of the grounds for the convenience of cemetery visitors, especially to provide shade from harsh sunlight and protection during rain showers, and to serve as a center for public functions. Another building was likewise constructed and served as an office and possibly as a makeshift chapel. Both buildings were designed to fit into the grounds in a pleasing manner. Also, work was undertaken to modify waterways to augment the cemetery's appeal.

During the 1870s through the 1890s, Mount Hope added a few ponds to its property. Tomb Pond, Stetson Pond, Fort Pond, and Garden (or Office) Pond were each created during the late 1800s to beautify the cemetery, and the brook was rerouted to provide water for two of the three ponds and to create a causeway. The City of Bangor deeded some of its land back to Mount Hope to allow for the construction of the most northern pond (Fort Pond), as well as to allow both the pond and a new dam there to fall entirely within the private cemetery.

Other grounds beautification likewise progressed. The existing road at the northern end of Mount Hope was rerouted in the late 1800s to provide a safer (for horse carriages) cemetery entrance and to create a more aesthetically pleasing cemetery approach. A new bridge was added over the confluence of the new pond and the brook. The cemetery also created new paths and avenues and built stone stairways ascending Cemetery Hill and at various other locations. The one leading up the front of Cemetery Hill contained more than one hundred steps, and was hereafter referred to as the One Hundred Steps to differentiate it from other staircases at Mount Hope and elsewhere. A stone staircase was also built from the top of Cemetery Hill down the side facing the main avenue and the current location of the office, although it does not go the entire way down the hill, as was a substantial staircase on one of the cemetery's undulations behind Cemetery Hill, close to what would become Stetson Park.

Mount Hope also continued to plant ornamental trees, shrubs, and flowers. It replaced numerous evergreens with hardwood trees deemed more suitable to the cemetery environment, as wet evergreen foliage had stained a number of marble monuments. During the same years, the cemetery purchased even more land and undertook its beautification, in some instances tearing down existing structures.

Then, with so much work undertaken in the more northern portions of the cemetery, plans were released for an extension of the northern, public road to the cemetery from Bangor to connect Bangor with the adjacent town of Veazie, which had separated from Bangor in 1853. The road extension would divide the private Mount Hope in two. The existing road led just to Mount Hope's northwestern border with the city grounds. The county road to the south already linked Bangor with Veazie, and the committee did not see the need for another thoroughfare. They fought the extension.

The cemetery lost the battle over the road extension much as it had its earlier eminent domain battle with the railroad along its southern border, and the "Highway to Veazie," later known simply as Mount Hope Avenue, was completed by early 1887. To prevent a small portion of its northern holdings from being isolated, the cemetery purchased additional lands north of the new road, and Bangor and Veazie agreed to move the boundary between the two municipalities such that all of Mount Hope Cemetery would lie within the city of Bangor. Some of the newly purchased land had been located in Veazie.

With the public road issue resolved and more land in its holdings, Mount Hope built another ornate building or pavilion to serve partially as a chapel for the newly laid out northern sections as the 1890s began. At the same time, it started laying out a "public park"—called Stetson Park for community leader and cemetery board member George Stetson—along the brook and near the newest pond. A bridge was added, a few islands created in the stream, and the site immediately became a popular spot for visiting people. Ducks, geese, the occasional blue heron, and other birds also enjoy the park.

By the 1890s, as observed by one of Mount Hope's presidents, "There is nothing in this country to which foreign visitors give more praise than to our [American] cemeteries. There is a constant and growing interest in them. Most of us remember when a cemetery would have been the last place to visit for pleasure." Times had changed.

Just as many people—Americans and foreigners alike—wanted to visit the new garden cemeteries, others requested burial sites in them for patriotic or other memorials, or for charitable organizations. Mount Hope began donating sites in the mid-1800s to various organizations and causes. These included gifts to the Bangor Female Orphan Asylum (later the Bangor Children's Home), the Bangor Home for Aged Women, and veterans of the American Civil War. Mount Hope was one of the more generous cemeteries in sharing its land.

While the Civil War was still ongoing, a group of Bangorites decided to build a memorial to the region's fallen soldiers. The citizens ultimately chose Mount Hope as the location for the memorial. The cemetery donated a large site in the old Garden Lot for the memorial and for graves for some of the fallen. (Ultimately, some 115 Bangorites would die in the war, with others later succumbing to their injuries.) The Civil War Memorial itself was built largely through subscription.

The obelisk-shaped Civil War Monument, as dedicated on June 17, 1864, was inscribed with the names of fifty-five of the dead. Two smaller stone monuments were also erected, and decorative high granite curbing was added to enclose the space. War hero Stephen Decatur Carpenter was initially buried at the site, but his family later reinterred his remains in their family lot at Mount Hope. Several other noted veterans—which, in truth, all the nineteenth-century freedom fighters of New England are—received burial near the memorial, which remains one of the cemetery's most frequently visited sites.

Other gifts were made to the public during the era. Mount Hope donated burial space at the front base of Cemetery Hill (not too distant from the Civil War Memorial) to the Bangor Female Orphan Asylum in 1863–1864. The home, established in 1835, immediately had eight bodies reinterred at the site, raising money for small granite grave markers by subscription. Other interments followed, and the home had a larger stone erected to honor all of the children. In 1874, the cemetery deeded the home—now at a new location and accepting boys—additional lots. In the 2010s, seventeen small grave markers remained at the site, dated into the early 1900s.

During the 1880s and 1890s, Mount Hope Cemetery granted the Home for Aged Women several lots. The original lot donations filled up rather quickly, and the Executive Committee granted others, all of them near the lots given to the Bangor Children's Home. Fifty-three individual stones were situated at the site in the 2010s, while a larger memorial honored the institution as a whole. Mount Hope also donated lots to the newer Home for Aged Men and to the Maine Charity School, later known as the Bangor Theological School, which features a tabletop ledger, among others, on the backside slope of Cemetery Hill. Over the decades, roads were built around the steep hillside, spiraling up almost to its summit. In the meantime, the seminary had a few bodies reinterred at its Mount Hope site, as well as having a few other people buried there upon their deaths.

Then, in the late 1890s, Mount Hope deeded land for another Civil War memorial and burial site, this time granting land north of Cemetery Hill and alongside its newly built pond. Known as the Grand Army of the Republic (GAR) Lot, the site was devoted to those who had served in the war—both those who were already deceased and those who might die in following years.

Work began on the GAR site in earnest at the turn of the century, and by 1901, the lot had been graded, flags and cannons installed, and a masonry tower constructed. A widely attended dedication ceremony in 1907 culminated the project in a festive spirit with noted speakers, performances by the Bangor Band, and military participation highlighting the day.

Some thirty veterans were buried on the GAR lot by the early 1920s, and in the 1960s, a third memorial to Civil War veterans was built at Mount Hope. Designed by Vernon Shaffer, a fifteen-foot bronze sculpture of a faceless angel bearing aloft a wounded man was dedicated to the 2nd Maine Regiment of (Civil War) Volunteers. Colonel Luther Pierce of Bangor, who had served with the 2nd Maine, made the memorial possible through a bequest. Mounted on a white granite setting fifteen feet high, the angel greets—if rather solemnly—cemetery visitors near the main, southern gate if they look to the left. The Luther H. Pierce memorial, like the other Civil War memorials, is popular with cemetery visitors.

In the 1990s, Mount Hope donated land for yet another war memorial, this time to veterans of the Korean War. The Maine Korean War Memorial Fund sponsored the memorial's construction and dedicated it to the 233 Maine men and women killed or classified as missing in action in the Korean War. Located close to the Mount Hope Avenue entrance just below the GAR Fort, the monument lists the names of all 233 veterans on a fifteen-foot-high black granite "wall." Flags from each of the twenty-one nations that participated in the conflict on the side of South Korea under the United Nations line a long, white granite approach. The approach is paved with inscribed stones commemorating veterans from various wars. Another popular site at Mount Hope, a 1995 candlelight service, marked the monument's completion. Meanwhile, burials at Mount Hope in the later 1800s had continued, as had cemetery beautification.

After decades of attempting to establish a regular water supply beyond that provided by the brook, in the late 1890s, Mount Hope finally acquired one by placing a water tank on one of the higher cemetery "bluffs" and building a windmill on the shore of the Penobscot River to pump river water. Pipes then carried the water throughout the cemetery. (The windmill system would not survive the twentieth century, however.) In the meantime, the cemetery added new faucets on the grounds and placed buckets at them for people to water their gravesites. Horses might be given water at the faucets also, and until 1896, dogs, too, were allowed to drink from them. In 1896, the board banned dogs from the cemetery. (Canines would be allowed in once again in subsequent years, but they were banned again in the late 1900s.)

Also at the turn of the century, the cemetery created a new pond to transform a recently acquired marshy plot of land. It then established lots nearby and fenced in about fifty acres of pastureland north of Mount Hope Avenue. It next developed another pond near the base of Cemetery Hill; the body of water was later known as Garden or Office Pond. Office Pond proved an especially popular spot for humans, birds, turtles, deer, beaver, and other creatures into the twenty-first century.

The cemetery soon built a new office near Office Pond (hence the more popular name of the pond), something the cemetery had long needed; the older, dual-purpose one was inadequate and in disrepair. To that end, the corporation purchased a small plot of land on what had been its southwestern border, and in 1901, it contracted noted Maine architect Wilfred E. Mansur to design a new office. Mansur also designed two new, probably wooden, waiting rooms near the main and upper cemetery entrances. These waiting rooms allowed visitors to rest while awaiting funeral services or transportation, especially at the upper entrance, allowing one to await a trolley car, part of the Bangor Street Railway and Electric Company that was established in 1889. One of the rooms would be replaced later and seemingly redesigned and used elsewhere as a gazebo. The office building, however, would long continue to be a source of pride.

By 1909, the new office building was complete. Of Old English design, it would grace the cemetery to the current day. Known as the Lodge, the building was finished with half-timbered stucco and Hull granite from Maine's Mount Desert Island. Originally, it held space for an office and a chapel. Large fireplaces grace each of the main rooms, and much of the original oak furniture remains in use. A second floor provided space for a drafting room initially, and later it was used for storage and other purposes. The building is essentially unchanged from 1909 except for a small addition made to house a crematory in the 1970s and then converted into a meeting room after the cemetery built a separate crematory in 1993. The Lodge is the first place most first-time cemetery visitors stop to obtain information and to tour the historical building.

By the time the Lodge was constructed, the cemetery had built wooden and other fences in many places and had erected gates, but they had since deteriorated. Mount Hope thus worked during the late 1800s and early 1900s to have ornamental, yet stronger, iron fencing and gates installed, as well as to place granite pillars at the main entrances.

It would take until 1923 to complete fencing of the cemetery, the completion made possible by a gift of iron fencing and new gates along the riverside by Mr. and Mrs. Franklin R. Webber. The gating system was concurrently modified to allow for two gated horse carriage and car entrances. (Cars had started to visit Mount Hope by the early 1920s.) A former vehicle entrance was simultaneously modified to accommodate only a footpath. Ornamental fencing would subsequently be added elsewhere in the cemetery, including near the middle gate, which is now the footpath gate, and the Webbers would soon construct one of the most intriguing structures at Mount Hope.

The Webbers donated the Webber Waiting Room in the early 1930s. Constructed of pink Maine granite and bronze, it replaced the existing wooden structure. George I. Mansur, brother of Wilfred Mansur, designed the circular building with its bronze door and other ornamental bronze-work topped by a conical bronze roof. Roughly fifteen feet in diameter outside (about ten feet in diameter inside) and twenty feet tall, the structure provided a lighted room in which people could wait for a trolley car or other transportation. Added to their gift of perhaps 4,000 feet of iron fencing, the Webbers had indeed been generous to the community and the cemetery. In the 1920s, the Webbers had also had a private mausoleum constructed on the grounds.

Before the Webbers died, numerous other notable—and, in some cases, disputed—burials had taken place at Mount Hope. One of those in the 1800s was that of lumber baron, railroad promoter, and Bangor's third mayor Rufus Dwinel. Dwinel died in 1869, and his monument inspired rumors and speculation in following years. Dwinel had had a large sarcophagus built on his burial site, one large enough to have held his remains. Granite legs (or feet) raised the sarcophagus above a stone slab. Rumors soon circulated that Dwinel might be buried in the stone sarcophagus rather than below it. According to one story, Dwinel, a millionaire, had stated that his wife would not receive one cent of his money as long as he was aboveground. In a variation of that story, Dwinel had purportedly stated that as long as he was aboveground, he would financially support his mistress. Other versions existed. However, the Dwinel sarcophagus is solid stone, not hollow, and Dwinel was buried below it, not in it. His lot continues to be a popular site at the cemetery, as does the nearby grave of Hannibal Hamlin.

Hamlin served as Abraham Lincoln's first vice president, and he was also a Maine senator and a Bangor mayor. Hamlin was a Maine native, having been born in the small town of Paris, and he was active in Maine railroads as well as in local institutions. He died in 1891 at age eighty-one while playing cards at Bangor's Tarratine Club, and thousands of people came out into the streets to watch his funeral carriage pass by. Hamlin's monument at Mount Hope, in the Riverside Lawn section near some other illustrious people's lots, remains one of the most visited cemetery sites.

Numerous local business and political figures chose to be buried at Mount Hope. Other people had less choice in the matter, such as the residents of the local children's home and of the home for elderly women. Still others were buried nearby just into the city section, at the Strangers Lot, also referred to at times as Pauper's Row, a popular nineteenth-century name for the burial lots for the indigent. One such person was James Babcock, who died in 1870 at age thirty at the Bangor Almshouse. His grave, like those buried near him, was unmarked. Another, more noted, grave would be located within the private cemetery, and it remained unmarked for decades. Before that happened, however, Bangor's most celebrated madam was interred.

Nancy (also known as Fannie or Fan) Jones lived in Bangor for sixty odd years, and she ran an infamous bordello on Harlow Street downtown, not far from the harbor during its heyday as a lumber port. She had numerous run-ins with the law, but by the time of her death in 1917, at age eighty-seven, she had become something of a local legend. Jones had purchased a large lot, and seven other people were buried there as well: five children, three women, and her escort or husband, John Thomas. Some of these were relatives; others were neighbors. Jones chose to be buried without a headstone.

Fan Jones or Thomas may or may not have been a soiled dove—a term prostitutes were sometimes called (doves, a symbol of peace and purity and sometimes of the Holy Spirit, graced two of the children's headstones on her lot)—with a heart of gold. However, the most infamous person to be buried in Mount Hope certainly did not have a heart of gold. Guilty of at least three cold-blooded murders as well as various assaults and numerous bank and other robberies, Alfred "Al" Brady was declared public enemy number one by the Federal Bureau of Administrations shortly before he and his midwestern gang came to Bangor in 1937 to buy guns and ammunition. They fell into a carefully orchestrated trap, and Brady and one of his men, Clarence Lee Shaffer, were gunned down in the streets of Bangor. A third gang member, James Dalhover, was extradited and later executed.

While a relative claimed Shaffer's body, no one claimed Brady's, and he was buried on a dismal day north of Mount Hope Avenue. No stone marked his grave until the early twenty-first century. Still, people found the site, and his was deemed "Mount Hope's most talked about grave."

Other graves, such as that of a "gypsy princess" and various children's graves, also became part of local lore. In addition, portions of Stephen King's *Pet Sematary* were filmed at Mount Hope in 1988, in the old garden lot near the One Hundred Steps. King made a cameo appearance in the movie, as is his wont, as the presiding minister at a female character's burial. Fred Gwynne, known for his starring role as Herman Munster in the 1960s sitcom *The Munsters*, also made an appearance, and he had recently appeared in another movie partially set in a garden cemetery. The cast interacted with cemetery staff, and locals regularly came to watch the filming.

Less famous people with some of the more striking monuments also attract visitors to the cemetery. The Amanda Skofield memorial, built in 1927, is one of Mount Hope's most photographed edifices. A stunning circular colonnade or classical open temple of rising white granite columns, it is topped with a band or rim of stone, engraved and dedicated inside to "A Beloved Mother." Another, smaller monument that lays flat within the temple marks Skofield's resting place.

Frequently photographed, too, is the Hill mausoleum, built in 1918 by Frederick Hill to hold the remains of his recently departed wife Marianne, those of her mother (whose remains were reinterred from Mount Auburn), and upon his death, his own. Marianne Hill had made arrangements for the mausoleum, and she had bequeathed money for its perpetual care. Frederick Hill made arrangements for fresh flowers to be delivered regularly and for the tomb's glass door to be open daily from spring through autumn. The circular white granite structure, similar to the rectangular Webber mausoleum built to hold Franklin R. and Martha Webber in 1922, remains popular, and each, like other cemetery monuments, has had to be under repairs from time to time. Each mausoleum had trusts established to that end and, in the Webbers' case, to maintain the fencing and the waiting room they had financed at the cemetery.

Another noted lot at Mount Hope is that of an adjacent part of the Webber family. The John Webber family lot contains several memorials as well as a small stairway flanked by intricately carved urns. The markers include a child memorial for Channing Webber, who died in 1881. The marker features an infant angel or cherub atop a shrouded urn or casket. The infant holds the large shroud that obscures part of the marker below it. The child seems to be clinging to whatever is under it, possibly a cross, yet he seems at peace. A mother's marker, for Anne S. Webber, wife of John Webber, is next to the child's memorial. It is inscribed simply: "More fondly we loved her than language can tell; stern death has removed her, yet all is well."

One can find other children's memorials at Mount Hope besides those for the Jones and Webber children or in the orphan's lot. One of these is the classic crib near the front of the cemetery, not far from the Jones lot. Worn with age and no longer legible, the crib marker features carved sides and headboard, and it was inscribed for Ella Wasgatt, who died at age three in 1868, and Freddie Harris, who died at age two in 1874. In the old garden area of the cemetery is another marker for a youth, one that would be popular in garden cemeteries as noted; it is a tree stump, one that almost resembles a broken column in its propor-tions. It was erected for the Job Collett family, and it was part of a family area. It has a number of broken branches as well as a dove on the top, but unfortunately, the dove has been damaged. Buried in the family lot, too, with their own small marker with a lamb resting on a tasseled throw, were Willie and Lillie, who died as young children.

Also, farther back in the cemetery, on a slope parallel to Stetson Park, two other child memorials are of interest. The first is a fairly simple stone, a small lamb curled atop it, for "Freddie" King, who died at the age of two in 1876 and is found next to his family marker. The small stone features the sculpture of a lamb.

Farther up the hillside, the memorial for the Atwood and Howard families is located. Stories have circulated about it over the years, either that, in one version, a child was trapped alive in her tomb, or that, in another, she comes out at night to haunt the cemetery. In reality, the memorial as seen from the avenue is a statue of a little girl, one enclosed in glass. She looks out over the cemetery below, and she serves as a family marker. In the later 2010s, vandals smashed the glass and broke the statue. Mount Hope has since had a new, identical (as far as possible) statue made in Vermont and mounted in new glass. The old marble statue is now part of the cemetery's archives. The first interment on the family lot was in 1876, for a two-month-old infant.

Mount Hope does not have the number of ornate memorials with angels, women-in-mourning motifs, bronze sculptures, and such as do some of the other garden cemeteries. However, it does generally have some of each type, and some of these are superb.

Mount Hope has a few zinkies (zinc memorials) and other metal markers. A fairly simple yet pleasing one is located on the lower back slope of Cemetery Hill. It marks the resting place of Horace Haynes, and it features a small obelisk atop a decorated base with symbolic plates, as well as one for family information. The obelisk is caped, has some shrouding on its sides, and includes garlands, wreaths, and a Masonic symbol. Mason symbols are found throughout garden cemeteries, sometimes many in one cemetery, sometimes just a few.

A more ornate zinc memorial is that of the Kelley memorial, located in the Garden Lot. The pedestal base of the marker is intricate enough with its nameplates, roses, and architectural embellishments, but it is the figure above that most captures the eye. It is a classic figure of "Hope": a woman with one arm resting on her chest, the other holding a large anchor at her side, her eyes cast upward, her smile subtle. She has weathered well, as have many zinc memorials in New England.

Mount Hope Cemetery has a great advantage in its layout, river location with waterways, and topography. It is the northernmost of the New England garden cemeteries, and like those discussed from northern New York and Vermont, the often bitter winters may have influenced the cemetery's development. All of New England has winter; some areas simply have harsher winters. Then again, there is spring, summer, and autumn. The trees and shrubs of New England cannot be surpassed in their beauty.

Gifts from families such as the Webbers helped beautify the grounds in some ways in the early 1900s, while Superintendent Harold S. Burrill designed new stone bridges over the brook during the 1930s, which likewise helped beautify the grounds. Three generations of Burrills would serve as superintendents and assistant superintendents over the twentieth century and beyond, each of whom, like those of the committee members, especially the Bragg family, held long tenures at the cemetery and stressed cemetery beautification as well as sound finances. Together, they made Mount Hope into a lasting, financially stable cemetery.

Cemetery beautification and modernization also continued over the decades. New land was purchased and designed for aesthetic appeal during the 1900s and into the 2000s. In the 1960s, paving the main roads began, and later, a maintenance building was erected for the necessary equipment and to replace an older carriage house.

Another modern development, community mausoleums—as seen in most of the garden cemeteries—allowed a person to purchase just one or a few niches for aboveground interment instead of building an entire mausoleum. At Mount Hope, the first ones were erected in the early 1980s, and others were added after 2000. Moreover, in 1995, Galen Cole of the Cole Land Transportation Museum in Bangor gifted the cemetery with a carillon bell system that played anthems, hymns, carols, and other music, sending it out from the top of Cemetery Hill throughout the cemetery, as well as through parts of Bangor, Brewer, and Veazie. This, like many other donations, gifts, and beautification projects, added to the aesthetic appeal of Mount Hope Cemetery.

Placed on the National Register of Historic Places in the 1970s, Mount Hope Cemetery is a regular stopping spot for guided historical tours. Moreover, hundreds of people visit the cemetery each year on their own, many of them visiting again and again. Mount Hope continues to hold great appeal for the general public well into the 2010s.

At Mount Hope, one can stroll around the grounds, watch wildlife, listen to carillon bells three times a day, visit the graves of both loved ones and famed individuals, and, of course, be buried there. Mount Hope continues to offer a resting place for the dead and a garden of beauty to the living.

Now that you've learned some of the basics about Mount Hope Cemetery, here are a few sources for further reading and information by the author, Trudy Irene Scee: Mount Hope Cemetery, The Complete History; City on the Penobscot: A Comprehensive History of Bangor, Maine; *and* Public Enemy No. 1, The True Story of the Brady Gang. *You may also consult the cemetery's website and visit and look around! Much of the author's original information came from Mount Hope's archives and interviews with staff.*

4

Valley Cemetery

And Her Daughter Cemetery, Pine Grove, Manchester, New Hampshire

Valley Cemetery from the first glimpse makes one wonder—wonder about how an encroaching city has affected it, wonder about how such a strong presence has been established in such a relatively small space, and wonder if there is something one is not seeing, if there is some danger here, or some mystery about the cemetery's history. And its history does indeed hold a few mysteries, and some would say the cemetery holds a few dangers. But walk in and look over the cliff, literally over a cliff, and you will discover something special and perhaps sense something lost. And just a few miles away, you will find Pine Grove, a larger cemetery, which is, one might argue, the Daughter of the Valley.

VALLEY CEMETERY IN MANCHESTER, NEW HAMPSHIRE, DIFFERED from many garden cemeteries of America when it was founded, in 1841, and opened in 1842, in what was already planned to be part of a busy downtown area. The location reflected a gift from a manufacturing company. Starting with a grant of almost twenty acres of land, within twenty years, the original site was filled close to capacity. Much like Springfield Cemetery, another small cemetery maintained by a municipality in a crowded area, Valley Cemetery had some challenges. Therefore, while activity continued at Valley, a new municipal cemetery, Pine Grove, was established to augment the original garden cemetery. Both cemeteries, along with seven others, are currently administered by the City of Manchester. Valley Cemetery or "The Valley," however, continues to stand out from the others.

Valley Cemetery enjoys a unique if sometimes troubled history. One may be perplexed when first encountering the cemetery, when walking around the site, and feel that something is missing or wonder exactly how the place fits into the overall garden cemetery movement and its design criteria. One may also be warned that the place can be dangerous. Both situations are explained by the cemetery's history.

Valley Cemetery's history started with the Amoskeag Manufacturing Company. Wealthy Boston citizens had reorganized and capitalized Amoskeag Manufacturing as a stock company circa 1830. The company would become an economic powerhouse in the region, ultimately manufacturing numerous items. According to the Manchester Historical Association, the company "transform[ed] Manchester into an industrial giant, and into the largest planned city in New England." The company purchased some 15,000 acres of land directly east of the Merrimack River and started a major textile operation along the riverbanks. In 1838, it started laying out town streets in a grid fashion and began selling off some 14,000 acres—the majority of its original land purchases. With the population growing rapidly and shifting to the east bank of the river, the community's needs changed.

Burial space in the growing—and, in some ways, physically shifted—community quickly became scarce. Recognizing this, the Amoskeag Manufacturing Company offered the Town of Manchester land to establish a public cemetery, the pertinent deed signed in February 1841.

According to the February 4, 1841, deed, "The Amoskeag Manufacturing Company for and in consideration of . . . one dollar to them paid by the Town of Manchester, the receipt thereof they do hereby acknowledge, have bargained and conveyed, and do by those present bargain, sell, [and] convey to the Town of Manchester a certain Tract of Land situated in Said Town containing nineteen and seven-tenths of one acre." A description of the boundaries of the rectangular plot followed. The adjacent streets of Pine, Elm, and Willow were already laid out and at least somewhat settled, and the deed spelled them out clearly in the description. The "old" Amoskeag Bridge and Merrimack Street also appeared in the grant description, as did various homes and other landmarks of the day.

Parts of the deed may seem puzzling to the present-day reader, but in summation, the company deeded the Town of Manchester and its successors the land "for the sole use or purpose of a Public Cemetery or Burial [G]round of Said Town." One portion was to be set aside as a "Common Burial place," seemingly for use by the poor. "Suitable walks or alleys" were to be established from "time to time" dividing the lots, and lots were not to exceed "six hundred square feet." A committee could set or adjust the price of lots as time passed. All monies received from lot sales were to go to "the sole purpose of enclosing and ornamenting said Cemetery." The State of Massachusetts approved the transfer.

A pleasing aspect at the Valley helped create a suitable setting for a garden cemetery. The location included a hillside offering a vista over the nearby landscape and the Merrimack River, and it had water—Miles Brook, later known simply as Cemetery Brook. The brook crossed the cemetery in a meandering fashion, entering at the bottom of a fairly steep ravine from near the southwestern corner and flowing to the northeastern edge and eventually emptying into the Merrimack River. The ravine divided the cemetery in half, into eastern and western sections with narrow strips of higher land uniting the two sides along the northern and southern boundaries.

The cemetery is bounded by Auburn Street to the north, Pine Street to the west, Valley Street to the south, and Willow Street to the east. The eastern half of the cemetery is largely flat except for the steep slope into the ravine, while the western side has not just the ravine cliffs but also a generally gentle but marked slope down to Pine Street. The topography offered both rewards and challenges.

The town acted quickly upon the receipt of the land. In early spring 1841, it established a committee to undertake the work of creating a cemetery. The committee was originally composed of seven men: Samuel D. Bell, George B. Swift, George Foster, Walter French, Hiram Brown, J. T. P. Hunt, and Alonzo Smith. These were men who were leaders in the community, and in some cases, they were influential well beyond Manchester. Hiram Brown would become the City of Manchester's first mayor after it incorporated as a city in 1846. Alonzo Smith would also become mayor, and other mayors would serve on the committee over time.

The committee sought the best way to create a new cemetery, and they had a survey of the grounds made. As it was "destitute of funds," to enclose the grounds with a wooden fence, the committee initiated a subscription drive and thereby raised $234, according to the earliest report on the cemetery, submitted by the "Committee on the Valley" to the City of Manchester in 1848. Citizens could apply their donations toward future lot purchases. Captain Walter French had "principal charge" of the design in the early years, and in 1848, the committee noted that "the grounds furnish much evidence of his good taste and careful attention."

In the summer of 1841, the new cemetery opened. The town held a dedication ceremony on July 5, one that included a religious service and a procession. More than 4,000 people attended the dedication, including children from local church Sunday schools. The dedication was held on the July 5, since July 4 was a Sunday and the town apparently did not want to interfere with Sunday church services and other events. The Stark Guard, named for Revolutionary War hero General John Stark, known as "The Hero of Bennington," led the march, and Reverend Gage delivered the religious services, which were chosen to include all local religious sects.

The new entity was named Valley Cemetery the following month, and the committee soon thereafter voted to fence the entire property, not just the portions of it citizens had already enclosed with a wooden fence. The committee also voted on lot prices and to purchase a hearse and a "hearse house." Some of the "choice" lots were bid off for $14 each in early September, and another twenty-six sold over the next several months. The first official burial, according to the National Park Service, occurred in 1841, that of Mary Baldwin, who had a marble stone on a granite base. Two young children were buried on the site before her, however, in 1839. As elsewhere, numerous bodies were reinterred from other locations.

The following year saw a road built into the cemetery from the eastern side of the grounds, as well as the planting of ornamental trees. The cemetery spent some $86 during the 1842–1843 fiscal year, according to town reports. A few other avenues—perhaps for walking, perhaps for carriages—were also established in the first few years. By the close of the

1844 fiscal year, which at the time ended in the early spring, the cemetery had also spent time "posting cautions against trespass." By the twenty-first century, various forms of trespass would prove major issues.

The cemetery soon established its main entrance at the corner of Auburn and Chestnut Streets, near the northwestern corner of the property. There, an iron gate designed by Moses Oliver, with a granite gateway added later, was constructed. Starting in the 1870s, stone and then concrete retaining walls were added along the boundaries, as in many places the elevation of the cemetery—situated on a hill—is higher than that of the surrounding streets. The entire cemetery was enclosed by iron fencing as the decades passed, with frequent repairs and additions needed, and various forms or styles were used over time.

Manchester grew at a rapid pace in the years following Valley Cemetery's establishment, as people came to work in the city's factories and in construction. The new cemetery immediately proved popular, and lots were soon hard to come by. However, interments and other activities and construction at Valley Cemetery continued for decades. The cemetery remained a popular place for residents, who held picnics on the grounds and strolled along the pathways. Carriage roads provided other means of enjoying and touring the grounds into the 1900s.

The years immediately following the dedication saw a thorn hedge planted to enclose the cemetery along with other improvements. Roughly 5,000 new plants were added to the grounds during 1846 and 1847, most of them planted to form the hedge. Fencing was later added in places to augment the hedge. The hedge, and not the wooden fencing, was initially intended as the cemetery's permanent enclosure. The Amoskeag Machine Shop purportedly later helped supply some parts of the perimeter with iron fencing. The initial iron fencing was ornamental along Pine and Auburn Streets, with plain iron bars erected along the other boundaries.

The committee members did have ongoing concerns in the 1840s and 1850s about how to best protect the cemetery, however. In early 1858, the committee reported that it was "impossible for those having charge of the grounds to keep watch over the whole twenty acres in such a way as to prevent or discover every possible breach of the rules and proprieties of the place." Yet, lest one fear that great criminal activities were taking place within the hedges and walls, the report continued: "However vigilant the keepers may be, our chief reliance for the safety of the trees, flowers, monuments, and other property must be on that sense of what is right and proper. . . . It is gratifying to know that rudeness of conduct, theft, thoughtless and malicious mischief have been of so infrequent occurrence."

One problem unique (possibly) to the cemetery was perhaps not a real problem at all. The 1858 report asserted that "the practice indulged in by some persons of plucking flowers from their own lots, ought to be abandoned. It is not in good taste to make a flower garden of a cemetery." Burial lots were meant for the "burial of the dead," so "if flowers are cultivated, it should be as a means of ornamenting a burial place, and not in themselves an end." Groundskeepers could not be expected to police the grounds for flower pickers; they could not be expected to know who had the right to pick flowers at a given lot and who did not. Growing flowers for the sake of growing flowers "ought to cease."

However, healthy flowers and other plants were crucial to the young garden cemetery. Committee members continued to look for ways to beautify the cemetery and ensure its financial stability. Sales of wood from unwanted trees as well as of lots had brought in money over the years, especially early on when clearing certain sections was ongoing, and in 1853, the committee proposed that the cemetery establish a nursery. A nursery might augment revenue as both trees and shrubs might be grown "for the convenience of the owners of Lots, for shade or ornaments, to be furnished at reasonable rates." The suggestion was followed by an appeal to keep the cemetery "a peaceful and quiet resting place for generations yet to come." It does not appear that the nursery became a reality, at least not at the Valley.

Trees, too, were of great consequence at the Valley. People were not to be allowed to simply remove trees from their lots because they wished to do so. That a tree failed to meet a human's standards was not reason enough to remove it, nor was a desire to have the same species, number, size, or quality as that of other lots or cemetery sections justification for the same.

The committee reminded the city in 1858 that, "the Valley can never be successfully reduced to a regular geometrical plantation. Even if that were possible the natural characteristics of the place would be found incompatible with such a plan." Moreover, they opined, "Let us hope that the day may come when all our people shall regard trees as at once the cheapest, the grandest, and the most appropriate ornaments of a rural cemetery." Trees would not waste away over time, but rather they would nourish the grounds and gain strength and beauty each year.

In a similar light, although upkeep was needed on the thorn hedge planted around the cemetery in the late 1850s, in 1848, after reviewing the cemetery's history, the Valley committee stated that the hedge previously planted along the western and northern sides of the cemetery was in good shape and was intended "to furnish a handsome, lasting and impervious fence when the present perishable enclosure shall have gone to decay." In 1848, the plants forming the thorn hedge were thriving.

In 1848, although tree-planting, flower-arranging, and other beautification continued, much had already been accomplished, and the committee stated, "The city may well congratulate itself in the possession of a cemetery so beautiful and ornamental, and so capable of improvement; in the spirit in which it has been sustained; and in the neatness and beauty of the monuments erected there to the memory of the dead." The committee recommended that the city acquire property owned by Amoskeag Manufacturing Company east of the cemetery and add it to the cemetery. "Such an addition . . . must be needed at no distant day, and perhaps at a future time cannot be procured."

Unfortunately, no land contiguous to the existing cemetery was added to the Valley's holdings, and the next two years added to the problem. Some of the land along the plain fencing came to hold the bodies of paupers and other people of little means, and the need for additional space was made evident just after the committee advised that the city purchase more land: in 1849–1850, a cholera epidemic hit New England, causing thousands of deaths.

In Manchester, the city set aside the northeastern corner of Valley Cemetery for those who died of cholera. Interments were purportedly made at night and in a mass grave. Few headstones marked the area and its dead. It was quite likely that the poor had only wooden markers, if any. Likewise, the northwestern corner of the Valley became the site of the pauper burials. Both areas remain relatively free of monuments.

Roughly a decade after the cholera epidemic, in 1858, records showed that 2,733 people had been buried at the Valley: 1,442 of them in regular lots and 1,291 in the public grounds. Space was indeed an issue, and it was one that needed resolving. In the meantime, in early 1850, the committee suggested that a receiving tomb be built at Valley Cemetery. In addition to the usual reason for having such a tomb—holding bodies over the winter months, which the report did not mention—it could be used "for the temporary deposit [sic] of the dead whose friends may at some future time wish to remove them. This would be a source of income, as well as convenience."

Unlike the nursery proposed in 1853, a holding tomb would be built on cemetery grounds in following years. A second tomb would later replace it when the first failed to provide sufficient room for community needs.

The Valley had become a beloved bit of green space in downtown Manchester by the 1850s, but it was also becoming crowded in terms of the numbers of bodies it might hold. Although lot sales continued and not all sold lots held bodies yet, Manchester, incorporated as a city in 1846, sought new burial grounds. By March 1852, the city had approved a loan of $1,000 for the "New Cemetery," with no name or location indicated for this "new cemetery."

No further action was immediately taken. Then, in 1855, according to an 1858–1859 report, the city purchased property two miles from City Hall, which itself is only a short distance from the Valley. In 1857, the city placed $100 at the disposal of the cemetery committee for work at the site, by then named Pine Grove. The next year, it decided to go ahead with preparing two and a half acres of the land for cemetery uses. The report noted that "it is the design of the committee to sell lots at a rate so low as to bring them within the means of all."

As of January 1, 1859, only one interment had taken place at Pine Grove. Committee focus on the new cemetery grew, however, and by 1860, the city was spending much more money there than at the Valley.

By 1861, some three miles of avenue had been built at Pine Grove, "but further improvements are required to make this an attractive burial place," the committee observed, and it recommended making those improvements. Moody Currier—who would serve as a New Hampshire governor and who would have a towering, granite obelisk memorial erected at the Valley—was on the committee, and he had been on the Valley committee since 1844.

For the next few years, the city focused on clearing more acreage at Pine Grove, and in 1863, they noted that "the entire absence of water here is much to be regretted, but to remedy that defect as far as possible it is hoped that at no distant day a supply will be introduced by artificial means sufficient to feed considerable ponds and for other purposes." The future would see additional land purchases for Pine Grove and the introduction of a pond near what became the main entrance for the cemetery, off Calef Road.

In 1863, the committee also noted that at Valley, "of all the original lots laid out in this Cemetery, only three remain unsold. Several have been laid out and disposed of during the past year on the slopes of the banks, which now afford the only available place to purchasers. A few more lots may be located here, but it will require considerable expense by the proprietors to properly grade and fit them up so as to ensure permanence."

By 1856, the Valley committee had been combined with the one managing Pine Grove Cemetery. That year, on February 5, the committee secretary noted, "This morning, all the Records of the Cemetery on the Valley were destroyed by the burning of Patten's building." Therefore, most of the early Valley records became unavailable to future historians.

The combined cemetery committee existed for some time after the city, which fortunately had kept its municipal reports elsewhere, added new cemeteries to its holdings, reaching nine by 2018. The municipal reports did not always include cemetery reports, or even detailed reports when they did include them, but at least they did preserve some information, including a copy of the original 1841 deed.

Interments at Valley Cemetery continued. Many people had bought lots in previous years, and as they and their family members died, their lots would be occupied. Most of the larger memorials and mausoleums at

Valley were constructed on the eastern side of the cemetery by the region's more wealthy citizens. This was true for the majority of the thirteen private mausoleums and tombs ultimately erected at Valley.

Besides Moody Currier, two other governors were buried at Valley Cemetery (as were two US senators and seven Manchester mayors): Ezekiel Straw, who died in 1882, and Frederick Smyth, also a former mayor of Manchester, who died in 1899. Smyth's mausoleum is one of the bigger attractions of the cemetery, perched as it is on the eastern edge of the ravine, overlooking the valley; its front is turned to overlook the ravine toward the western bank. A twenty-foot white granite base built into the hillside supports the mausoleum and makes it even more omnipresent. The mausoleum, also made of white granite, is visible from the valley and from the opposite hillside.

The Smyth mausoleum is just to the left of straight ahead when one enters the cemetery from the entrance on Willow Street. Built in a Greek or Ionic temple style with four columns on the front overlooking the valley and decorative pilasters on the remaining three sides, the large mausoleum is visible from numerous locations in the cemetery. It is thirty feet high, with decorative bronze doors now boarded over. Smyth had a varied career, serving in numerous capacities not just locally and statewide but also internationally, and he established the Manchester Library as well as otherwise contributing to the city and region.

Another one of the more interesting tombs or mausoleums is the E. W. Harrington mausoleum. Located near the ravine on the Willow Street side of the cemetery, yet facing at an angle away from the valley, the white mausoleum was built in an Egyptian revival style of large, white stone blocks. It features slanted sidewalls, a tiered flat roof, inscribed columns flanking a bronze doorway, and a winged orb with a snake symbol above the doorway. Classical urns on the step leading up to the door offer planting spaces.

Immediately upon entering the cemetery from the Willow Street entrance, the visitor encounters one of the other most-noted mausoleums in the cemetery, and it certainly is the most eclectic one. While ahead one sees the Smyth mausoleum, just to the left of the decorative gates at the junction with the first cross avenue is the Aretas Blood mausoleum, an extremely ornate structure. New York sculptor Alexander Doyle designed the building using a Greek cross shape—one that has four equal arms.

The Blood mausoleum has been classified as High Victorian Gothic, with stylistic features common for the late 1800s. Each side has a gabled façade with a lancet window, a lintel supported by small ionic columns, and an ornate finial. The mausoleum also has a Renaissance-style dome that elongates the mausoleum visually, and its embellishments further capture the eye. This is a structure one simply needs to see to appreciate, and in a sense, it has a relative in the Hill mausoleum located in Pine Grove.

Aretas Blood, for whom this intriguing edifice was built, lived from 1816 to 1897 and rose from a mechanic's position to be the founder and principal owner of the Manchester Locomotive Works, where he developed new designs in railroad engines and parts. The company purchased the Amoskeag Locomotive Works in 1859, where Blood had previously worked. (As noted at the outset, Amoskeag Manufacturing would come to produce a wide range of products.) His company continued to expand, and after his death in 1897, Blood was interred in his mausoleum at Valley, which he had built at the cost of $40,000 a few years earlier. His wife was also interred there.

Blood's wife, Lavinia Kendall Blood, started the Manchester Woman's Aid and Relief Society in the 1870s, and his daughter Eleanora would marry Frank Pierce Carpenter, president of the Amoskeag Manufacturing Company. The Carpenters would eventually be interred at Carpenter's mausoleum at Pine Grove. Carpenter would donate funds for a new public library in Eleanora's name after she died in 1910.

Also at Valley Cemetery, the 1856 Gale mausoleum was built to resemble a miniature chapel with buttresses, and although smaller and less ornate than the Blood mausoleum, it is still one of the most unique monuments on the grounds. It is relatively diminutive but quite distinctive and has stone curbing around it as well as individual family gravestones. It blends a variety of architectural styles, and it was built for physician Amos Gale, who died in 1856, and his wife, Mary Ayer Gale. Mary Gale established the Gale Home for Aged and Destitute Women in Dr. Gale's name in 1891, and it remained in operation until 2002.

On the other side of the cemetery, near the northwestern corner and facing Pine Street, one of the earliest tombs in the cemetery features a somewhat simple face constructed of granite, as its retaining walls and the four pilasters "support" its large granite lintel and capstone above. The George W. Bailey Tomb was built in 1857, and its doorway is now filled in with cement blocks.

Another noted vault is the Nathan Parker mausoleum, dated 1860. It sits mostly aboveground and features a gabled roof with "N. Parker" carved in relief above the iron door. A square urn on a square granite base sits atop the roof. Nathan Parker was a Manchester politician and banker, elected to the state house of representatives and state senate.

Other tombs and mausoleums also exist at the cemetery, including the Ayer vault, constructed in the early 1850s. It features an obelisk atop the roof and was built for Richard H. Ayer, the first president of one of the local banks and owner of an important local brickyard. The vault is largely aboveground. In addition, into the hills facing the valley, a few other tombs were also erected.

Several interesting family lots were established at the Valley, some of them overlooking the ravine. For example, the Elliot family had one of the handsome yet simpler lots with curbing. They had a fairly large memorial dated to 1880 with an architectural base (granite and, farther up, marble) topped by a draped marble urn. The front panel of the memorial is inscribed for "Mary E. Elliot, The Founder of the 'Elliot Hospital.'" The feature panel or inscription being devoted to a woman is refreshing, and Elliot was one who certainly deserved this early—in terms of historical timing—recognition. Mary Elliot was married to physician John S. Elliot, and the hospital she started still serves the city of Manchester, with the first extant building completed in 1896. The name Elliot is accompanied by that of Harvey in raised letters on the base of the memorial. The embellished curbing also encloses four smaller stones.

A more unusual family marker is set nearer the Willow Street side of the cemetery. The Edward L. Custer memorial, named for a fairly well-known landscape and portrait painter, was erected in 1881. Sometimes described in mathematical terms, the octagonal main section is set on a square base and supports a hexagonal, angled, two-section dome. Greek key design carvings are situated underneath an embellished cornice that separates the two major sections. The dome is topped with four small-ish Celtic crosses, each facing opposite directions. Various panels around the memorial are inscribed for family members, with the Custer name sculpted with raised letters on the "main" side of the rather squat memorial.

Valley Cemetery is rich in mausoleums and tombs for its small size, as well as with obelisks and architectural markers of various stones and styles. It has memorials for some of the poorer members of society—excepting those that died in the epidemics—and for veterans, a washer-woman who helped fund the Tuskegee Institute, a mill girl who designed her own monument, and a memorial for the Manchester Fire Department from the mid-1800s.

Older, Gothic memorials are plentiful, as are obelisks of various sizes, many of them marble and weathered, some of them capped or other-wise embellished. However, the cemetery has fewer statues or figures than other garden cemeteries do, with the memorials built for the Eastman and Haynes families being exceptions. These memorials are both classic in design and feature female figures, and similar statues would be found in other garden cemeteries. Pine Grove, however, would see its share of sculptural funerary art, perhaps because its years of interments extended beyond those of the Valley.

In 1862, the city widened Pine Street near the brook crossing at Valley Cemetery to allow for a sidewalk of standard width to extend "entirely across the Valley at this point." Two iron gates had recently been erected at "the foot entrance on Chestnut Street, and wooden ones placed at the other foot walks, enabling the Superintendent of the Cemetery to exclude all persons from the grounds after sundown, or at such other times as may be deemed important." The cemetery had also sunk a well in the south-western part of the grounds for the use of lot proprietors.

Although lots were becoming scarce by the 1860s, Valley Cemetery continued to hold an important place in the city. In 1868, Decoration Day, later known as Memorial Day, was established to honor Civil War veterans. At Valley, where some 120 veterans were buried, processions were held with great numbers of local citizens participating in parades or in laying flowers at the gravesites, according to the Manchester Historical

Association. Schoolchildren decorated the graves with flowers and evergreens, and some sang songs or read poems to the people assembled for the occasion. The Louis Bell Post of the Grand Army of the Republic fired off a twenty-one-gun salute, and local bands played patriotic music.

It was at about this time that the city started to explore the idea of truly landscaping the land in the ravine. In 1864, the committee had reported that "the subject of building an avenue to wind along the bottom of the banks on either side of the brook, has received some attention. It is thought that such an avenue neatly graded and turfed would add to the beauty of this part of the Cemetery. It would supply a large number of lots, otherwise of little value, and increase the revenue sufficiently to outset the outlay at least. We leave the question to our successors to determine whether such an undertaking is advisable." The ravine was roughly fifty to eighty feet wide at the bottom, depending on one's exact location, and roughly 800 feet long, so it was clearly a significant amount of space not currently used for burials.

As the committee was voted in yearly and there was little turnover, the successors for this and the gate project were essentially the same people, and the carriage road or avenue project was soon underway, most of it complete by late 1865. The avenue started at the gate on Chestnut Street, passed the city tomb, and then divided "to the right and left by winding drives along the banks, descending at a rate of ten feet fall to one hundred feet in length, until they reach the bottom land." The balance was nearly level and raised five feet above the general ground level. Overall, the road seems to have been a "loop" one. Drainage pipes were laid along with the avenue. Burial rates at Pine Grove had remained low, and the committee said it would take time to make the new cemetery popular, as opposed to Valley, where "these grounds are already enshrined in the hearts of our people." Lot sales at the Valley remained brisk, and they were still sufficient to support the ongoing work there.

Work on the "New Avenue" was completed in 1867, by which time two "substantial bridges" had been built—apparently avenue bridges. In addition, a resurvey had been made, and a new cemetery plan was being developed. The costs of all this work had just about expended existing Valley funds, but new lot sales along the avenue were expected to refurbish the coffers. Several tombs had recently been added to the cemetery, and lot owners were decorating their holdings in an agreeable manner. Few or no lots were available for sale in Valley Cemetery by 1869, except, it seems, in the ravine, where the committee noted there remained room for several tombs. Additional footbridges and walkways were also constructed at Valley during the era, and by the next decade, a network of paths and carriage roads connected all sections of the cemetery, pedestrian gates had been added along each side of the grounds, and sidewalks now surrounded the cemetery.

The city also undertook further beautification of the valley itself, landscaping the ravine between the two higher sides of the cemetery, the eastern and western hilltops being divided by a one- to two-hundred-foot space across the ravine, depending on one's location. Staircases were built into the sides of the hills, leading down into the ravine. The new walkways or avenues ran along either side of the brook and were surfaced with peastone. The brook itself saw additional work, mainly the addition of stone retaining walls and the creation of at least one "island"—an almost teardrop-shaped island with its own retaining walls. Ornamental shrubs and trees graced the valley, as did, eventually, flowering or trailing plants in flower boxes built into or set upon the side walls of a pedestrian and carriage bridge, and "summer houses" were built at the bottom of the ravine.

Surviving photographs and postcards taken in the ravine show at least two different "summer houses" or gazebos. These had partially open sides, one with a round stone base, stone arches, and a conical roof seemingly finished with tile or shingles in different colors in an alternating pattern. A wooden pedestrian bridge over the brook was near it. The other "summer house" was a more angular building, seemingly with a stone base also, with squared, wooden walls and a dormered roofline.

Photographs taken soon after the turn of the twentieth century show the network of paths in the valley as well as the completed carriage road. One postcard shows railings along the roadway winding down into the valley, and another highlights a stone retaining wall at the base of the western slope. Graves had been added near the base of the slopes, and the ravine as a whole had a wonderful park quality. The entire landscape was meticulously maintained. If the designers of Valley Cemetery had hoped to create an environment the living could enjoy, they had certainly succeeded. Moreover, landscaping the ravine did open up more burial space.

The 800-foot-long ravine at Valley Cemetery has a winding quality that makes it difficult if not impossible to see the entire ravine from one vantage point. Its generally steep walls—forty to eighty feet in height—also make it difficult to see out of the ravine when inside of it. With its winding brook, gazebos, and bridges, as well as its avenue and stone stairways—numbering more than forty steps on the western side—and walkways, the Valley, with its ravine, was unique on the urban landscape in the late 1800s, and it was something special in the garden cemetery movement.

Still, modernity encroached. In late 1871, the committee noted a problem with the increasing Manchester population. "A high and close fence" was needed around the entire cemetery, for, as the committee reported, "the growth of the city in buildings and population in the immediate vicinity of the Valley begins to be felt by those having charge of this ground as a serious and growing inconvenience." The cemetery considered erecting rugged fencing along one or two sides during the coming season, with the balance to follow. An appropriation from the city would be needed for this, as lot sales in the now crowded cemetery could not be expected to cover the expense.

Waterlines were added to Valley Cemetery in 1880, and drinking fountains soon graced the cemetery as well. Water was a great asset to the Valley, but it also became something of a problem as the years passed. Heavy rains caused runoff, and dirt and silt sometimes spilled into the brook. Earlier on, it had caused problems with the new avenue into the ravine. Adding drainage pipes had seemingly resolved that problem, although they may have furthered the problem with the brook.

In 1888, based on ongoing need, the cemetery erected a new receiving tomb. It was a masonry structure built into a hillside just north of the brook, and it was situated, in terms of city streets, "between Chestnut and Pine Streets." As with the tomb at Mount Hope, it was utilized by the entire region, not just for bodies slated for burial at Valley. The new tomb was sixteen by seventeen feet inside, with ten-foot ceilings, and it had racks for seventy-five caskets, according to cemetery records. Two metal doors continue to provide access to the tomb, which is now used primarily for storage. The cemetery removed the old holding tomb after completing the new one.

The new receiving tomb necessitated raising the existing road into the ravine four feet in one area and required new drainage measures. This may have added to the problems with water runoff into the ravine. It was at this point that the cemetery graded the brook's banks "and walled it with stone." A new carriage bridge was also built, and a pedestrian one was moved. Additional "shrubs, plants, and trees" were then "set out." Some "ladies" also asked to have the care of particular lots, and permission was granted to them. The 1880s also saw an enlargement of an existing "lodge-house" to allow an octagonal-shaped office for the superintendent.

However, even after the brook had been lined with stones and drainage completed for the new receiving tomb and carriage roads, the cemetery could not resolve its runoff issues. After a major storm in the early 1900s caused serious erosion along the slopes, the city hauled out load after load of silt from the brook. Erosion and silt continued to be a problem, and the cemetery removed soil from the brook as needed. In 1915, during which there were fifty-four interments at the Valley and money coming in for perpetual care increased, the cemetery "straightened" the brook "the entire way."

Meanwhile, at Pine Grove, things were finally picking up. In early 1888, the committee noted with pride that Pine Grove was meeting their earlier predictions and becoming a preferred place of burial. There had been some recent problems, but work was continued at an incredible rate. At Valley, however, "once an object of rare beauty and full of auspicious hope to a prosperous village just bursting into cityhood," things had declined, such that it was "now suffocated by the growth of a laboring population and the encroachments of mechanical industries," and it seemed some of the lot owners at Valley were looking to Pine Grove for burial needs.

"Monuments of great value and rare artistic beauty" were being erected and vastly enhancing the attractiveness of Pine Grove. It was determined that Pine Grove was where the city should direct most of its money for cemetery needs. Small onsite nurseries were growing plants for the grounds, and by 1909, a greenhouse or two would be added. The existing pond "built" just off Calef Road was completed, thus finally giving the cemetery a water aspect. Little was being done by the city at Valley Cemetery by the 1890s, but many of the lots had come under perpetual care provisions.

By 1894, the garden cemetery movement had spread throughout New England, and that year, the cemetery committee and the city engineer traveled to Boston to tour cemeteries and to look for ways to improve the landscape and increase efficiency at Manchester's cemeteries. They reported that they had met with Superintendent John Barker at Forest Hills Cemetery, and he "escorted [them] over the grounds." They "saw many things that they thought would be a vast improvement if carried out at Pine Grove, especially the grass walks and iron numbers."

The group next visited "Mount Auburn, but there was nothing seen [there] that could be improved" over what they had seen at Forest Hills. They visited the nearby Lowell Cemetery, but it, too, failed to surpass Forest Hills Cemetery. In their eyes, "nothing of importance worthy of mention was seen. On the whole," they thought, "the visits of the Committee should produce some good as it should help them to do some work in better shape and at less expense." One thing they definitely did after the trip was purchase 600 iron markers of the "pattern" they had seen at Forest Hills Cemetery. Some of these may have been used at the Valley, but they seem to have been intended primarily for Pine Grove.

Still, how to balance the popularity of the Valley with the need to shift burials to Pine Grove remained problematic. People continued to request burials at the Valley even though there was simply no room. However, as seen at Mount Hope Cemetery, people who had been able to secure Valley lots did not always pay for them, and sometimes people were buried in unpaid-for lots. This was an ongoing problem, and it also became one at the now more frequently used Pine Grove.

In January 1895, in a rather startlingly action, the committee responsible for both cemeteries voted to have bodies buried on the lots that had not been paid for removed for burial at the public grounds if the lots were not paid for by April 1896. This specific motion may have applied to both cemeteries, but it was at largely focused on Pine Grove. There is no evidence that it ever transpired.

A chapel had been built at Pine Grove by the end of the century, and even though office space was also available at Valley, most meetings of the early 1900s convened at City Hall. A superintendents lodge was also built during the era at Pine Grove—which now boasted 265 acres—as well as greenhouses and other outbuildings.

In 1918, the problem of unpaid-for lots was still not satisfactorily resolved, and the committee voted that those who had "purchased" lots prior to 1861 but who had not yet paid for them were to do so within three months or the lots at Valley would be "removed to the common ground and then be put into the market again for sale." The lots could be expected to sell quickly. It is unclear if some of the lots were already occupied and, if so, the bodies may also have been part of what was under consideration for relocation, much as they had been in 1895. It is unclear if any bodies were moved due to unpaid bills in the 1890s or in the early 1900s.

While some people failed to pay their bills at the Valley as elsewhere, others went out of their way to contribute to the cemetery. In 1907, Hannah A. Currier, the third wife of Governor Moody Currier, paid to replace the original gate designed by Moses W. Oliver at Auburn and Chestnut Streets. The cemetery thankfully received the gift of the new ornamental gates. Hannah Currier donated the granite and wrought iron gateway to honor her late husband, a former governor of New Hampshire as well as a cemetery committee member. Granite urns top the cut stone gateposts, and pedestrian gates open to either side of the vehicle entrance.

The main gate—and the entrance was originally the main gateway to the cemetery, also—is located near the northwestern corner of the cemetery along Auburn Street. It opens onto a downward hill on the right side, as well as the graves of the poor. Almost straight ahead—and perhaps the reason Hannah Currier funded this particular restoration—is the monument to Governor Currier; it is a tall obelisk, and it is the tallest memorial on the grounds. The memorial has a tapered base with stylized pendants where the base and shaft meet, and the lot also has individual granite markers for the governor and his family. In 1914, Hannah Currier also agreed to pay for new iron fencing along Willow Street, after the cemetery made some changes to the brook and the nearby slopes at that location.

In 1915, the Green family likewise made a generous gift. They donated a new gate at Pine Street in memory of builder Stephen D. Green (1806–1880). The gate still stands and, like the Currier gate, it is built of white granite with its posts topped by ornamental urns. It, too, has arched, delicately wrought gates, this time surmounted by the name "Valley," whereas the words "Valley Cemetery" surmount the Currier gates. The bronze plaque notes that the gate was erected for Stephen Green at the bequest of Frank and Sarah Green. However, Eliza Green was also part of the generous gift, donating the money to carry out the wishes of her recently deceased husband, Frank Green, who sought to honor his father, Stephen Green.

In perhaps the last significant building project at Valley Cemetery, in 1932, a stone Gothic-English-revival chapel was constructed, replacing an older wooden chapel or lodge house that had stood at the same site and that was used by the superintendent for some years. Local architect Chase R. Whitcher designed the new irregularly shaped, seam-faced stone edifice, built of uneven-size, varicolored granite stones. The building has narrow buttresses.

The 1932 chapel is "fenestrated with lancet windows framed with Gothic labels," as described by the National Park Service. Above the double-door front entrance an ornate pediment features three carved angels, one reading while the other two kneel in prayer. Above that is a tripartite lancet window "capped by Gothic stone tracery," one essentially duplicated in a barely projecting wing to one side of the chapel, while a small window set high in the rear wall, the apse, has similar stone tracery. A door to the opposite side, facing the Smyth mausoleum, is simpler yet also handsomely detailed. The building cost $12,000 to construct and had electricity, stucco interior walls, and asphalt floor tiles. It was dedicated to Hattie Jenkins York (1855–1934). The new chapel also fell into disrepair in its turn, however, and is currently closed. Soon after the chapel was erected, the cemetery began a slow decline.

The focus of municipal cemetery committees had shifted by the 1910s, but they still maintained an office at Valley Cemetery. The Valley office was used in general by Superintendent E. C. Smith, but it only saw occasional board meetings. In 1918, foreshadowing problems to come, the superintendent had the committee "examine some new fence on Willow Street" and also fencing on Valley Street, calling attention "to the damage done apparently by boys in smashing off the small ornaments thereof." Smith told the men that at one time the staff had picked several hundred of them off the ground. Records for Valley Cemetery are scarce after 1920; however, it is clear that problems continued.

In 1936, the Amoskeag Mill, which had given and sold so much property to the city holdings beyond that of Valley Cemetery, closed its doors. That same year, a major flood damaged much of Manchester's riverfront, and a few years later, in 1938, a hurricane struck New England, damaging and uprooting many of the Valley's mature trees.

A decade-plus later, in the 1950s, continued problems with the brook led to a city decision to essentially redo—or undo—the ravine landscape: it constructed a large, two-chambered culvert to capture the brook's water and buried it underground. The city also removed the gazebos—or summer houses—and the ravine bridges. It then buried the entire bottom of the ravine with backfill. It buried the brook, with its carefully constructed retaining walls and channels, as well as the roots and bases of the trees in the valley. There may have been practical reasons to reroute the brook and cover it over, but the process destroyed the garden cemetery aspects of the ravine. A few photographs taken circa 1959–1960 show the redone valley; a retaining wall seems to have survived along one wall, but little else of the elaborate construction and landscaping of earlier decades remained.

According to the later Friends of Valley Cemetery and some other supporters, the ravine could be redone and could be cleaned and restored, but part of its history, its magical aura, was buried. The upper slopes of the valley and the perimeter remained, and most of the road into the valley survives, but the park-like ravine landscape was destroyed. Responsible renovation may be possible; restoring what it once was is not. You cannot restore what no longer exists. However, the brook can be brought back aboveground, and historic photos could guide some form of refurbishment.

Neglect of the overall cemetery followed. In part, it was financial straits and the demands of maintaining nine municipal cemeteries plus changes in the urban landscape that caused the problems of the 1950s–1960s and thereafter. Some of the mausoleums fell into disrepair, and some retaining walls began to collapse. The city at some point decided to direct storm and wastewater into the valley below the holding tomb, creating additional problems. The double culvert in the ravine had already begun to fail. The later 1900s and early 2000s saw the stench of sewage become a recurring problem, especially in the summer months, according to a group established in the early 2000s.

Vandalism also began to spread by the late 1960s, and in the 1980s, a vandal took an ax to the chapel's back door. Graffiti soon followed. Indigents also made campsites in the valley, and by the 2000s, drugs and possible drug trafficking made an appearance. Things were not good. However, in light of its historic significance, its many surviving memorials, and its general historic integrity, as, among other things, few modern markers are found on the grounds, Valley Cemetery was added to the National Register of Historic Places in 2004.

Manchester is New Hampshire's largest city, and Valley View is a noted green space, but it is one with some obvious problems, within a neighborhood that includes the city jail as well as numerous stores, apartment houses, and small businesses. About twenty wild turkeys make the cemetery their home, as do, it seems, some living human beings. Dogs also visit.

Wild turkeys also enjoy the grounds of Pine Grove Cemetery, which has a much larger acreage and is removed from the city's most congested areas. The occasional fox, deer, and, more rarely, even a moose have been spotted on its grounds. Canada geese regularly visit the pond at Pine Grove during their migrations.

Pine Grove had opened in 1851 to meet growing community burial needs as Valley Cemetery began to reach the end of its available lots for sale. In some ways, Pine Grove seems like an extension—or a daughter—of the Valley. Its Victorian-era funerary art is clustered primarily in one small area, the one where the initial lots were established. Had the city acquired an additional ten acres or so for Valley Cemetery when first advised of the need, Pine Grove might well have a very different character than it does, as might the Valley.

Pine Grove began to really take off in popularity by the early 1900s, by which time there were essentially no lots for sale at Valley. The wealthy started building mausoleums at Pine Grove in the late 1800s, many of them located near the chapel, such that by the twenty-first century, they almost resembled camps around a lake, albeit majestic camps.

Some aspects of the front portion of the cemetery improved greatly after the creation of the aforementioned pond in 1907. *Park and Cemetery* covered the project, noting that its "artificial lake not only adds a very attractive landscape feature to the grounds, but does away with an unsightly spot that had long been an eyesore." The article carried photographs, including one showing the fountain that would entertain humans and wildfowl alike into the next century. The area had been a bog or swampy area. The city appropriated money to dredge the swamp, construct an island in the middle of the new pond, add a fountain, and build small bridges.

Like Valley Cemetery, Pine Grove would come to hold many of the same types of funerary art seen in other garden cemeteries, but it would see proportionally many more statues as well as more mausoleums, whereas the Valley held more of the older-style monuments, as some had been moved there for reinterments and others were more reflective of the early years of the garden cemetery movement. Most of the more noted statues, mausoleums, memorials, and other markers at Pine Grove would be erected in a relatively small section of the newer cemetery, located near the chapel area and the front portions of the cemetery near the main gate. It almost seems as if that one section should be considered a direct extension of the Valley, both in time and in space. Ornamental shrubs and other plants were added, and an avenue was laid around the pond.

A number of New Hampshire governors would seek interment for themselves and their families at Pine Grove as Valley Cemetery began to reach capacity. James Weston, for example, served as governor during the years 1871–1872 and 1874–1875. His background was in civil engineering, but he returned to another of his professions, banking, after his terms as governor. He was buried at Pine Grove following his 1895 death. In comparison to some governors, his marker was less extravagant but still quite stately. There is also a Weston mausoleum at the cemetery.

Another governor of New Hampshire, serving from 1893 to 1895, John Butler Smith, who died in 1914, would have an Egyptian-revival-style mausoleum built at Pine Grove. A white granite mausoleum, it features heavy blocks and resembles, in some ways, the Harrington edifice at the Valley.

Governor Charles Miller Floyd would fall somewhere in the middle of Weston and Smith regarding the ornateness or size of his memorial. He would have a smallish, classic Greek temple or canopy memorial constructed to mark his and his family's remains. The canopy rests on a tiered base, and an urn in the center provides space for ornamental plantings. Floyd served his state in several capacities, including his time as governor from 1907 to 1909. He died in 1921. His memorial is close to the Manning memorial, a large, eight-column, curved colonnade on a tiered base.

However, the Hill mausoleum, slightly removed from many of the others, is perhaps the most commented-upon memorial at Pine Grove, and it is certainly one of the most striking. The gray granite structure is two "stories" high with small columns, decorative archways, and stained glass windows. Similar to the Greek cross format used in the Blood mausoleum at the Valley, its side projections and dormers are rather narrow but of equal length in terms of how far they project, with the center section once again taking up most of the architectural footprint. The dormered doorway features a set of columns flanking the ornate entrance.

There are eighteen private mausoleums at the cemetery as well as a public mausoleum—a structure which most garden cemeteries have added over time. The Carpenter family has two of the mausoleums at the cemetery: one of them is constructed in a more classical design, the other was built more along the lines of the Hill mausoleum, but neither is as tall nor as ornate, except for their doorways.

The older 1800s chapel was replaced at Pine Grove in 1904 by a donation from Ursula Riddle. Her only stipulation was that the bodies of both herself and her mother, Fanny Riddle, be walled up within the new chapel. They were, and a plaque hangs in front of their interment spot. The cemetery held a dedication ceremony for the new chapel on August 15, 1905. Opposite to the resting place of the mother and daughter, the cemetery has made use of a small wing to house the administrative offices of the superintendent, who is in charge of the grounds at Pine Grove, Valley, and the city's other municipal cemeteries.

The original land holdings at Pine Grove were augmented with additional purchases in the 1800s and 1900s. Some 175 acres of the cemetery are currently developed, and another one hundred acres remain undeveloped. Pine Grove has ample room for current and future interments. Pine Grove also has a number of appealing statues, and most of them, like the mausoleums, are clustered close to the chapel. The ornate larger family memorials with statues, so popular in the late 1800s to early 1900s, however, are no longer the norm at Pine Grove or in New England's other rural cemeteries, although the cemetery continues to prosper.

However, as indicated, Valley Cemetery fell into serious disrepair or decline by the late twentieth century. In 2002, to address this issue and rooted in the Southern New Hampshire University's Education Continuum, the Friends of Valley Cemetery was established. The nonprofit community organization was dedicated to the purpose of raising funds to be used to restore Valley Cemetery. Partnered with the city, it raised hundreds of thousands of dollars in grants for restoration projects.

In 2003, the group established a "Strawberry Festival" much like the ones seen in many communities for fundraising purposes in the 1800s. The festival took place in Valley Cemetery. Other activities followed, and the Friends had the cemetery designated as an arboretum, something the managers of the mid-1800s would have greatly appreciated. The University of New Hampshire printed a walking tour pamphlet of the cemetery trees, complete with descriptions of the twenty-nine species found among the cemetery's 350 "significant trees," as identified in 2002. Small plaques were added to the trees identifying their common and Latin names, and these remain in place; hence, the Valley is also an arboretum. In 2004, as one of the Friends' initial projects, the Currier Gate was restored. That same year, Valley Cemetery was added to the National Register of Historic Places.

However, the impetus for restoring the cemetery, and the funding, soon ran out. The project, after making some important improvements, fell by the wayside. By the 2010s, complaints were coming in about the burial grounds being used for drug transactions and drug activities such as shooting up heroin. Graffiti defaced some monuments and buildings, while other monuments, mainly smaller ones, were destroyed or allowed to decay. In addition, homeless people made use of the cemetery as a place to find shelter; they were not necessarily a direct threat to the grounds but something the cemetery was not created to encompass. If nothing else, the lack of restrooms and trash receptacles would indicate one unsanitary aspect of the practice.

Then, in 2017, another movement was underway to clean up the Valley and to return it to its historic use as a place of beauty where the living could enjoy nature, visit the resting places of the dead, and admire cemetery monuments without fear. Motor vehicles and bicycles are forbidden at the cemetery, and walking is therefore encouraged. Local citizens came out for cleanup days, and the cemetery seemed to be back on track. However, the city's now combined cemetery and parks department noted that it simply did not have the funding needed to maintain its cemeteries at the level some people might desire without substantially raising city taxes. Improvements above the minimum would seemingly have to depend on the public for funding and execution.

The author received more than one warning about the possible danger of going to the grounds alone in late winter and summer 2018, and although there were no major issues, she would advise other visitors to go with another person, and during daylight hours. She could not tell exactly what a couple of groups of people she saw were doing in the cemetery when she visited, but they were not touring the grounds. There are indeed people using the grounds for shelter, and there is associated litter. The cemetery crew that maintains numerous cemeteries is unable to keep up with the nighttime residents of the cemetery, as well as the daytime visitors who are there for other reasons than to enjoy the vista. Hopefully, the future will prove brighter.

However, Valley Cemetery is worth visiting even now; just be careful. And look at the trees as well as the monuments and stairways. There is still great beauty at the Valley, even though some of it has been buried.

Also, drive over to Pine Grove Cemetery. "The Daughter of the Valley" holds some wonderful monuments and mausoleums, and Ursula and her mother remain entombed in the walls of the chapel, which has been "certified" as haunted. At Pine Grove, one can walk freely from dawn to dusk, and there are miles of avenue to explore.

Sources for the history of Valley View are scarce, but you might enjoy and glean more information from the Manchester Historic Association and the online articles of Aurore Eaton. Manchester municipal sites and Wikipedia contain some information, although that information is essentially the same, sometimes word for word. See also local newspapers on the revitalization actions from 2002–2017 and Across New Hampshire Patch. The most thorough source of information, however, is the Manchester City Archives at City Hall, as well as the office of the superintendent of municipal cemeteries at Pine Grove Cemetery. The "Master Plan for Valley Cemetery" is also useful, and it seems to rely heavily on the Historical Association's records for its history sections. The 2004 Registration Form for the National Register of Historic Places provides a great amount of detail on many of the markers as well as some basic background information. Park and Cemetery *carried an article in 1907 about Pine Grove, and made a few other mentions over the years.*

5

Between the Walls

Springfield Cemetery, Springfield, Massachusetts

When you first approach Springfield Cemetery, entering through the main gate, you may think, "Oh no, modernity has truly encroached here. Even the main gates are squashed in between two big apartment buildings." But go through those gates, and suddenly the buildings, smaller ones, are visible only on one side; go a bit farther, and the apartments and other buildings are lost. And then a valley opens up, and you see greens or golds or whites and browns, depending upon the season. Look above you, and you will see that this is indeed a cemetery. Natural hillsides and landscaped terraces serve as gravesites, while the valley itself remains largely open.

SPRINGFIELD CEMETERY, ESTABLISHED IN 1841, WAS AMONG THE FIRST cemeteries in America, perhaps *the* first, to incorporate a long "approach" in its original design. Mount Hope in Maine, the second recognized American garden cemetery, does have a long open space on one side after you enter its gates, and in actuality, Springfield has only a long enclosed approach. However, there are no graves on either side of the Springfield approach, just distant buildings to the left beyond a small rock wall and, to the right, a hill with a steep-walled incline, which together create almost a tunnel feeling on "Cemetery Lane," as the approach is called. The approach, however, may have been the result as much of property acquisitions as it was of landscape design. Either way, Cemetery Lane soon opens onto a valley. Unfortunately, although it remains beautiful in and of itself, as with the ravine at Manchester's Valley Cemetery, something is missing here.

Springfield is essentially the third or fourth garden cemetery in New England—or the fifth, if the New Haven Burial Ground is included in the list. Springfield was in the planning stage at the same time as Valley Cemetery but held its dedication ceremony a couple of months later. Containing only forty acres, it is one of the smaller—though by no means the smallest—of the early garden cemeteries.

It might be easy to overlook Springfield for a larger Massachusetts garden cemetery such as Forest Hills—established in Boston in 1848 and now containing 275 acres—or for a few others in the eastern part of the state. However, Springfield Cemetery has qualities beyond its size and early date that make it a good inclusion here: it is an ongoing private-proprietorship garden cemetery; it embraces another, more distant part of the state than Mount Auburn and the other Boston-area ones; and it has other unique attributes, to be discussed herein, including that long approach.

After the establishment of Mount Auburn in Massachusetts and Mount Hope in Maine in the early 1830s, the garden or rural cemetery movement was on. Springfield Cemetery opened in 1841, as did Valley Cemetery of New Hampshire (with its daughter cemetery, Pine Grove, opening in 1851). The Albany Rural Cemetery of New York would open in 1844; Swan Point Cemetery in Providence, Rhode Island, opened in 1846. In 1854, Mount Green would open in Montpelier, Vermont, and in 1856, Evergreen Cemetery would open in Portland, Maine, as well as Brookside Cemetery in Watertown, New York, and Elm Grove Cemetery in Mystic, Connecticut. In 1866, Cedar Hill Cemetery would open in Hartford, Connecticut, while Lakeview Cemetery opened in 1871 in Burlington, Vermont. These cemeteries, along with some discussion of a unique transitional cemetery in Barre, Vermont, established near the close of the century (and that of the much earlier transitional New Haven Burial Grounds), constitute the garden cemeteries of New England discussed at length herein.

However, other garden or rural cemeteries did open in New England and New York during the era, and some of these will be discussed in the conclusion. Outside of New England, Laurel Hill Cemetery opened in Philadelphia, Pennsylvania, in 1836, and Green Mount Cemetery in Baltimore, Maryland, in 1838. By the mid-1840s, garden cemeteries were starting to appear in the upper South and the Midwest, followed by other regions of the nation. The birthplace of the garden cemetery in America, however, was definitely New England and the Northeast.

Springfield Cemetery opened in 1841. Its site was originally known as Martha's Dingle, a location with hills, ravines, and brooks, which served as a natural bird sanctuary. The land included roughly twenty acres. A surviving 1891 letter from landscape designer William Elliot reports that the land was originally "a steep-sided and branching hollow drained by several brooklets and shaded by fine forest trees." It had several advantageous features, and more land would soon be added. The "dingle"—a dingle being a small, deep, wooded valley—and its surrounds had once belonged to Martha Ferre, hence the name Martha's Dingle. Ferre had sold the land to Alexander Bliss to raise a dowry, according to the most prevalent story.

According to a short history written by the cemetery proprietors in 1857, "On the 4th of October, 1840, an informal meeting of a group of gentlemen was held for consultation on the subject of a 'rural cemetery.'" This informal meeting led to a formal group being established to investigate the possibility further and to form an association to prepare a report for the association. The association then voted to acquire the twenty-acre property from Bliss. The association secured legal access for the land, and in early May, they secured a "warrant" to hold an organizational meeting on May 9. According to one source, the desire to secure a new burial site had been voiced as early as 1833. By 1840, the community at Springfield held about 10,000 living people, and its graveyard was overflowing with the dead.

On May 9, 1841, the association adopted a new organization with seven trustees, including a president. The first president was Unitarian Minister William B. O. Peabody, who had long advocated that Springfield establish a new cemetery. Peabody remained the president until his death in 1847. The new organization, a proprietorship, decided to raise money through subscription, and to that end, it charged $10 for each share in the cemetery organization and was able to raise more than $3,000 by June 1. Shareholders were to have a share in the lots laid out, according to the number of shares they had purchased.

With some of the money raised, the proprietors started laying out and improving the grounds. Early improvements included planting ornamental flora, fencing the grounds, and grading as needed. Fountains were also added. Apollos Marsh served as superintendent for at least the first sixteen years of the cemetery's existence and added greatly to the layout work, according to cemetery documents. A 1991 essay written by Donald J. D'Amato credits Peabody and portrait painter Chester Harding with overseeing the work and doing much of the planting themselves. Artist John James Audubon also may have helped with the planning, according to D'Amato, as Audubon stayed with Peabody a few times in 1840 and 1842 while selling subscriptions to his own "elephant folio." Peabody and Audubon certainly shared an interest in birds and nature, and they may well have shared a roof for brief periods.

Either way, on March 28, 1841, the founding members of the Springfield Cemetery had voted to purchase the land from Alexander Bliss, and six months later, on September 5, the new cemetery was dedicated. The grounds were consecrated by religious services, and the president of the association, Reverend Peabody, delivered "an appropriate address." A great number of people attended the dedication, and Peabody stated that when he saw so many people "winding up through the glades of the cemetery," he was affected by the thought of "how soon we will take our places in the dust below." Reverence for the dead was in the heart of every person, he said, and at Springfield Cemetery, they had found a worthy place to lay their dead. The local population had grown substantially and had long needed a worthy place for burials, he reiterated. As if to emphasize the need, a child was buried at the cemetery the day after the dedication. Reflecting Peabody's long involvement with the cemetery, local people would often refer to the cemetery as "Peabody's Cemetery" in the following years.

The proprietors purchased additional grounds over the years, such that the cemetery consisted of thirty-five acres at a total cost of $8,271 in 1857. The newly acquired property included a house adjoining the burial grounds on Mulberry Street in 1848, purchased for the use of the superintendent, and a barn was soon added. Also, the board secured a six and a half–acre lot formerly known as Peach Orchard on the southern side of the cemetery, as it was currently supposed that it was the only direction in which the cemetery could possibly expand. That land was held in reserve for future burials, and until that time, it would only be planted with some shrubbery and trees before eventually being laid out with paths and drives.

The cemetery set regulations as early as 1841. These included forbidding visitors from picking flowers or firing guns. Visitors were not allowed to bring in wagons during some years, and they were not to stray off the paths and roadways.

The cemetery erected a receiving tomb in 1841. Located at the edge of the valley and built into the hillside near the end of Cemetery Lane, it was subsequently found to be too small, and several years later, the cemetery doubled its holding capacity. It would be used primarily for storage in the twenty-first century, and it had sunk into the ground somewhat over the years.

In addition to beautifying and expanding the grounds over the years, the association also decided to have a suitable gateway constructed along Maple Street. The trustees voted to do so in March 1845. Reverend Peabody designed the gateway. The sandstone gate was meant to symbolize the division between life and death, between the "city of the living" and the "city of the dead." Peabody had already developed a plan for the gates, and the association proceeded to secure estimates on the cost of building it. The gateway's construction started, and the entrance it covered became the official one for the cemetery. However, for unknown reasons, construction costs far exceeded what was expected. In 1857, trustee and board president George Bliss could only say that it had involved "great expense," but other than that, he had no explanation. At one point, a new builder was brought in to finish the project, at a cost not to exceed $300. The newest work was soon suspended, however, and the gateway remained incomplete in early 1857. Peabody's arch may have never been totally finished, but it did serve as the cemetery's official entryway for decades.

Bodies were originally carried under the archway into the cemetery by pallbearers, followed by mourners on foot, the Maple Street entrance being close enough to the center of town to make this feasible. A black-and-white photograph dated circa 1905 captured the beauty of the fairly simple Gothic gateway with ivy growing on portions of it with its main arched entrance for vehicles or horses flanked by smaller pedestrian arches. The so-called arch overall, however, was not a simple rounded entrance-way, but rather it was a rectangular one in a medieval style with "towers" above the walkways. Meanwhile, many people continued to use the entrance off Pine Street, as the superintendent's house was located closer to that entrance, as was a greenhouse. This led some of the proprietors to complain about the "back" entrance being used as the "main" entrance. This dual entryway situation was not limited to Springfield Cemetery, however.

Meanwhile, besides purchasing new property and building a gateway, the cemetery acquired more bodies—thousands of them—and not just original interments. In 1848, the trustees entered an agreement with the First Parish of Springfield to remove remains from their burial grounds on Elm Street, property fronting the Connecticut River, in exchange for that property. The cemetery was to remove any remains not claimed and moved by family or friends of the deceased. The disinterments were to be done "carefully" and then moved to a section specifically laid out for them at the new cemetery near Pine Street. Any old monuments were to be moved with the bodies. Hundreds of them are still located near the upper Pine Street gate, many of them featuring smiling death heads or winged cherub heads, and some have hourglasses, like those seen in New Haven's Grove Street Cemetery, most of them of sandstone or brownstone.

The disinterments and reinterments took place that same year, 1848, and a ceremony was held to mark the occasion. Some 1,624 bodies were moved from the "old North Burying ground" and another 810 bodies from "the South Burying grounds," for a total of 2,404. Thirty of the bodies were reinterred elsewhere. Just over 500 monuments were also moved. All remains that did not have monuments or were not otherwise identified were buried in a mass grave, two "common graves," or, at least, "together," according to cemetery sources, with a common monument built for them. A hedge to honor them was also planted. The transfer of the bodies meant that Springfield Cemetery, in effect, became the resting place of many of the region's seventeenth- and eighteenth-century pioneers.

THE DEAD SHALL BE RAISED

Built in the early 1840s at the 1796 New Haven Burying Grounds or Grove Street Cemetery in New Haven. Connecticut, this sandstone, Egyptian style gateway would be one of the more substantial of the garden cemetery gateways, and gateways would be important for many of the cemeteries, although they would range greatly in style and building materials.

This simple arch at New Haven highlights the emerging desire to create aesthetically appealing memorials, and the benches seen around it highlight that as well as the desire to make cemeteries comfortable for the living. There are a number of stone benches in this cemetery as in others.

Seen here at Grove Street is one the "zinkies" which would become increasingly popular. This is a fairly ornate one, complete with a statue, as would be one at Mount Hope in Maine, with, fittingly, a version of *Hope* seen as its statue. This one marks the passage of a child and includes symbols associated with the death of a child or young person. Grove Street would come to hold many of the same types of memorials as would the garden cemeteries proper.

Built of granite at Mount Auburn Cemetery in Cambridge and Watertown, Massachusetts in the 1840s, the Egyptian style gateway is a celebrated one. Its design and a wooden prototype were in place in the 1830s. Its orb with snakes on the overhanging cornice is an especially fine rendering, and the gateway is 60 feet long.

Entitled *Grief*, the Thatcher Magoun marble memorial features a woman comforting a young girl at Mount Auburn. Variations of this theme are seen in a few of the garden cemeteries, including Swan Point, Cedar Hill, Albany Rural, and Springfield Cemeteries. The Cheesebro memorial at Elm Grove Cemetery features a woman comforting and reading to a young boy, both of them dressed in Victorian apparel.

One of the most recognized memorials at Mount Auburn, the Sphinx was donated and designed by Joseph Bigelow and dedicated to those who helped abolish slavery in the United States.

The Washington Tower sits on the highest point at Mount Auburn and is fully accessible during the summer season. The tower is granite and 70 feet tall, with a granite circular staircase leading to a galley on top which offers a stunning view over the cemetery and the region.

The Mary Baker Eddy memorial at Mount Auburn is one of grandest open temple memorials in the New England garden cemeteries, with flights of stairs on each side leading down to the pond below.

The James Bartlett family memorial at Mount Auburn features one of the child models the author calls "Florence" and who has seemingly had "her" image rendered on statues in the various cemeteries. This particular marker is larger than most, and includes two lamb carvings, a classic symbol for children's memorials. This is one of the more complex renditions of the type.

The Francis Calley Gray memorial features one of the most moving dog statues at Mount Auburn Cemetery. Dogs are found in other cemeteries also, generally portrayed as loyal guardians of the graves of their people who have passed away. A number of dog statues are located at Green Mount Cemetery in Vermont. Some such statues, however, also commemorate the dogs themselves.

When walking through Mount Auburn, statues seems to appear almost like magic from the luxurious landscape, with paths frequently crossing and providing glimpses of new marvels just around the bend or across the way. These two are the Louie and Dutton statues.

The Neoclassical sarcophagus of Henry Wadsworth Longfellow continues to attract visitors at Mount Auburn although it is one of the simpler memorials. Longfellow has his marker here, as do a number of family members on the same lot.

The One Hundred Steps at Mount Hope are seen here, although the true number of them may not show. This set leads up the front of Cemetery Hill, another set, about half as long, leads down one side of the hill, while yet a third set leads up a smaller hillside further back in the cemetery. Swan Point Cemetery in Rhode Island also has a noted set of steps of its own, equally enticing, the Forty Steps that lead to the Seekonk River.

The Grand Army of the Republic or Fort Memorial is one of the most visited sites at Mount Hope. Built at the turn of the twentieth century, the fort has canons and flags, as well as graves of men who died in or as a result of the Civil War. This is one of three Civil War memorials at Mount Hope; the first was built while the war was ongoing, and the third was added in the 1960s, with a bronze angel bearing a loft a wounded man.

The often photographed Classical open temple, white granite, Amanda Skofield memorial at Mount Hope was built in 1927, and is inscribed for her.

Seen from the valley below, the Smyth mausoleum at Valley Cemetery, built for New Hampshire Governor Frederick Smyth, remains beautiful but has suffered from graffiti in recent years, while the valley itself has become overgrown. A flock of wild turkeys makes its home there.

The Egyptian Revival white granite mausoleum at Valley Cemetery also sits near the edge of the ravine, but faces the upper level of the cemetery at an angle. The French memorial is seen just in front of it, as is, unseen, the cemetery chapel.

The family lot at Valley Cemetery for Governor Moody Currier features a soaring obelisk, a Classical monument common in the garden cemeteries in the 1800s. These are seen in all of the cemeteries covered herein, especially in Brookside, Elm Grove, and Mount Hope Cemeteries.

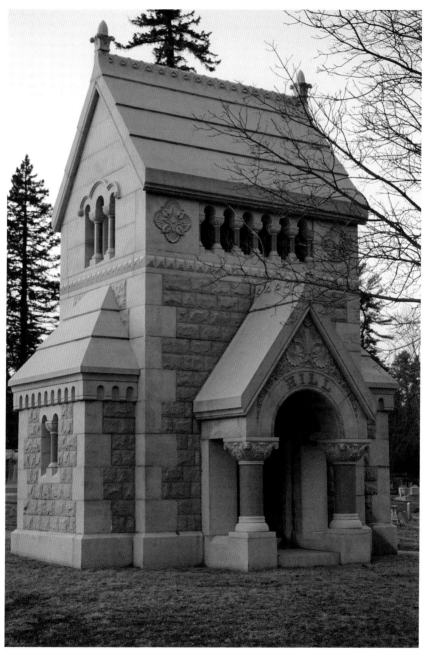

The Hill Mausoleum at Pine Grove Cemetery, which is, in essence, in its historical section, an extension of Valley Cemetery, is one of the most appealing and unique mausoleums of the many located there, or, indeed, in the garden cemetery mausoleums throughout New England.

Springfield Cemetery, like Valley Cemetery, is located in a major downtown area, but, with a long approach on one side, and a varied terrain, it too holds quiet areas and is much worth exploring. Seen here are one of three gateways, the eastern gateway.

One of the most remarked upon memorials at Springfield Cemetery is that erected for Winthrop and Elizabeth Fuller. The bronze figure emerging from the doorway faces a hillside upon the edge of which rests the cemetery chapel and a memorial to the Civil War.

The Soldier Rest Memorial sits atop one of the lower ledges at Springfield Cemetery. Donated to the cemetery, its style is similar to those found in a number of garden cemeteries, including those at Albany Rural and Evergreen.

The Case marker at Springfield illustrates another Classical statuary type found in a few of the garden cemeteries, including Elm Grove: a male angel, some with and some without wings, carrying a trumpet or other horn instrument.

The Prescott memorial at Springfield features a female in mourning, one hand crossed over her breast with the other hand holding flowers, in this case lilies.

The Hilton mausoleum at Albany Rural features an amazing bronze bas-relief covering its face. The sculpture portrays the Angel of Death giving poppies to a warrior.

The Burden tomb at Albany Rural was built into one of the ridges and features superb stonework and retriever dog statues mounted above the pillars that flank the doorway.

The Burden book memorial is made of marble and so large that steps are provided so that the visitor might climb them to look down at the book. The book, like the family vault, faces the Hudson River.

The 1868 Banks *Angel at the Sepulcher* is one of the most noted memorials at Albany Rural. The marble male angel has been heralded for its artistry, and its unique characterization for its day. A similar male angel is found at Cedar Hill Cemetery, where the angel sits at the top of a long exedra bench, one of a few at the cemetery.

The Dalton circular cinerarium of white Vermont granite at Albany Bural Cemetery holds the cremains of the Dalton family and with its Corinthian columns is one of the more remarkable buildings of its type in New England.

President Chester Arthur chose to be buried at his family's lot at the Albany Rural Cemetery. His large black granite sarcophagus marker does not actually hold his body—nor do the sarcophagus markers found in the other garden cemeteries hold those of the deceased, although some, like Arthur's, are certainly large enough to have done so. Wide stone steps lead up to the memorial, which is guarded by its bronze angel.

The Meyers book angel located near Willow Pond is another piece of bronze funerary work found at Albany Rural. Like that at the Chester memorial and another one at the Parson's memorial nearby, the Myers angel is larger-than-life, and she stands between the open pages of a granite book.

The Masonic broken column at Albany Rural marks an organizational burial lot. Broken columns tend to symbolize a life cut short. Sometimes they are draped with "cloth" although this substantial column is not. Individual stones for Masons spiral out from the memorial on its tiered base.

Hundreds of stones were moved with the bodies. The oldest stone, according to current records, was that of Mary Holyoke, who died in 1857 and whose remains purportedly crumbled to dust when she—and possibly her husband—were being disinterred. Her remains are quite likely not the only ones to have suffered this effect, either at Springfield or in other cities where the dead were moved to new locations. In some instances, remains were not even located.

According to D'Amato, proprietor George Bliss oversaw the movement of the bodies and stones to their new location. As D'Amato wrote, seemingly referencing a cemetery source, "Workmen, moving slowly in a line across the grounds, probed the sandy soil with long poles. The dirt was also carefully sifted. These remains were of ancestors—the founders of Western Massachusetts—they were considered sacred." As elsewhere, some of the bodies may have been left behind.

The trustees calculated the cost of moving the old remains and used that as the price paid for the old burial grounds: $2,046. The cemetery then sold the old grounds off in a number of parcels, which by 1857 had generated a $5,098 profit. The scope of what acquiring and moving the old remains meant can be seen in the fact that in addition to those 2,404 reinterments, the cemetery had sold just 730 lots in the sixteen years since it opened. Springfield Cemetery also reinterred 220-plus additional bodies. Altogether, from the reinterments, regular burials by the superintendent, and a few burials by local clergy, there had been a total of 4,213 burials in the first sixteen years. Included with the total sum, the cemetery had buried 170 people classified as "principally paupers and strangers" on "the common ground owned by the cemetery."

Springfield Cemetery was to all appearances on solid financial ground in May 1857, even with its many improvements and expenses to date. New lots were approved for development in 1857, and the trustees were authorized to purchase additional lands for cemetery use should such property become available. A monument to William Peabody, who had done so much for the cemetery, was recommended, the memorial to be placed in a prominent place. George Bliss, in the 1857 history, credited Peabody as being essentially the founder of the cemetery as well as its steadfast friend. He also acknowledged the work of George Eaton, Esq., who had also worked hard on laying out and ornamenting the grounds and to whom, with Peabody, the cemetery was "mainly indebted for the great beauty of the drives and winding walks and fountains which elicit the admiration of all strangers, and constitute this cemetery the pride of our citizens."

Peabody died in Europe in 1847, and his body is interred there, but a memorial was erected for him at Springfield. Dedicated in 1861, an estimated 3,000 people attended the ceremony. The monument is located next to the chapel. It is of a Gothic "architectural" style with pilasters and columns and an ornate canopy, and it is made of "soft yellow-tint freestone" imported from Nova Scotia. Jacob W. Mould of New York City designed the memorial, and its "soft" nature makes it appear almost wooden in photographs, although it has stood up well over time.

The cemetery continued to prosper as a private cemetery. It acquired small parcels of land and reached its present size, thirty-nine and a half acres, by 1866. It continued to make improvements, including adding or developing fountains and small ponds and brooks that no longer exist. Like the stream that had run through the ravine at Valley Cemetery, these were later piped under the surface or simply removed. A surviving ink drawing of the history of Springfield by William Clogston shows a Victorian couple, the woman with a parasol opened above her and the man sporting a top hat, walking over a wooden bridge in the cemetery, with trees lining the brook below. The drawing is labeled, "The Bridge," and it seems to be of the same bridge captured in a photograph circa 1906.

In 1885, according to cemetery records, Dorcas Chapin, widow of Chester W. Chapin—a noted businessman and US representative from 1875 to 1877—donated funds for the construction of a cemetery chapel. It was created in the English Gothic style of East Longmeadow sandstone—the same stone Peabody's gate had been built with—and Milford pink granite. It still contains original stained glass windows from the L. C. Tiffany Company of New York City. The Dorcas Chapin Chapel can seat fifty people and is located at the edge of the slope overlooking the valley, the front of it obscured by the trees from most vantage points. In 1908, the cemetery added a crematorium to the chapel. The Chapin family also has an impressive memorial on the eastern side of the cemetery.

In 1887, the cemetery dedicated its Soldier's Rest Civil War Memorial. Located near the chapel, the monument depicts a Union private cast in bronze standing at rest. Graves of fallen soldiers—at least 200 Civil War veterans are buried in the cemetery, according to one source—surround the monument, and some are buried at the base of the nearby slope. Local women, who had earlier formed the Soldier's Rest Association to help support returning veterans and their families, provided the money for the memorial. They used surplus from the funds to commission the statue. The monument once had four canons, which were melted at the armory during World War II.

Later in the century one of the board members contacted a noted design architect to see what else might be done to improve the grounds. The cemetery was running out of suitable interment space by 1890 and wanted to determine the best way to proceed with laying out any future lots.

The proprietors wrote to Charles Elliot, born in 1859 in Cambridge, Massachusetts, whose family also had ties to Maine and other New England states. Elliot's grandfather, Samuel Atkins Derby, and two of his other immediate forebears had been among the earliest members of the Massachusetts Horticultural Society, the society that had incorporated in 1829 and helped establish Mount Auburn Cemetery in 1831. By 1890, Elliot referred to himself as a landscape architect, a term only introduced in America with the development of garden cemeteries and public parks and closely tied to events in the New England and the Northeast. Elliot's career reflects the development of the field.

In 1869, Elliot's mother had died, and soon thereafter, his father became the president of Harvard University. Elliot later entered Harvard University, developed an interest in lighthouses, and in Mount Desert Island in Maine. He even wrote a short history of Mount Desert as well as sketching several New England lighthouses and writing about them.

Elliot had a great appreciation of the outdoors, and he learned of developments in landscape design from a neighbor of his uncle in Brookline, that neighbor being the renowned Frederick Law Olmsted. Elliot's grandfather was himself an architect and did business with Olmsted from time to time. Elliot was uncertain as to just what the new profession of a landscape architect would entail, but he decided that it would suit his tastes and skills. Therefore, he began a series of studies, some of which were undertaken at the Harvard Department of Horticulture and Agriculture.

Elliot's father spoke with Olmsted about which courses might best prepare young Charles, and Elliot was able to meet Olmsted in person on April 22, 1883. Olmsted offered Elliot an apprenticeship at his offices, which Elliot accepted, leaving his university studies. Olmsted was then about sixty years old and had had a hand in many of the major public park and related developments in the nation, including co-designing Central Park in New York City. Elliot accompanied Olmstad to various sites, and he wrote correspondence and did drafting work for Olmsted. Elliot also worked with other designers at the firm.

In early 1884, Elliot realized that there was not always sufficient work to keep himself and "Mr. J. C. Olmsted" busy at the office. They were currently working on a project involving Boston's Back Bay, and Elliot used any spare time to continue his book studies and for outdoor excursions. On April 1, 1885, he noted that he was done with drafting and ended his apprenticeship. He remained in contact with Olmsted, however, and other Olmsted associates would design some of America's garden cemeteries during the nineteenth century.

Elliot traveled widely in the mid-1880s, studying his craft in America and in Europe. He studied buildings, parks, and public places of all sorts. Elliot would return to America to work in the private sector, consult on public parks both large and small, and become involved in the movement for public reserves. In 1902, his son would publish his "memoirs," including many of his design plans, letters, and reports, with a small amount of biographical material mixed in. Olmsted himself had urged Elliot to write about his work, and write he would.

When Elliot returned from Europe in 1886, he set up his own offices in Boston, and it was there that the letter from Springfield Cemetery reached him. Dated June 27, 1891, the return letter from Elliot to the cemetery provides a contemporary view of the Springfield Cemetery as seen through a designer's eyes, as well as providing some factual information about the cemetery, then almost fifty years old. The introduction to Elliot's answer, seemingly written or edited by his son, states that

Springfield had been "one of the earliest of the American garden cemeteries, and had at the beginning a very diversified surface and many fine forest trees." Moreover, Elliot's advice had been "conservative, yet it outlined a distinct policy for the future, which would in time produce valuable results."

Elliot wrote to the cemetery in June 1891 that he had "studied the condition and circumstances" of the cemetery. He had toured the grounds with a board member and had made a few suggestions while there. He also noted that over the years the land had been "terraced and sold as lots; until there is now but little ground belonging to the corporation, except such as is either too wet or too steep for burial purposes." Existing roads and avenues easily reached what usable burial land remained. He would have liked to have seen some different lines in the existing roads—perhaps he meant the upper-level ones that were grid-like, similar to the avenues at New Haven—but too many graves now surrounded them to change their courses significantly.

In general, Elliot wrote, the cemetery was so hemmed in by existing conditions and graves that there was little it could do to improve things. However, more low shrubbery might be planted, especially on the upper-level portions where many monuments "stand close together, and tend to remind one of a stone-cutter's yard." This was not a very flattering statement, but many of the smaller cemeteries did bury people closer to one another than some landscape artists might prefer. Moreover, the early garden cemeteries, which Springfield had been, had operated without an historical guide.

Elliot also recommended that the cemetery plant periwinkle or moneywort in shady places where the grass was not faring well and that "masses of shade-loving bushes . . . [as] shrubs used intelligently will add variety and interest." Wilder plants might be used along some of the steeper banks.

Most of the work that still remained was "to be in the perfecting of the cemetery on its present lines." Moreover, speaking from a time and perspective that did not exist when Springfield Cemetery and other early garden cemeteries were founded, Elliot could look to the newly established public parks in America and write that the proprietors at Springfield should keep in mind that "the resort to the cemetery is hereafter to be chiefly for its quiet and peacefulness. Your new parks will draw away the mere holiday-makers. You should, I think, do all that may be possible to emphasize the retired and restful character of the place." Therefore, the cemetery should "avoid all appearance of endeavoring to make a show."

As part of this emphasis on the quiet beauty of the place and its perhaps overcrowded character in a few spots, Springfield cemetery should also "obtain and preserve in the hollows the greatest possible extent [lawns] of uninterrupted turf. These hollows are too wet for graves," Elliot wrote. "I would put in new lots in any and all of the other available places, before I should permit a single lot within the valleys. Indeed, I hope they may never be permitted there." It appears this advice was heeded, as more than one hundred years later, the valley remains largely undisturbed by graves except for a few along its edges.

Elliot recommended that existing banks be graded, as they currently resembled "railroad banks." Shrubbery should be added along "the brink of the hollow slopes, and the moist levels of the bottoms should be preserved as rich and unbroken sheets of greensward." Leaving the valley unbroken would make it the focal point of the cemetery, upon which visitors would "look with pleasure and relief." Everything to keep the sight lines clear should be done. This included removing a few paths across the area near the fountain basin (they were removed, as the fountain would eventually be) as well as some flower gardens and leaving the valley free of shrubbery with only overhanging trees from the banks above to frame the green space. No currently reserved lands were to be sold for gravesites.

Elliot also recommended that some other, unoccupied ground be left to simple grass, with possibly some framing trees. The road near the main entrance should be set "into the hill," as he had suggested when he visited. It seems as though the main entrance has not moved appreciably since its establishment, however.

Elliot summed up his letter by saying that he did not think the cemetery needed to do much in the future other than those things he had proposed. The cemetery was nearing its occupation capacity, but it had been "endowed by Nature with an unusually interesting shape and character." What the cemetery truly needed was not a good landscape architect but a good superintendent. He would be glad to consult with a cemetery superintendent.

It is unknown if Elliot ever returned to the cemetery or had further communication with the board or staff. He died in March 1897 in Hartford, Connecticut, where he had been working on plans for a public park. The cause of death was diagnosed as cerebral meningitis, while his mentor, Frederick Law Olmsted, was hospitalized elsewhere for quite different reasons. Neither man lived to see the new century.

It seems that the cemetery has not greatly changed since Elliot toured the grounds and made his suggestions in 1891. The valley remains a focal point of the cemetery, although there are noted memorials and such on the grounds also. The cemetery currently contains forty acres, and thus the proprietors were right in 1857 when they felt they would not be able to secure much additional land. A new gateway was, however, built after Elliot's time. Three gates currently exist at Springfield cemetery, one on each of the three streets along which the irregular-shaped cemetery has frontage: Maple Street, Pine Street, and Cedar Street. Two have fairly ornate posts and surround walls. Each has iron gates. One is not currently open to the public. In some places, the cemetery still has cobblestone roadways.

Springfield Cemetery has many interesting monuments besides those already mentioned. It has the whole array of statuary art seen in other garden cemeteries, although some are more limited in number or fame. It has its share of simple yet tall obelisks, urn-topped monuments—both shrouded and un-shrouded—"architectural" memorials, table monuments, a few mausoleums, and angels and figures of mourning in various guises.

One of the most intriguing memorials in the cemetery is that of a shrouded bronze figure walking through a stone doorway, holding a rose or other flower. The marker is dedicated to Winthrop and Elizabeth Fuller. The memorial was sculpted by Heinrich Waderé and installed in Springfield in 1910. Located at the base of the hill on which the Soldier's Rest Memorial and the chapel are located, the larger-than-life figure faces the hill and not the valley that opens behind it. The memorial has an exedra wall flanking the figure and doorway with pilasters and steps that the figure is posed stepping down.

Near the Fuller memorial is a now headless statue of a young angel that attracts the eye on the Southworth lot. The head and most of the wings have been broken off the statue; indeed, the small bits of wings are visible only from behind. A number of other markers are located on the site.

Also near the Fuller memorial is the Morgan family monument, created by Henri-Michel-Antoine Chapu in the late nineteenth century. It features a bronze bas-relief of a seated woman, seemingly holding a shroud aloft, with a stack of books at her feet. The "face" of the memorial is turned away from the valley, and the marker is shadowed by trees.

Farther down the valley from the headless child and the Fuller memorial is the Josiah Gilbert Holland memorial. Created by Augustus Saint-Gaudens in 1881, the memorial features a bas-relief portrait of Holland by the well-known sculptor and the Latin inscription *Et vitam impendere vero*, or "to devote life to truth."

Holland was a novelist and poet who published under the name Timothy Titcomb. He also helped found *Scribner's Monthly* with Charles Scribner and Roswell Smith. Holland served as the journal's first editor starting in 1870. Holland had started out in a poor family, worked in a factory to help support his family, and then put himself through medical school before entering practice in Springfield. Although his early years as a writer proved difficult, it diverted him from his medical career. He soon married Elizabeth Luna Chapin, and the couple moved away to teach.

Writing continued to call to Holland, and he returned to Massachusetts to edit the *Springfield Republican*. In addition, his essays were collected into a book that brought him recognition, and several publications followed, including a history and an advice book for young people. After he helped found *Scribner's*, Holland published a few novels and continued writing until his death in 1881 at age sixty-two.

Saint-Gaudens not only created Holland's memorial but also created the statue *The Puritan* found in downtown Springfield. Concerning other funerary art, he created the Adams memorial at Rock Creek Cemetery in Washington, DC, featuring a shrouded bronze figure, one of the most famous works of the day and possibly an inspiration for a stunning memorial in Green Mount Cemetery in Montpelier, Vermont, which is covered in a later chapter. Also, if one were to follow that line of thinking, it was also an inspiration for the Fuller shrouded bronze figure and exedra wall at Springfield.

Also located at the eastern edge of the valley is the Daniel L. Harris sculpture of a male figure adorned in classical garb. Harris was a civil engineer who specialized in building bridges and railways, and he served as the president of the Connecticut River Railroad, as well as being a Springfield mayor. A large number of smaller markers surround the central one.

Other statuary funeral art is seen at Springfield cemetery, especially in the upper levels. One that stands alone on the western side of the valley, almost at the edge of the cemetery, is the Prescott memorial, a classic female figure with a wreath and one hand crossed over her chest. On the opposite side of the valley, on the uppermost level, are most of the remaining statuary memorials not already mentioned.

The H. N. Case memorial on the eastern side of the cemetery features a male angel carrying a horn, likely Gabriel, but perhaps not, as a number of male angels with horns can be found at the cemeteries, and not all of them are identified as Gabriel. Not far distant in this lawn of funerary art, the Clark memorial features a seated figure with a lyre atop a large sarcophagus-style base. Decorative curbing surrounds the family plot, which features other markers as well as the central one.

The Wright memorial features another noted but less common theme in Victorian funerary art, which is that of one woman comforting another, generally a younger woman or, but much more rarely, a boy. For the Wright memorial, a young woman rests against the lap of another, who is a seemingly older woman. This is a unique version, however. The older woman looks nun-like with her style of covered hair, and the whole sculpture sits upon a large, capped, architectural-style base girdled with pilasters.

Springfield Cemetery also has one of the mourning-woman-with-wreath sculptures that would become popular in many of the garden cemeteries, and it is located at the Alfred Day family lot. Most of them have small variations, although a few essentially identical ones have also been identified, largely, it seems, a result of the growing stonecutting business in the late nineteenth century, especially in the granite business. The woman-in-mourning—sometimes also called a "weeping woman"—memorial at Springfield has a different expression on her face than others do. It is a subtle difference, however: she seems as much reflective as she is mournful. She rests her head on one hand, while in the other hand she holds a floral wreath. Like many such statues, she has no shoes and is classically robed with her hair unbound.

A unique setting of three female figures is seen with the Dickinson memorial. The central, standing female figure is perhaps the youngest, and her robe is tucked around her waist with her upper torso exposed. The sitting woman to one side of her appears to be in her early years of adulthood and holds flowers, while the third figure, sitting and leaning forward, seems of a more advanced age. Together, they illustrate the stages of life. The Dickinson is perhaps the largest of the statue memorials at the cemetery, with a large ornate base and short columns supporting the trio of women. As with a few other memorials at the cemetery and elsewhere, especially the marble ones, the effects of weathering are apparent. Behind the Dickinson memorial and facing a different avenue is a simpler memorial with a single female figure, who is standing, her hair down, holding flowers, on the Perkins memorial.

Other interesting memorials are located in Springfield Cemetery, many of them in the upper levels of the cemetery, especially in the eastern section, including the Titus memorial and the Smith memorial. The Titus memorial is the more unique of the two, as it is a model of a Victorian house.

Andrew Titus enjoyed a successful career in real estate in the Springfield area during the mid to late 1800s. He died in 1896. His memorial reflects his career, as it is a solid, tall carving of a two-story Victorian home, complete with windows, doors, and the name "Titus" inscribed near the front door. Titus had lived in a Victorian home just opposite the memorial and the nearest cemetery gate, on Cedar Street. The steps to the Titus marble house are made of Longmeadow brownstone. The stone house is also a monument to Titus's three wives: Louise, Mary, and Pamela. Individual smaller, less-detailed "house" stones also mark the graves of various family members. House memorials are found in other garden cemeteries as well, but the Titus house is an intriguing one.

The cemetery likewise holds a few zinkies (zinc memorials) and other forms of funerary art, including ledger markers, broken columns signifying a life cut short, and draped urn memorials in a variety of stones and on various bases. One of the zinc memorials of note, which is one of the smaller ones, is that which marks the resting place of Catherine Davidson. Seemingly placed there by her parents, the marker notes that Catherine died in 1883 at age forty-four. Written on the zinc memorial, too, are the words, "The Last Enemy That Shall Be Destroyed Is Death."

Haunting words are inscribed on many rural cemetery markers, even on some of the smaller, less-costly ones. Some, like the smaller broken column of Lieutenant James Smith, speak profoundly and quietly. Other memorials soar to the skies, it seems.

One of the larger but relatively non-ornate family plots in Springfield Cemetery is the final resting place of one of the city's most noted residents. Horace Smith may not be immediately recognized by his name alone, but add the name of his most famous company, Smith & Wesson, and the situation rapidly changes. Born in 1808, Smith was an inventor and a gunsmith as well as an astute businessperson. He formed two companies with his main business partner, Daniel B. Wesson. For one of these companies, the two were joined by Oliver Winchester as an investor after a company reorganization, with an accompanying name change from the Smith & Wesson Company to the Volcanic Repeating Arms Company in 1855. That company was eventually reorganized as the Winchester Repeating Arms Company, a company that has its own place in history.

Smith and Wesson soon formed another company, the Smith & Wesson Revolver Company, in 1856. They then began manufacturing a small revolver with the first self-contained cartridge—the rimfire cartridge, which Smith and his partner had patented in 1854. The cartridge was seemingly *the* cartridge of the American Civil War. The men then patented the revolver—best known as simply the Smith & Wesson revolver, which was a marvelous success—and continued to introduce other gun innovations. The company established a new factory in Springfield in 1860 to meet the demand for their guns, and soldiers on both soldiers of the Civil War purchased Smith & Wesson revolvers for their personal protection.

Smith alone, who had previously worked for an armory, had created other weaponry before joining in his partnerships with Wesson and others, and he was critical in creating the weaponry his companies had produced, along with going up against perhaps the other most well-known gun manufacturer, Samuel Colt. Smith had invented the "explosive bullet," used initially to shoot whales, and Wesson also made whale guns. Smith and Colt soon became competitors.

Smith had invented his Volcanic cartridge in 1854, as well as his rimfire cartridge. Colt, who would be buried at Cedar Hill Cemetery, another garden cemetery discussed herein, had a patent on his revolver design set to expire in 1886. Knowing this, Wesson had begun working on a prototype for his own cartridge revolver. He was aided by the discovery that an employee of Colt held the patent to one of the gun components he would need to use in his revolver, and it was at this point that he realigned himself with Wesson. Smith and Wesson reached an agreement to pay the former Colt employee a royalty on every revolver they made. The two business partners would enjoy great success in their new company until Smith retired from Smith & Wesson in 1883. Smith worked on other business interests thereafter.

Smith married three times and left a sizable estate. Portions of the estate went to relatives, and other portions he designated to be used for the public good. A scholarship program, the Horace Smith Fund, was created in 1899 from this endowment. Smith died in 1893, and his burial lot features a tall obelisk and curbing, as well as individual small stones. Wesson would live until 1906 and be buried in Oak Grove Cemetery in Springfield.

Another interesting memorial, a large, white-roofed colonnade or open Greek-style temple memorial has been called the "Chapin Temple of Love." Located near the intersection of Pine and Cedar Streets, the memorial was constructed in 1926 of Westerly granite, according to the Babcock-Smith House Museum of Westerly, Rhode Island. Stonecutters who worked with Westerly granite included the "temple" in advertising during the era. The Joseph Coduri Granite Company served as the contractor for the memorial, which features a large colonnade complete with fluted columns with Corinthian capitals on a tiered base that creates steps leading up to the temple.

A number of mausoleums and family tombs are scattered throughout the cemetery. A few tombs or vaults were built into the slopes along the valley, or into the levels above, while the mausoleums are primarily on the upper levels of the cemetery. They are worth seeing.

The Robert Wolcott Day vault located between the two upper gates of the cemetery is an early example of an Egyptian-revival-style tomb, and it is a fairly large one, although it does have elements of a later era. The Day vault features large stone blocks, and the family name and a winged hourglass symbol are inscribed above its double doors. A column flanks either side of the doorway. Unlike the Egyptian-style mausoleums at Valley Cemetery and Grove Street in New Haven, the Day tomb, which is mostly aboveground, has a gently peaked roof with embellishments. A stone approach leads to the tomb, with rhododendrons and other shrubbery providing a serene setting. The mausoleum holds the remains of Robert Day (1852–1926) who served on the cemetery board as its president from 1912 to 1926 and otherwise contributed greatly to the institution.

The cemetery trustees decided to widen Cemetery Lane in the 1920s. They also decided to demolish Peabody's archway and to construct a new gateway at the Maple Street entrance. A new gate, its funding donated in honor of Robert Day, was constructed at the entranceway, located where the cemetery enters the street, and completed by 1928. For a short time, both the new gate and the old archway stood, one a fair ways beyond the other. The 1928 Georgian gate still exists, squeezed in between two large apartment buildings, as does another stone entrance on Cedar Street, and an iron gateway is located farther up on Pine Street.

The cemetery used East Longmeadow sandstone—as it had with its 1880s chapel—when it built a new office building in the early 1930s. Like the chapel, also, it is Gothic in style and contains a columbarium as well as office space. Leaded glass windows, hardwood furniture, and oak plank doors and trim adorn the building. Bronze was used for windowsills, frames, and other hardware and adornments. Tennessee marble was used for the flooring, and wainscoting was installed of Italian marble or oak, depending on the location. The outside is interesting, more so the longer one looks at its fine workmanship, but the inside is more compelling, one might argue.

However, there is something missing at Springfield Cemetery. As well as removing the fountains that had proved popular in the nineteenth century, the cemetery reworked its waterways so as to make none of them visible. There are no brooks or small ponds in or leading into the valley at Springfield any longer. In some ways, the topography resembles that at Valley Cemetery, although at Springfield the valley floor holds the main entrance into the cemetery. The valley in Springfield Cemetery is well-maintained even without the fountains and paths and waterways once there, so the absence is perhaps less noticeable. However, one might still regret the loss of the nineteenth-century landscaping and the water that once nourished Martha's Dingle.

Still, there is so much more to this cemetery snuggled between apartment buildings. The multilevel aspect, the winding road through the middle, the mausoleums lining the valley and slopes, and the variety of monuments pulls one in. Go through either of the two stone gates or through the iron gateway and (depending on which are open) you will find something worth seeing, and just what you see first will vary greatly with the entrance you choose.

You may wish to read the entire 1857 "Historical Memoir of the Springfield Cemetery, Read to the Proprietors at Their Annual Meeting, May 23, 1857, by George Bliss, Their President," printed by Samuel Bowles and Company of Springfield. This includes the cemetery's dedication address and a few other documents worth perusing. A few short articles about the cemetery are available online. In addition, Charles Elliot's memoirs, including his letter to Springfield Cemetery, have been preserved in Charles Elliot, Landscape Architect, a Lover of Nature and His Kind, Who Trained Himself for a New Profession, Practiced it Happily, and Through it Wrought Much Good, *edited by Charles William Elliot, 1903. In addition, the cemetery has a short, 1991 article written by Donald J. D'Amato, titled "Springfield Cemetery, 150 Years of History." There is also an article online, titled "Horace Smith and Daniel Baird Wesson Biography," as well as other publications about the two men, including a biography of Smith by R. J. Neal and G. Jinks, seemingly self-published in 1966.*

6

The Northeast's Largest Garden Cemetery

Albany Rural Cemetery, Menands, New York

Admiration—and then awe—is something one might feel when entering the Albany Rural Cemetery: admiration for its monuments, its rolling hills, its "residents," and its situation near the Hudson River. Like Springfield Cemetery, its designers incorporated a long main approach into the burial grounds proper, or rather, two of them. There are two major entrances to the cemetery, each has a distinct feel, and each has a rather peculiar and intriguing edifice near its gates. These are, in effect, foregrounds to the cemetery proper, to the cemetery's burial sections. And, after one travels either approach, one soon begins to see distinguished memorials or mausoleums, depending on one's exact route. No matter which entrance one takes, one is soon surrounded by fine funerary art. And there is water: two brooks and a pond—or two—and space and size; Albany Rural Cemetery is immense.

WHILE PLANNING WAS UNDERWAY FOR THE VALLEY AND SPRINGFIELD Cemeteries, plans were also underway for a new garden cemetery just across the Massachusetts and Vermont borders into eastern New York: the Albany Rural Cemetery. By far the largest of the garden cemeteries discussed herein at some 467 acres, Albany Rural Cemetery has a special place in history. And not just for its size.

Established in 1844, Albany Rural Cemetery has three sections, identified by the ridges on which they are located: the North Ridge, the

Middle Ridge, and the South Ridge. However, for the casual visitor, the names of the avenues and the corresponding numerical designations may be just as useful, if one is looking for a specific memorial. And, memorials there are indeed here, scores of thousands of them, in an extensive variety. They vary greatly in style and in age, as the cemetery is now more than 175 years old with more than 140,000 interments.

On December 31, 1840, following a sermon by Reverend Bartholomew T. Welch about the deplorable condition of some local burial grounds, according to an 1884 history of the city, *The Albany Handbook, A Strangers' and Residents' Handbook* by Henry P. Phelps, a group met to discuss creating a new cemetery. The assembled group then appointed thirteen men to "carry the plan into effect." On April 20, 1841, the group incorporated to establish a new cemetery for Albany.

As elsewhere, many of the city's burials were taking place in overcrowded churchyards as well as in one particular city cemetery, the State Street Cemetery. Flooding at the State Street location created several difficulties as time passed and helped spur the call for other burial grounds. The association was charged with establishing a rural cemetery outside of Albany's city limits. On April 20, 1844, the association agreed on a site for the cemetery, located nearby in what would become the village of Menands, on a plateau overlooking the Hudson River. Portions of the property had once held a school and a mill.

According to Phelps in his 1893 history, *Albany Rural Cemetery, Its Beauties, Its Memories*, securing two parcels of land totaling more than one hundred acres from Thomas and John Hillhouse and from "Governor Marcy and others" proved financially difficult. The association held a subscription drive, but they still needed to secure a mortgage for part of the purchase. One banker, encountered outside his bank, "openly and roundly denounced the whole project, bringing his cane down upon the pavement most emphatically, and declaring it was the height of absurdity to expect anyone to bury their dead in a 'mortgaged lot.'" Time proved him wrong.

Reverend Welch served as the first president of the association; Thomas W. Olcott would serve as the second president, and Erastus Corning was the third. Each of these men—involved since the association organized—would play a strong role in the future of the cemetery.

Philips credited Welch, with his oratory skills, and Olcott, with his financial acumen, at overcoming the major obstacles to the cemetery's creation.

Welch and Olcott had also been entrusted with finding someone to improve the grounds. They secured the services of Major D. B. Douglass to that end. Douglass was instructed to create a cemetery where people could stroll along winding pathways and enjoy nature as well as fountains and other human creations of beauty. He could add ornamental plantings where desired. The association first decided on "The Evergreens" as the name of the new cemetery and so advertised it, but they soon changed the name to Albany Rural Cemetery. After that, the discussion of changing the name to a more poetical one arose from time to time, but nothing came of it.

The land purchase and preliminary designs completed, the cemetery was consecrated on October 7, 1844. The dedication was well attended. Citizens lined the streets and marched in a procession to the new cemetery. Local and state dignitaries, military units, fraternal organizations, firemen, and others participated in the procession, and hundreds, perhaps thousands, of people attended the four hours of festivities and addresses.

At the cemetery, a chorus of more than a hundred people sang, a poem was read, and clergy members delivered religious exercises in "Consecration Dell." Then, it was time for the main address.

The Honorable Daniel D. Barnard delivered the dedication. He started by telling his audience, "This, my friends, is an occasion and ceremony of most uncommon interest. We have sought out a pleasant location for the dead; and having chosen our ground, and secured its possession, we come here now to dedicate it and devote it solemnly to that purpose forever." For the dead, those assembled were setting aside the ground to be "their separate dwelling place as long as time shall last." He left no doubt that the place should be a permanent cemetery.

"The purchase is ours, the inheritance belongs to them," Barnard continued. Regarding those still living, he stated, "Here we expect to bury our friends, and here we expect our friends will bury us. . . . We choose, so far as the choice depends on ourselves, this field for our last resting place."

Religious sentiments followed, as well as observations about how the dead had often been treated in the past. "Sometimes they have been sank in deep waters. Sometimes they have been reduced to ashes by fire. . . . Sometimes they have been huddled together in barrows and cairns, or in grottos or catacombs." Three million bodies, Barnard said, were now buried under the street of Paris. In Naples, up to the present day, because of their sheer number, the dead were "thrown in undistinguished heaps, into vast charnel pits."

Moreover, in some places, even where interments were the practice, there was a "revolting haste in terminating tenancy of the body in the narrow strip of ground which it has been allowed to occupy." In some of these places, substances were thrown onto bodies to hasten their decomposition, and in some instances, a fixed amount of time was set, often at only five or six years, before a new tenant was brought in.

"It is difficult to say where the dead have received the greatest wrong," Barnard continued, reviewing practices as far back as Egypt in his speech. However, he opined, perhaps the greatest insult to the dead was that "in our own times, cadavers may be seen, sometimes comprising many hundreds of desiccated bodies, sitting in ghastly mockery of life, dressed in gay attire, and tricked off with glittering ornaments, or bearing the symbols of earthly rank, authority, or command." It was more natural to bury the dead, to let them return naturally to the earth in a peaceful place of sepulture. This peaceful return to the earth was what the living overwhelmingly desired, Barnard asserted.

The practice of respectfully adorning the places of the dead—as seen with the Greeks, Hebrews, Egyptians, and others—was natural, and it had lately become popular again, hence the rise of the rural cemetery. Other American cities had set the example Albany was now following.

The acres for the new cemetery had been "happily chosen," Barnard continued. "We can see and know what they are, but we can scarcely know what they will be—how full of incomprehensible beauty—when the forming hand of taste shall once have been laid upon them." The grounds were beautiful with their trees and dells, their "soft toned, gentle, living waters," their gentle slopes and hills and knolls. He asked his audience to "think of all this natural beauty brought out and softened by the hand of art—at once brightened yet subdued by the civilizing and humanizing processes to which it may be subjected—and then think of it inhabited only by the dead," by individual graves and groups of graves "marked by every variety of modest memorial which affection can suggest. What scene in nature could be more beautiful, more attractive, more impressive, more approving!"

Barnard noted that the cemetery would be open to everyone, regardless of class, race, or religion. The dead would not be moved once interred. "This will be a common burial place where all will meet on terms of common fellowship and brotherhood," he envisioned. "Friend shall meet friend here; and enemies, too, shall meet, their enmities all forgotten." The cemetery would be a refuge from hatreds and "from shivering misery and squalid want, from secret griefs [sic], from penury, oppression, injustice." The young and the old would lie there, as would the wise, the distinguished, and the humble.

It was hoped that the cemetery would help assuage "the bitterness of the mourner's grief." Friends could watch over the graves of their departed and adorn them. Nature would help the mourner contemplate life, commune with nature, "with the spirits of the departed, and with God, the Author of all." The new cemetery would be a place of beauty and healing.

Following Barnard's dedication, the Lothian Band performed, a doxology was read, a chorus sang, and a benediction was performed. The ceremonies thus concluded; the large gathering dispersed.

Subscription books for lot sales were issued the following June, with those who bid the highest for lots having the first choice. Bids ranged from $1 to $80. Welch and Orcott were both given free choice of a lot, in consideration of their work in establishing the cemetery. Lots sold for $25 for a sixteen-by-sixteen-foot parcel, and in May 1845, the first interment took place. Lots regularly sold to people from Albany and surrounding towns and cities, but the cost of improving the grounds up until the late 1860s left the association financially strapped.

Major Douglas, who had previously designed Greenwood Cemetery in Brooklyn, New York, continued work on the cemetery's layout in 1845 and 1846. Once the initial planning and work were completed, John Hillhouse stepped in until 1848, followed by Burton A. Thomas. Thomas's son, Jeffrey P. Thomas, next took over that responsibility as well as becoming cemetery superintendent, serving into the 1890s.

The main avenue through the cemetery is named the Tour, and if one follows it, one will indeed experience a tour. By the 1890s, visitors could reach the cemetery via trains that arrived and departed throughout the day. Carriages likewise carried visitors around the grounds, while those who came by trolley could stroll. Many, no doubt, followed the tour around the cemetery, the avenue already being eight miles long with many more miles of connecting avenues and walkways. The main approach to the cemetery, the eastern entrance, featured a long, stately drive that was lined with "majestic elms," as Phelps described the scene in the early 1890s. Postcards of the cemetery were available.

Today, if one uses the eastern entrance, three roads lead up to the three major sections of the cemetery: the North, Middle, and South Ridge areas. If one enters from the southern entrance, the main road leads to various intersections and roads, some leading to avenues that curve around and down the hillsides, others to the main pond, Willow Pond, via a row of mausoleums and fine statuary. In the early twentieth century, more monuments were constructed in the area, and cemetery buildings were added in the 1890s. Now as then, whichever way one enters, there is much to see.

Visitors in the 1800s enjoyed looking at the monuments and having picnics on the grounds. The cemetery has two creeks, waters that were dammed for a while to create four ponds, one considerably larger than the others. Eventually, these were taken away via removal of the dams. One small area is still dammed, it seems, while another pond, Willow Pond, continues to attract attention with its water fountain, surrounding avenues, and nearby, often exquisite, funerary art.

Superintendent Thomas created "Cypress Water" in what was essentially a swamp in about 1870. Phelps described it as a "pear-shaped lakelet" and said that in the 1890s it looked as if made by nature. The twentieth century would see further changes at the small body of water, including a name change to Willow Pond. As seen at Mount Auburn, the land around the pond seems to have been "prime real estate."

Like other garden cemeteries, Albany Rural would see reinterments from other locations. In 1866, according to cemetery sources, the Albany Common Council approved the disinterment of the remains at the State Street Cemetery and at all churches within the city limits and their reinterment at Albany Rural. Some were so moved in 1868. Bodies reinterred from the churchyards were buried in a section known as the Church Ground. Later, in 2002, another large reinterment process occurred when the former Albany Poor House was redeveloped, and the bodies buried there were removed. Those reinterred at Albany Rural Cemetery included former inmates of the poorhouse, of the Albany Orphanage, and of the Albany Jail, plus a few unclaimed bodies. The 2002 reinterments were far off from the mid-1800s, however, when the initial reinterments occurred.

Immediately popular with the public, enough bodies were being buried at the cemetery by the early 1850s, or awaiting burial there, that a holding tomb was needed. The cemetery built a large receiving vault in 1853. By 1858, however, the 1853 vault was no longer sufficient to meet community needs, so the cemetery built a new one. The two vaults flow naturally into one another in style, size, and situation. They are located immediately next to one another, built into the hillside along the main road closest to the southern cemetery entrance. Although no longer in use, they are well worth seeing, and at the time of this writing, one can look into the 1858 section, just as one can look into a few other tombs on the grounds, generally the older ones.

A few early tombs, mausoleums, and memorials indicated just how the future might go with regard to lot demands and the ornate nature of some of them. The Burden Family vault was one of these.

Built in 1850 of grey granite just above the eastern gateway off Broadway, the mausoleum faces the Hudson River. Inside rest the remains of twenty-two people, including the industrialist who built it, Henry Burden. According to Paul Grondahl in *These Exalted Acres*, it was Burden's wife, Helen, who designed the much-admired mausoleum and the open-book memorial in front of the family lot.

The book memorial is marble and much, much larger than life; so large is it in fact that two stone steps have been provided so that the visitor might climb them to look upon the pages of the book, inscribed with family genealogy. The book is displayed on a stone pedestal, with a stone cushion or cloth underneath the book, complete with tasseled stone corners. Another large stone book is located across the cemetery—one that has a bronze angel standing among its open pages.

The large Burden vault—built into the ridge—features an ornate iron door flanked by double pillars, with two life-size retriever dogs carved above them, almost at the top of the tomb, facing outward, seemingly guarding those within. According to Grondahl, the dogs were modeled on family pets, and the carved face above the doorway was modeled after Helen Burden, or, at least, bore a marked resemblance to her. The stonework on the face of the tomb is more detailed than most seen elsewhere—or anywhere.

Henry Burden was able to build his impressive vault because he made a fortune during his lifetime. Burden was an industrial giant in the region in the mid-1800s. Born in Scotland in 1791, he would found Burden Ironworks in Troy, New York, where he would harness the energy of a nearby waterway to use in producing the first mass-produced horseshoes in America, as well as boiler bolts and railroad spikes, using innovative machines he had invented himself. His products played critical roles in the Civil War.

However, Burden made an enemy in Erastus Corning, who founded the New York Central Railroad, over a water dispute. Corning tapped into Burden's water supply, and Burden sued him over it. Both men would be buried in the Albany Rural Cemetery.

Corning's is the largest private family lot in the cemetery, located on a promontory perhaps most easily reached via the southern gate, the Menands Road entrance. The Corning lot is circular in shape, featuring numerous pink granite markers. However, the most commanding marker is that for Erastus Corning himself. The family patriarch has a bronze cuneiform sarcophagus as his marker. A number of sarcophagi are located in the various cemeteries, some of them cuneiform or cross-shaped, but Corning's is not only cross-shaped and bronze all over—instead of just having bronze ornamentation—but also modeled on an Albany cathedral. Corning and his family had donated the land for the Episcopal Cathedral of All Saints of Albany and endowed it in other ways, and he chose the church as a model for the sarcophagus.

According to various sources, including Phelps, Corning had started out as "a poor boy who sold oranges in the streets of Troy [New York]." His spine was injured at birth, and he could not walk upright, but nevertheless, he became one of the wealthiest men in New York. He speculated in land, became an iron magnate, and founded the New York Central Railroad. He then merged his railroad with several smaller ones and built his company into the largest corporation of his day.

Burden feuded with Corning, and the two are really not too far apart in death, but it is not Corning who rests beside Burden at Albany Rural. Immediately next to Burden at the cemetery, in terms of non-family interments, is the McCoy tomb.

The McCoy vault is built into the hillside alongside the Burden tomb. Built of gray granite blocks, it has a rock archway above its arched double doors. A Celtic cross is mounted at the peak of the vault, above the family name, and stone vines grace its outer edges. Near either side of the doorway, a primitive face carved in stone protrudes slightly from the face of the tomb.

Bypassing the Burden lot and winding up the hill, one comes to markers for other eminent families and individuals and some child or baby stones, before winding again and going downward, where one finds other memorials. There are intriguing memorials here of all sorts, but there is also a dankness in the air and more shade than in much of the cemetery.

Down in an often dark valley near the middle of the cemetery, at the end of the cemetery's Middle Ridge and not too distant from the lot known as the Church Grounds where some of the oldest stones, including those of slaves, were placed after the cemetery opened, and near a small plot with old blackened stones, which is the Townsend family lot, is the tomb sometimes considered the most frightening one in the cemetery: the Douw vault. Certainly, if one looks inside, beside the dank smell, one can see old crypts. It also seems there might be things one should not see, but that is perhaps as much the atmosphere of the vault as anything else. Somehow, the Townsend lot, just slightly down the slope and enclosed by a falling-down fence, might seem to be at the deepest part in the cemetery, but that is not true. One of the brooks—Moordenaer's

Kill—runs right next to it and eventually runs farther downhill to the eastern entrance road.

However, it is dark at the bottom of this valley, and that "eerie" mausoleum just above the stream was built for Volkert Petrus Douw and his family. Moreover, it would be the setting for a scene in the 1987 movie *Ironweed*.

Douw's years of life, 1720 to 1801, precede the establishment of Albany Rural Cemetery. Douw's father had married into Albany's prominent Van Rensselaers, descendants of the Dutch patrons. Douw married and had nine children with Anna De Peyster. He ran the family store for a time, and then he entered politics, first local and then colonial and later state politics. According to Paul Grondahl, he became one of the wealthiest men around, and he owned fourteen slaves in 1790. He was buried in a family cemetery, but years later, his remains were moved to Albany Rural. Other family members would be interred there, both his immediate Douw family and Rensselaer relatives, who had a strong impact on the history of the region. The Douw vault was actually built for John De Peyster Douw.

In 1987, when filming *Ironweed*, starring Jack Nicholson and Meryl Streep, part of the movie was filmed at the Douw tomb as well as in the adjacent Saint Agnes Cemetery. The vault, built in an Old Dutch style of grey and brown stone, requires repairs. The sandstone cross mounted on the roof has broken off, with part of it still near the vault steps and one section resting against the front of the tomb. The rusted door hangs open, and the vault needs a fair amount of masonry work. It is this deterioration, and the great sense of age and atmosphere added to by the old stone bridge over the brook and the deteriorating Townsend plot, that made the site an appealing one for the movie. Interestingly, as in the filming at Mount Hope Cemetery of Stephen King's *Pet Sematary*, Fred Gwynne, star of the 1960s sitcom *The Munsters*, made an appearance in *Ironweed*, too.

The Douw tomb is not the only one in that low valley. There are others, too, including the Stanford vault built for Josiah Stanford, a tavern and hotelkeeper who became prosperous and had nine children with his wife, Elizabeth Phillips. The Stanford children did well, especially Leland, who became the governor of California and then president of the Central Pacific Railroad. Stanford built the western portion of the

Transcontinental Railroad, and it was he who drove the famous spike connecting the two halves of the nation in Utah in 1869. He also started the college that became Stanford University after the death of his son. He had wanted to build such a memorial first at Albany Rural, but could not acquire the hundreds of acres he requested. His wife, who ran the university after his own death, was subsequently murdered.

Leland Stanford built the tomb at Albany Rural for his father after his 1862 death and paid for the Lathrop memorial—one of the largest in the cemetery and topped with a Greek goddess in mourning—for his parents-in-law. The vault features an ornate cast-iron door, long and curving wing walls, steps leading up to the door, ornate lettering above the door, and a portico topped by urns. The tomb underwent a restoration in the early 2000s. Other tombs are located nearby, as are numerous interesting memorials of other forms.

Two specific mausoleums at the cemetery are likewise rich in detail and could be mistaken for small chapels, although ones of widely different styles and sizes. One of them, some people think, also resembles a small castle or a cathedral.

The Winslow mausoleum is the largest at the cemetery, is ornate, and was built for John Flack Winslow and his wife. Winslow, born in Vermont in 1810, was the first to produce structural steel in the nation, and he managed the Albany Ironworks while his partner at the time, Erastus Corning, was concentrating on his railroads. Of major importance to the nation, Winslow partnered with John Ericsson to build the first iron-clad Union warship, the USS *Monitor*, a project that Winslow ended up financing himself. Winslow built his final resting place, with room for another forty-seven interments, during the Civil War, in 1864. Winslow lived until 1892.

Winslow's mausoleum is also known as the Winslow Mortuary Chapel. It sits high on a large terraced lot facing the Hudson River. Steps lead up to the mausoleum from the front, while other steps lead down to the lot at the rear. Built in a Gothic style, it features a copper roof and copula, ornate carvings, windows, and a rough, granite exterior. The structure underwent a restoration in the early 2000s and holds a place of pride in the cemetery.

Across the cemetery, closer to the southern entrance, the G. C. Hawley mausoleum sometimes confuses visitors as to its purpose. Built in 1917, the mausoleum holds the remains of George and Theodora Hawley. Constructed of gray granite, the mausoleum has an almost medieval look to it, like that of a church or a castle. It features four miniature peaked "towers," an ornate arch over a rectangular doorway with windows, and a turret-like addition or apse with windows on the backside.

Between the two more noted mausoleums is the Visscher mausoleum, a simple one built a little higher on the hill as the Winslow one. The building may be more simple in its architecture than the two just mentioned, but like the other two, it is a true mausoleum—built all aboveground—and it has wonderful stonework, especially around its double-arched doorway, which features detailed metalwork depicting a rising or setting sun.

Mausoleums and tombs abound at Albany Rural Cemetery, but so do other forms of statuary art. A number of memorials for—or at least partially for—children are located at the cemetery. Some feature animal sculptures or carvings; others do not.

Because those who are memorialized by the child markers generally did not reach adulthood and have lengthy careers, less is known about them. Although only a few are noted here, there are also others worth viewing, including statues of lambs, resting infants, and angels.

Located near a long line of mausoleums sometimes referred to as "Millionaires' Row" near Willow Pond is a simple child angel named Florence. One of her hands is broken off, but in the other, she holds a flower, or flowers, the arrangement also aged. Not too distant from Florence, the marker for Henry V. Heck, who lived and died in 1911, is a small boy angel, one of his hands also broken off, and he, too, holds a wreath of flowers. A simple, graceful child angel memorializes Arthur Oden, who died as a small child. The male child angel wears a simple shift, his eyes cast down and his hands together, seemingly in prayer.

Another child angel, a larger one, stands atop the Rufus Clark memorial. The child angel holds a trumpet close to his or her chest and gazes skyward. This statue served for an entire family, however.

Writing years after the children's deaths but still long before the twenty-first century, Phelps noted in his history of the cemetery that there were fashions in grave markers. He noted, "The pitiful representations of lambs, and children, and miniature angels are no more called for than the winded faces found on the slabs of the eighteenth century. Italian marble itself is no longer used much, chiefly because it cannot stand the weather." So, too, was the red sandstone seen elsewhere no longer much in use, and granite was seemingly the preferred stone of the 1890s, especially Westerly granite, which was replacing Quincy granite in demand. However, angels, lambs, and children's memorials of all types and in various stones are located in numerous places at Albany Rural and other garden cemeteries. Phelps, although he might not have known it, was writing at the end of the garden cemetery movement, but in his commentary, he included several aspects of the movement.

Other angels, most added before Phelps wrote his history, memorialize entire families and feature "adult" angels. One of these is considered the most celebrated monument in the cemetery, although another angel would seem to garner as much attention. Others are lesser known but perhaps just as compelling, including those of the Hascy and Sanders families, as well as the one that adorns the grave of Josephine Smith. Each of these and others are worthy of notice.

There is also a stone angel perched atop the Root mausoleum along "Millionaires' Row" worth seeing. Josiah Goodrich Root made his fortune in textiles. Starting out as a worker in a woolen mill, the Massachusetts-born Root would rise through the ranks and eventually run one of Stephen Van Rensselaer's mills. He then started his own company, which became a huge success in knitting thermal underwear and other goods. Root died in 1883, and his current marble angel—one holding her hands in prayer, eyes cast upward—replaced an earlier one in the 1890s. Photographs of the older angel show it seated and possibly male. The newer angel was on order from Italy at the time Phelps wrote.

Perhaps the most spectacular stone angel for a family, however, is that which tops a towering, ornate pillar and base. High on the plinth above, an angel holds a child aloft. The child has his or her arm raised, seemingly in salute or farewell or victory. The statue has a Romanesque feel to it, and it was carved for Franklin Cleveland and his wife, Gertrude. As seen elsewhere, individual stones are dispersed at the base of the towering memorial for individual family members.

Perhaps the most celebrated angel at Albany Rural, however, was sculpted by a man who would himself be buried in the cemetery. Erastus Dow Palmer was an acclaimed American sculptor who started out as a carpenter and lived between 1817 and 1904. He was born and raised in Pompey, New York, just south of Syracuse. After he became a sculptor, Palmer maintained studios in Albany but worked in numerous locations. He created two statues on display at the US Capitol Building: *Peace in Bondage*, and a statue of Robert Livingston. In addition, Palmer's full-length sculpture *White Captive* is on permanent display at the Museum of Modern Art in New York City.

Palmer created a number of the memorials at the cemetery, including the stunning white-marble sculpture known as *The Angel at the Sepulcher*. Created in 1868 and located on the hill above Willow Pond near the Corning lot, it is considered one of the most profound sculptures at the cemetery. Its subject is a seated male angel whose expression and intent have been widely commented upon. Inscribed around the upper base of the monument are the words: "Why seek ye the living, among the dead?" These were words the biblical angel at the tomb of Christ had asked the women who approached him—Mary Magdalene and Mary, the mother of Christ—followed by the words, "He is not here, but is risen." These words, especially "He is Risen," appear on several garden cemetery memorials but generally not with the question that preceded them.

Phelps devoted five pages to the statue, including commentary that in the decades before Palmer carved his angel, "angelhood had become singularly demoralized"; a peculiar choice of words perhaps, but he added an explanation of sorts. He stated, "An angel meant a female figure . . . much spiritualized . . . and weakened accordingly, till there was little left but sloping shoulders, flat chest, a featureless face, impossible wings and a Grecian gown." This ideal had been so impressed upon people by the 1860s that Palmer was taken to task by a studio visitor as to on whose authority Palmer had chosen a male angel. Palmer had purportedly replied that there was no "inspired authority for anything else"—biblical passages identified that specific angel as male.

Palmer described the completed angel as having a face "of wondrous beauty—etherialized, but strongly and strangely human." The *London Art Journal* of 1871 stated that the sculpture was "the outcome of an original and earnest mind, a statue which the greatest living sculptor might acknowledge with pride as his own." Visitors to the cemetery did, and do, regularly seek out the statue.

The seven-foot figure, *The Angel at the Sepulcher*, memorializes the Banks family and its patriarch, General Robert Lenox Banks. Banks had graduated from Princeton and moved to Albany as an adult, after having served as an aide-de-camp and quartermaster general during the Civil War, according to his obituary. He became a prominent Albany citizen and served as a treasurer for the New York Central Railroad as well as on the board of Albany Rural Cemetery. Banks commissioned the angel sculpture for his wife, Emma Rathbone Turner Banks, who died in 1866. Banks died in the 1890s at the age of seventy-two of senile dementia, according to cemetery records. His second wife, Mary De Camp Banks, died at age ninety-one in 1935. Both of his wives and other family members are interred on the lot.

Palmer sculpted a few other memorials at the cemetery as well, including his earliest one, the Olcott memorial. The memorial features a marble sculpture of a youth seemingly writing and leaning over a bit to do so in front of a draped urn. The statue rests atop an ornate pedestal base—one panel of which features a bas-relief of a mother rising to meet her babies in heaven. One of the people interred here was Emma Olcott, who died in 1865 at age sixteen. Time has stolen some of the detail from the memorial, which remains compelling just the same.

Interred across the lane from this memorial is the one for Thomas Worth Olcott and his wife, Carline, who died in 1880 and 1867, respectively. Olcott had been a president of the cemetery association, and his memorial includes a bronze frieze portrait by Palmer.

Palmer died in 1904, and he was buried at the Albany Rural Cemetery, not far from his most acclaimed memorial sculpture. His own monument—a large, embellished sarcophagus—was designed by Albany architect Marcus T. Reynolds. Unlike most funerary torches seen during the era, the eight torches on the Palmer memorial are not inverted; their flames burn toward the sky. Palmer's son, an acclaimed landscape painter, Walter Lunt Palmer, is buried in the same lot, his life memorialized on the back of his father's sarcophagus. The work of both men can be found at the Albany Institute of History & Art, as well as other places.

Although Palmer was still alive in the mid-1890s, his lot had been "well-chosen" but as yet "unmarked," according to Phelps, who wrote of Palmer as being "the sculptor, whose genius, more than that of any other man, has made both famous and beautiful this cemetery, of which he is a trustee."

Two noted bronze works by Oscar Lenz also adorn the cemetery. These include the *Angel of Resurrection* and a frieze on the Parsons family monument, as well as the relief of a seated warrior, the warrior receiving a bouquet of poppies from the Angel of Death, on the George Porter Hilton mausoleum. The bronze work on the Hilton mausoleum takes up almost the entire front of the edifice, and carved under the stunning frieze are the following words: "I Have Fought a Good Fight, I Have Finished My Course, I Have Kept The Faith."

Lenz's *Angel of Resurrection* features, as one would anticipate, an angel. The angel is a bronze angel, one that is larger-than-life but nonetheless occupies only about one-third of the entire height of a towering cross. A more Roman angel than some others, Parson's angel wears a simple robe with vine rope twined around her waist, her arms slightly raised, and palms facing upward. The patina on her surface is such that she appears to have tracks of tears running down from her eyes.

In the center of the cross arms of the Parson memorial is carved a wreath, and in the center of that is an urn. In the arch above the angel's head are carved the words: "He is Risen, He is Not Here"; hence, the name of the statue. Other angels in various cemeteries represent the biblical resurrections also, but not all are so clearly marked so as to express this identity. The "wraparound" frieze of the memorial was intricately cast, and it shows people, many people, Roman soldiers and citizens, seemingly in awe of the resurrection.

Another noted sculptor also created monuments for Albany Rural Cemetery and was also buried there himself: Charles Calverley. Calverley, in terms of the cemetery, is best known for his bronze statue *Meditation*, which is located on the Boulware lot. Calverley had worked as a stonecutter in his youth, then for Erastus Dow Palmer, and eventually achieved his own recognition as an artist. According to a short biography of his life, *From Stonecutter to Sculptor* by Elizabeth K. Allen, in all probability, Sara J. Kidd Boulware commissioned the bronze *Meditation* memorial for her husband, Dr. Jeptha Richard Boulware, to rest atop a sarcophagus-style base sometime after his death in 1887. Calverley had also, soon after the physician's death, made portraits of the couple in bronze relief.

Calverley was close to seventy when he undertook the *Meditation* statue, installed in 1902. It features a seated woman, her pose not unlike many of the seated woman-in-mourning figures found in the garden cemeteries, but she holds no flowers or wreath and her expression is more one of quiet reflection than of mourning. Deemed a neoclassical and allegorical statue, Allen stated that the statue would have been deemed already passé when it was installed but that the "quiet restrained pose and exquisitely modeled surface impart to the figure a timeless quality," one that causes the viewer to ponder "the transience of life."

Calverley made a bust of himself that was later installed as part of his own memorial after his 1914 death. (A bronze relief of his wife who died before he was already in place by the mid-1890s.) In the late 1900s, the bronze bust was stolen and not located for more than a decade, and it was only found by coincidence, according to cemetery staff. It was returned to the cemetery and mounted more securely than it had been originally.

Not far from the Calverley's Boulware memorial, the Greer memorial features one of the woman-in-mourning-with-wreath stone figures. Seated and barefoot, she, like most but unlike the Calverley *Meditation*, has her gaze cast downward.

Another variation is found on the Kibbee memorial. On it, the woman has her hair held back and wears a decorative headband. Her body faces the front of the memorial, unlike many, and she has one bare foot almost dangling in front of the substantial base, her eyes cast down, her hands folded and holding a wreath.

The Jones memorial also features a seated woman in stone, but she is of another type. She holds one hand gently across her chest while in the other she holds not a wreath or flowers but a book, upon which is carved an anchor. Her hair is arranged in a classical mourning style, her eyes cast upward. A similar styled figure is found on the Johnson memorial, although the female figure on it stands atop a tall base, and she holds a large anchor at her right side, the attached rope draped across her body and the far end held in her left hand. The Hinckel memorial likewise has a standing female figure with her hair arranged in mourning holding an anchor, but this is a small one.

Another exquisite example of a woman with a large anchor is at the Temple lot. This one is again standing but with a flower garland wrapped around the waist-high double anchor, the other hand across her chest and her hair down and arranged in a classical flowing style. Lilies are carved around the large base of the memorial.

Concerning Greek colonnades and mausoleums, the Dalton and Boyd lots are not to be missed. William Dalton served as the chief engineer for the American Locomotive Company. In 1928, after the death of his wife, Dalton hired Marcus T. Reynolds to design his mausoleum, or more specifically his circular cinerarium, to hold the cremated remains of himself and his family. The Dalton Cinerarium is one of the most striking structures at Albany Rural. Constructed of white Vermont marble with detailed carvings on six Corinthian columns, a bronze door, also detailed, allows one to look in to see the marble and bronze tablets that list the names of those whose cremated remains are interred inside. The domed roof adds to the classical beauty of the memorial.

The Boyd memorial is another classical monument, although it is an open edifice with five classical columns mounted upon a large, circular, tiered base that rests upon an even larger foundation. Individual markers are set directly against the base for John Scott Boyd and his wife, Sarah Anna Root, with other markers spread farther out. The Dalton memorial underwent a restoration in the early twenty-first century, and some work at the Boyd memorial would no doubt enhance its appeal, too, although it remains a compelling marker.

The Albany Rural Cemetery is the burial place of many noted individuals. Perhaps the most noted person buried at the Albany Rural Cemetery is Chester Alan Arthur, the nation's twenty-first president. He and his wife were both interred at the cemetery, in what some might consider a rather modest manner, considering that he was a US president. His wife, Ellen Lewis Herndon Arthur, had predeceased him, having died in 1880.

President Arthur, born on October 5, 1829, died in New York of Bright's disease on November 18, 1886. A native of Vermont, besides serving as president, Arthur had served in the Civil War, ultimately becoming a quartermaster general, and he had later served under President Ulysses S. Grant as collector of the Port of New York. There were purportedly some irregularities while he was in charge, but President James A. Garfield chose Arthur as his Republican running mate in the 1880 elections, the year President Arthur's wife "Nell" died of pneumonia.

Months after taking office, President Garfield was shot. When he died of his injuries on September 19, 1881, Arthur became the nation's president. He served out Garfield's term—without a vice president—but did not secure the nomination for the 1884 election. He thus returned to his earlier career in law.

Henry P. Phelps, in his 1893 *History of the Albany Rural Cemetery*, wrote the following about Arthur just a few years after the former president's death:

It was right of course that Mr. Arthur should sleep among his kindred and his grave was therefore made there [in the lot his father had purchased] before any testimonial was projected. This [was] the free, cheerful, almost unlooked for contribution of his friends, resident largely to the state of New York. With few words, with little publicity, and no solicitation, a handsome sum of money was promptly raised, sufficient to pay for the monument and also for a statue in New York City. The whole proceeding was conducted in the generous, gentlemanly way so much in accordance with the life and manner of the man whom it was sought thus to honor.

Kind words indeed, but President Arthur's remains were closely looked after by his friends, and the memorial they built for him is a striking one. In addition to his much-visited memorial at the cemetery, his friends contributed $10,000 toward a memorial built for him in New York City.

President Arthur's memorial was designed by Ephraim Keyser and dedicated on June 5, 1889. His sarcophagus somewhat resembles that for Napoléon Bonaparte, which has caused some comment, but the resemblance is largely in the cut of the lower portion of the sarcophagi and the stone used. Both have square-cut feet and a full body, and both are a distinctive black color. According to cemetery staff, President Arthur's sarcophagus is made of black granite, and he is not buried in it but rather slightly behind it near the marker for himself, his wife, a son, and three daughters.

Unlike some funeral art, however, there truly would have been room to entomb one or more bodies in President Arthur's substantial sarcophagus. Also unlike many sarcophagi, his has both a bronze nameplate and a bronze presidential seal, and an American flag flies at the site. There is no doubt that a president is interred here.

Standing at the front and slightly to the left side at the head of the sarcophagus is an angel cast in bronze. Her face and hairstyle are unique; they are truly unusual for an era of angels cast in images of classical beauty. Her wings are ornate, delicate, and flowing, and she holds a palm branch in one hand, seemingly in the process of laying it upon the tomb.

An angel stands guard over the final resting place of this American president, and as noted, another marker is slightly behind the sarcophagus: a combination tablet and smaller white sarcophagus are inscribed with President Arthur's and other family names. A wide, decorative stone staircase frames, as it were, the entire memorial. Each year, on President Arthur's birthday, October 5, American veterans place a fresh wreath at the graveside, a gift from the current president.

Chester's memorial was deemed "one of the most interesting and artistic monuments" in the cemetery by Phelps in 1893. This was a fine and deserved endorsement, but it also shows something else: Albany Rural Cemetery was getting some close attention by the late 1800s, and it was enough attention that a guidebook or two was published discussing its merits and the cemetery locations the public might like to visit. It

already had many fine memorials, both of local citizens and of some well-known individuals and national players.

Not only a president but also sons of presidents are buried at the cemetery. In addition to President Chester Alan Arthur, his son, Chester Alan Arthur II, is buried at the cemetery, as is John Van Buren, or "Prince John," the son of President Martin Van Buren. He died at sea in October 1866, and his body was later interred at Albany Rural. An Italian marble cross marks his grave.

The cemetery holds the remains of eight presidential cabinet secretaries, as well as five US senators, thirty-two members of the US House of Representatives, two US Supreme Court justices, members of the Assemblymen of the New York Colony, and six members of the Continental Congress.

One early dignitary buried at the cemetery is Major General Philip Schuyler, who served in the Revolutionary War on the side of the colonists. He also served as a delegate to the Continental Congress, and General George Washington appointed him to command the northern district of New York. A falling out with General Horatio Gates led to a court-martial proceeding, from which Schuyler was acquitted with honor. He served until the end of the war and was later elected one of New York's first two senators to the new Congress. A native of the area, Schuyler died in 1804, and a thirty-six-foot-high Doric column with a square cap marks his grave.

Albany Rural Cemetery had voted in 1870 to set aside land for a memorial to Schuyler, and eventually, one of his descendants, a Mrs. Miller, paid to have the memorial erected. Schuyler had died in 1804 and was originally interred in a family vault at another cemetery, then moved to an unmarked lot, and later moved to Albany Rural.

There is another Schuyler interred at Albany Rural, however. According to *These Exalted Acres*, no one has been able to link the two memorialized Schuylers, one of whom was a free black man and the other a man who had owned thirteen slaves. Captain Samuel Schuyler came to Albany in the late 1700s and died in 1842. He was a ship captain and an entrepreneur, operating particularly along the Hudson River. He founded Schuyler Tow Boat Line and operated a coal yard and a feed and flour store with his sons. His memorial is a thirty-foot gray, rectangular-capped obelisk with a bas-relief anchor. His family has a number of stones and is located in what was considered a highly desirable location facing the Hudson River.

In addition to these leading men, General Stephen Van Rensselaer—an industrialist as well as a veteran and community leader—who founded the Rensselaer Polytechnic Institute, is buried at Albany Rural. So is William Paterson, a US senator and a governor of New Jersey. Paterson is buried on the same lot as is Van Rensselaer. Paterson signed the US Constitution, and he served on the Supreme Court until his death in 1806. James Manning served as secretary of the treasury under President Grover Cleveland and is also buried at Albany Rural.

Another celebrated "resident" of the cemetery is William Learned Marcy. Marcy served as a US senator, a three-term governor of New York, secretary of war under President James K. Polk, and secretary of state under President Franklin Pierce. Marcy died in 1857, and his relatives choose his resting place for him, recalling that he had "frequently expressed the wish to be buried where he had spent so much time in reading and in contemplation." And so he was.

In addition to separate individual memorials for those who fought in the American Civil War and other wars, the Albany Rural Cemetery has a Soldiers Lot. According to the National Park Service, the site holds the remains of 149 Union soldiers. Many of the soldiers died in Albany area hospitals of their injuries or illness during the Civil War. The city—the cemetery remaining a municipal one—donated the site to the federal government in 1862. The last burial on the lot took place in 1897. Central to the Soldiers Lot is a memorial built by the Grand Army of the Republic (GAR) for all of the soldiers, although the soldiers also have small, individual, white marble markers. The monument features a life-size bronze statue of a Union soldier topping an immense granite base, much like similar statues donated by the GAR in other places. A bas-relief, bronze portrait of President Abraham Lincoln is attached to the base, however, as well as bronze plaques with the names of the fallen soldiers.

With more and more interments taking place, the cemetery needed more work space, in all senses of the phrase and for all sorts of workers. By the 1880s, the need was abundantly clear, and construction began.

The cemetery built its office, or lodge building, in 1882, based on plans by R. W. Gibson, who also designed Albany's Cathedral of All Saints. A visually unusual building, it features a Potsdam red sandstone and Croton brick exterior along with a red tile roof, making it highly visible on the landscape. It has been described as Romanesque and just as eclectic as the building located at the other gateway. It sits just inside the main or eastern entrance off Broadway. A bell tower was located nearby and used heavily in the first years of cemetery operations, but it was used less so after burials became more frequent. The lodge has a porte cochere at its front entrance.

Not too distant from the office, the cemetery constructed a superintendent's house in 1899. It was designed by Marcus T. Reynolds, an eminent Albany architect who, as noted, also designed a few of the more noted markers at Albany Rural. According to cemetery staff, the house, after being occupied for decades, would then sit vacant for forty-five years. The cemetery in the late 2010s was raising funds to restore the building.

Reynolds also designed the rather eclectic caretaker's cottage near the southern gate. He would serve on the board of the cemetery and otherwise contribute to it, and he was buried on a family lot at Albany Rural.

In 1884, the cemetery constructed a chapel for burial services. Designed by R. W. Gibson, who also designed the lodge down the avenue a bit, it also features a red Potsdam stone exterior. Its steep roof is likewise tiled, and it also has a porte cochere. Two wings were subsequently added onto the chapel.

Also on the same level and road as the lodge and chapel, as well as the earlier holding tombs, is the barn complex. Built to meet cemetery needs, the barn is immense, having two major wings, with one side on the inside of the L-shaped structure essentially open, roofed as though for horses.

New and noteworthy memorials continued to be added to the cemetery during and after the cemetery-building construction of the late 1800s. On the lawn near the pond, the Albany Masonic Burial Plot memorial rises above many others, a tall, white, broken column with a grouping of individual stones spiraling out from the center. The plot—purchased in the late 1800s—measures seventy-six feet in diameter, with burial space for 129 graves, according to Phelps in his cemetery history.

The column, erected in 1933, rests on a large, tiered base that creates three stone steps leading up to and surrounding the memorial. Farther away stands a monument to the Brotherhood of Railroad Trainmen, a tall obelisk with bronze plaques. Each organization had many members in the region.

Also near the Willow Pond section of the cemetery are several statues of note besides those already mentioned. The Godfrey memorial has a variation on the theme of a woman consoling another person, in this case, identified as *Religion Consoling Sorrow*. On the memorial, a figure in the throes of grief rests against the knee of a seated female who holds a book in one hand and gazes upward. As Phelps described the sculpture, "The positions, the expression, the drapery are all natural; the whole treatment is dignified, artistic and satisfying. There are few better designs in the cemetery, and few better executed." A nearly exact replica of the Godfrey sculpture, although not the impressive base it rests on, would be found in another rural cemetery, as would, at the same location, a statue of a male angel very like Palmer's *The Angel at the Sepulcher*. As the granite industry grew in the late 1800s, many themes in funerary art would be repeated in cemeteries across the region, some of them with unique twists, others without.

The Glazier memorial, however, is one of many that are unique to Albany Rural. A rough-cut stone overall, finely carved details stand out, and the two features together create an immediate sense that an explorer rests here, perhaps a Spanish one from the 1600s, in view of the style of the two swords, two bugles, shield, and length of cloth draped over the edge of the memorial. But no: although the Glazier memorial was erected for an explorer, it was carved for one who lived from 1841 until 1905, one who was also an author and a Civil War veteran.

Willard Glazier grew up a poor boy in northern New York, bought a horse with the money he earned as a trapper, and then went to Albany, where he attended the State Normal School (a teaching school, as they were then known, which is now the State University at Albany). He enlisted in the Union Army in 1861, and he and his horse joined the cavalry and the 2nd Regiment of New York, according to Grondahl and other sources. Glazier was captured during the war, but he escaped. Later, while exploring the American West, he was captured by Native

Americans. Glazier married Harriet Ayers, who supported his desire to explore the American West and to write. Glazier wrote several popular books involving adventure and his time in the army.

Built of Hallowell and Westerly granite, according to Phelps, and with the figure of *Hope* pointing upward, the Fort monument and family lot also memorialize, in part, an author and publisher of books, this time one who focused on the paranormal and satire. Charles Hoy Fort, whose most well-known work was *The Book of the Damned* in 1919, was buried in his family's lot—his father having been a successful real estate speculator and grocer—after his death in 1932. His fans—he inspired the creation of the Fortean Society—regularly visit his grave near Willow Pond, some reporting mystical or other odd occurrences.

Moreover, for one last, stunning angel figure, the bronze Myers memorial is worth visiting. Located near Willow Pond also, the simply robed female angel standing atop a polished rose-tinted marble base commemorates the life of John G. Myers. Myers built one of the largest department stores in the region, one that became an iconic institution in Albany, and suffered a disastrous collapse in 1905, a year after Myers died. Thirteen people died in the collapse, and others were injured, but the store rebuilt and lasted until the 1970s. The angel's hands are turned down in what is considered a sign of mourning, and her face, too, is somber and resembles in its patina and expression the Parsons bronze angel. She stands between the open pages of an immense stone book.

Full of marvelous statues, mausoleums, tombs, and buildings, the Albany Rural Cemetery was placed on the National Register of Historic Places in 1979. It is the largest garden cemetery in New England, linked to the rest of New England geographically and historically, as is another lovely garden cemetery farther north. Both are worth visiting, as are some of the state's other rural cemeteries. However, be prepared to spend an especially long time at Albany Rural; its many memorials and attributes have only been touched upon here.

The Albany Rural Cemetery holds a wealth of information in its archives, and it has a few books available for purchase, including the 2013 book These Exalted Acres *by the* Albany Times Union *(with Paul Grondahl being the primary author), which provides basic material. Henry P. Phelps's 1893* History of the Albany Rural Cemetery *includes the dedication address and offers the reader a tour through the cemetery as it was in the 1890s. His earlier inclusion of the cemetery in his 1884 history of the city,* The Albany Handbook, A Strangers' and Residents' Handbook, *also provides some information as well.* From Stonecutter to Sculptor, *by Elizabeth K. Allen, published by the Albany Institute of History and Art, provides some information on Calverley and his relationship with Palmer. In addition, the cemetery's application for the National Register of Historic Places gives some information about the cemetery up until 1979. The* Albany Times Union *regularly carries articles about the cemetery, and its archives yield additional information. And again, the cemetery itself, the physical cemetery, is a huge repository of information.*

7

The Garden of Ethereal Wings

Swan Point Cemetery, Providence, Rhode Island

Swan Point is one of the most mystical of the garden cemeteries, especially if one first visits in early spring on a rainy day and, if in the breaks of rain and along the river, one sees the mist and sees the angels—angels or otherworldly beings—winged creatures carved and sculpted and formed in whites and blacks, in stone and metal, perhaps guarding the dead, perhaps protecting the living. And perhaps, in the gloom of evening, they are warning those who seek out the place as the night is falling that there will be no incursions here. And then again, during some seasons, there are the other winged creatures that give the cemetery its name: the swans. The swans also visit the cemetery just over the wall, one that, with its own atmosphere, only adds to the feeling of both wonder and mystery. There are the other birds too, including the fantastical long-legged great blue herons who seek the shores of the Seekonk River. Go to Swan Point; you will be intrigued or enthralled.

SWAN POINT CEMETERY IN PROVIDENCE, RHODE ISLAND, IS ANOTHER active garden cemetery, and it is one not to be missed. Established in 1846 with sixty acres, the cemetery would become one of the favorite green spaces for the general public in the region, ultimately reaching some 300 acres and currently holding about 200 acres. Even today, people express surprise when they first go to Swan Point, according to the cemetery staff, expecting to encounter something gloomy or small. Instead, they find a large, well-maintained, pleasant burial space, albeit, one might argue, a rather mystical one.

Like most of the garden cemeteries discussed herein, Swan Point remains an active cemetery, and like them all, it is a nonsectarian entity, open to everyone regardless of religion. Like most of the other rural cemeteries also, Swan Point would become a favored burial place for the elite of its city and state, although some cemeteries would see such patronage decline over the passage of a century or more.

Unlike Mount Hope and Mount Auburn—America's first two official garden cemeteries—Swan Point was not established in association with a horticultural society. Nor was it a municipal cemetery like Albany Rural, Valley, and Pine Grove Cemeteries. However, a few other private garden cemeteries had been successfully established by the mid-1840s, without a horticultural society's aid, as had the private Springfield Cemetery, and the possibility of making a financial success of such an endeavor had been recognized. Swan Point has proven financially successful, but it is still a nonprofit corporation. The money earned by cemetery services past and present is invested for continued cemetery care and operations, much as it is with the other private nonprofit garden cemeteries.

As with some of the rural or garden cemeteries, Swan Point—located on the shores of the Seekonk River and extending to what was once known as Neck Road (now Old Road) and the newer Blackstone Avenue to the west—underwent a few transitions in its early years. In 1840, the cemetery had its genesis when one man decided that Providence needed a new cemetery, a healthy cemetery, a cemetery that would be an improvement over those already existing in Providence. He took action, just as several people had done before him in other towns and cities in New England.

In 1840, Thomas C. Hartshorn, a prominent Providence educator, started to advocate for a new cemetery for the city. Hartshorn stated that the time had come for the city to have a new burial ground, and he wished to locate one on property that combined, according to cemetery records, "beauty of situation, amplitude of space, and capacity for improvement." In these ten words, he essentially urged the city to create a garden or rural cemetery. Few people listened to Hartshorn in 1840. He waited for five years and tried again. This time he was able to convince enough people and to sell enough subscriptions to attempt to purchase land near the Old Burial Grounds, but this fell through when the newly incorporated Providence and Worcester Railroad acquired the land first. This setback, however, would prove a positive one.

Hartshorn soon set his eyes on acquiring property on Rhode Island's Seekonk River. With the subscription money raised thus far, he purchased two tracts of land: one from William Morris and the other from Edward Perry et al. It was located off Neck Road, but there was no easy way to reach the property from downtown Providence. After raising the initial money to purchase the land—some fifty-nine and a half acres—Hartshorn had a difficult time proceeding further.

In 1846, six years after Hartshorn started his endeavor, however, the Swan Point Cemetery Association was established, and it was so recognized on July 6. Hartshorn would serve as the secretary and actuary of the new organization, with John Stimson as chairman. The board had four other members, and according to the cemetery's National Register of Historic Places application, the men were all friends of Hartshorn, and he had convinced them to join him.

Swan Point Cemetery engaged the services of a Providence group of engineers, Atwater & Schubarth, to design the cemetery. The company had recently designed a new section of Providence's North Burial Ground, and at Swan Point, they were to lay out winding paths and roadways as well as groups of burial plots in a manner to best take advantage of the rolling landscape. Schubarth would subsequently break his partnership with Atwater, but the Norwegian-born Schubarth would be buried at Swan Point in 1889 near the original entranceway at Swan Point.

Atwater & Schubarth ultimately mapped out 109 groups of plots, each with surrounding paths or avenues and each divided into a number of burial lots. Each group of plots averaged 4,000 square feet. The cemetery held a meeting of its subscribers on October 20, 1846, at which time 860 burial lots in eighty-six of the groups of plots were sold or distributed for $13,000 total.

Off to a solid start, the Swan Point Cemetery Association was chartered as Swan Point Cemetery Corporation in May 1847 as a stock company with a board of trustees. Lot proprietors were to be trustees of the company, and the corporation was empowered to hold requisite property as well as buildings and other structures.

The cemetery held a consecration ceremony on July 2, 1847. Local clergy of various denominations spoke, as did the president of Providence's Brown University, Francis Wayland.

According to an article published that September by the *Providence Daily Journal*, the dedication ceremony was well received. Moreover, when the chosen location for the new cemetery was first announced, the choice was greeted happily, for, "besides the beauty of the place, there was something suitable in the name which it had always borne. As well as of purity, the spotless bird was an emblem of peace and repose." The author continued to praise the location and said that "from the pure chalice of innumerable flowers, unsullied by false human lips, bees and insects with song shall partake mystic communion."

While the cemetery opened for business and the first interments occurred, Schubarth continued to do design work for the cemetery until as late as 1863, including designing a few newer sections in the same manner as Atwater & Schubarth had the initial ones. Swan Point continued to further "improve" its grounds after the dedication in various ways. It built a holding tomb (still standing) and a keeper's lodge (razed in 1909), both designed by Thomas A. Tefft. It also constructed a bridge over the grounds' "great ravine," laid out graveled carriage roads, and established a nursery with 1,000 trees. In addition, cisterns were soon dug to irrigate the grounds. The cemetery was off to a good start and in the manner envisioned by Hartshorn.

It is unknown exactly when the first burial occurred on the grounds, and the identity of the deceased is also somewhat unknown, or rather, conflicting claimants exist. An early history of the cemetery written by Edwin M. Stone in 1870 identifies William T. Grinnell, who died in Scotland in 1835, as the first interment. An extant monument, however, claims that its "resident" Timothy McLaughlin was "the first person buried at Swan Point Cemetery." The boy was born in 1843 and died in 1845. Perhaps both claims are valid, one being for the first reinterment and the other for the first regular interment.

Like Mount Auburn, Swan Point soon saw a need to regulate visitors. While most anyone could visit on weekdays and Saturdays, on Sundays, only lot owners and their guests could enter the grounds. Lot owners could also secure tickets to allow them to enter with carriages or ride horseback. All visitors had to display decorum appropriate to a burial place, desist from in anyway injuring the trees and shrubs, and resist "plucking even the violet that springs up by the grave of a child, for it is an emblem of immortality, for the consolation of bereavement and sorrow," according to cemetery records.

As true elsewhere, many reinterments occurred at Swan Point soon after its establishment, including a number of them by the First Congregational Society (now known as the First Unitarian Church). The society acquired a large—five-acre—oval tract of land at Swan Point and transferred remains there from their older burial grounds, some of them dating back to 1722, according to cemetery records.

The First Unitarian Society Grounds would be relocated to Swan Point with a large collection of Federal-era slate markers. It would also have the associated Pastor's Rest site for the burial of First Unitarian Church ministers, with a large circular monument being its most prominent marker.

During the 1850s to the early 1880s, Swan Point acquired some older burial grounds within the same group of private cemeteries (the conglomerate known as the West Burial Ground) as where the First Unitarian Church had previously had its grounds, and workers removed those remains to Swan Point also. In Providence, as in other large cities, burial space had become scarce and, in some instances, was wanted for other purposes. Most of the reinterments at Swan Point were made close to the Seekonk River, with many of the old headstones also relocated. Some of the reinterments were of remains a hundred years old, giving the cemetery a glimpse further into the past, much as would be true at some other garden cemeteries such as Springfield Cemetery and at New Haven's transitional Grove Street Cemetery.

In 1858, Rhode Island granted the cemetery a new charter, making it a nonprofit entity entitled the Proprietors of the Swan Point Cemetery. The original company released its stocks, land, and other assets to the new corporation. The new entity then established its own bylaws, elected a board of six directors, and was authorized to hire a superintendent. Within a few years, it was acquiring additional lands.

The cemetery would gain additional land over the years until it extended past modern-day Blackstone Avenue, which itself was made possible by gifts of land. Initially, there was no direct road to reach the cemetery. A meandering or zigzagging road or route did exist, and in the early 1870s, an omnibus following this route provided the first public transportation to Swan Point. However, this was still not sufficient for easy access to the grounds.

In the mid-1880s, therefore, the cemetery hired a New England landscape architect then based in Chicago, Horace W. S. Cleveland, to redesign the property as needed. Cleveland would become a well-known and respected landscape designer over the years, with some people considering him only slightly behind Frederick Law Olmsted—if behind at all—in the place of landscape-design history. Cleveland and Olmsted would work together for a time after the Civil War, and they developed a great respect for one another as well as a strong friendship.

Cleveland had also been the grounds designer for the Butler Hospital for the Insane, which abutted Swan Point Cemetery, in 1859. Also, according to the hospital's application for Historic Sites Recognition, the Olmsted brothers would do further work on the grounds in 1906. Swan Point's neighbor also had property extending to the river, and its property, too, would be deemed "park-like."

Cleveland had previously worked on Providence's Roger Williams Park, as well as designing two cemeteries in Massachusetts in the 1850s: Oak Grove in Gloucester in 1854 and Sleepy Hollow in Concord in 1855, as part of the firm Cleveland and Copeland. The two submitted an entry to design Central Park in 1857, which Olmsted and his often unnoted partner, Calvert Vaux, won. Cleveland later designed Eastwood Cemetery in Lancaster, Massachusetts, which opened in 1876, with his son. Moreover, in Chicago in 1872, after the Great Chicago Fire, he was hired to help rebuild South Park, originally designed by Olmsted and Vaux. Cleveland published a book on cemetery design in 1881, titled *A Few Words on the Arrangement of Rural Cemeteries.*

By 1886, Cleveland had made a strong name for himself. It is no surprise that the proprietors at Swan Point found him a worthy person to aid them in their design dilemmas. Since 1876, the cemetery had had a superintendent as well as a board of directors, and its superintendent, Timothy McCarthy, would work closely with Cleveland on the new project.

As part of the redesign project, to further cemetery access, the cemetery deeded Providence a 200-foot easement through the property. This effectively cut off about twenty-two acres from the western side of the cemetery, once Blackstone Avenue, designed by Cleveland, and was built into the cemetery.

Cleveland designed Providence's Blackstone Boulevard in 1886 to pass through the edge of the cemetery, and under Cleveland's supervision, the cemetery added a boulder wall to enclose the property along its new boundary using indigenous rock and established a new entryway on the avenue. A boulder wall surrounds much of the cemetery to the current day, and Swan Point retained its early rock gateway, one of granite boulders, although iron gates open and close from the rock entranceway. Beyond the gateway stretches one of the two straight roads on the grounds: Holley Avenue, which extends into the heart of the cemetery.

In 1900, *Park and Cemetery* (later called *Modern Cemetery*) published an article about Swan Point, written by Phelps Wyman and featuring a photograph of the new stone wall and gateway. In the photograph, the massive boulder that bears the nameplate for the cemetery is shown perched atop a substantial rock wall or pile, the tip of the boulder exceeding the tallest parts of the adjacent walls. The entryway is little changed since that time.

However, the journal went far beyond praising the new boulder wall and entranceway. It also praised the choice of trees and shrubbery at the cemetery, giving numerous specific examples, and stating that "Swan Point's good qualities are not necessarily its most conspicuous; one has rather to search to find why it pleases him. He discovers its site well chosen, its natural features simple but full of charm, its horticulture inconspicuous but developed tastefully." A few late-nineteenth-century articles in the local press or local histories had likewise praised the beauty of the cemetery.

To discover the cemetery's charm, Wyman urged, one should visit more than once and go the first time in the early morning when the mists are still in the air. The grounds were beautiful in many ways, "but the glory of the place is in the descent, broken by ravines and covered with the same woods which make all New England beautiful."

The countryside around the cemetery was less-developed at the turn of the century, and Wyman noted that the cemetery was entered by "a beautiful country road shadowed by overhanging trees." The visitor would soon see the Seekonk River and encounter an avenue below the cemetery's ridge, one that runs near the river, and one without which Swan Point would not be Swan Point. "Across the shifting lights of the river one sees nature seemingly but little changed. . . . The calm and quiet of the place is of that stillness which satisfies our imagination as a fitting place of repose. When our time comes for rest, we should lie the more peacefully for this nearness to Nature's quietness," Wyman wrote. Finding the location for Swan Point was a wonderful thing, but it was its development that was key, and such "development" of a great feature like the Seekonk River view was something other cemeteries might emulate with their own best features.

Speaking specifically of the wall, Wyman noted that the cemetery had been full of huge boulders and rocks and had made "sensible use" of them by creating the wall. "As long as the individuality of each stone is merged in the general mass of the wall, the effect is excellent," the article observed. The wall was already covered in places with vines of two varieties.

Furthering the admiration rendered the cemetery, Richard M. Bayles stated in his 1891 *History of Providence, Rhode Island* that "Swan Point is the most beautiful and costly [cemetery] in the city." Bayles noted the lovely river, and then he stated, "The beauty of the place is in its landscape, and a great deal is the result of artistic landscape gardening." However, "there are the most and finest memorials here of any ground in the city, among them that of Senator Anthony, that of the Barnaby family, and that of the Nightingale family. Hundreds of others are the equals of any work which could be produced." Bayles also noted, "The wealthy modern people of the city have placed their loved ones here." At the time he wrote, most of the development and burials had taken place in the sections close to the river.

Work still remained at Swan Point at the turn of the century. Little progress had been made on building a new receiving tomb, as well as a chapel and crematory as planned in the 1890s, largely because the expense of creating the boulder wall and the new entrance had monopolized cemetery resources. The superintendent, however, had managed to squeeze several years worth of work into one during the building of the wall. The cemetery entered the new century on solid footing, according to the annual report of the proprietors.

In 1903, one of the city's trolley car lines was extended along Blackstone Boulevard to provide transportation to the cemetery at Swan Point's new entryway. The cemetery then erected a fieldstone shelter for public use, much as Mount Hope had been able to add its ornate trolley waiting room.

Swan Point benefited from having one superintendent, Timothy McCarthy, serve for thirty-five years from 1876 until his death in 1911. He was followed by Daniel Thurber, who had been with the cemetery for about thirty years, eleven of them as assistant superintendent, according to *Park and Cemetery*, which published McCarthy's obituary.

The journal noted of McCarthy that "for more than a third of a century he had labored to make his the most perfect cemetery, from a landscape point of view, in the country. Original in methods and ideas," over time, the names McCarthy and Swan Point (consisting of 150 acres at the time of his death) "became synonymous as well as famous through out the land." The journal stated that McCarthy had "accentuated rather than conventionalized the natural features of the grounds under his care and framed his masterpiece with the boulder wall—the finishing touch of the artist." McCarthy's brother had worked with McCarthy for much of his tenure, until his death earlier in 1911.

Timothy McCarthy had been active in such organizations as the Association of American Cemetery Superintendents, and in a second article, the superintendent's association referred to McCarthy as "the original and artistic superintendent" of Swan Point, identifying him as a "magnetic and vigorous leader" in cemetery and association affairs. The Gardeners

Chronicle of America that year also commented on McCarthy's passing, noting that he had been born in Ireland and had worked at Forest Hills Cemetery for a short time before his 1876 move to Swan Point. He and his father-in-law were both members of the National Association of Gardeners.

With a new superintendent, things went on at Swan Point. A few years after the trolley cars had reached the cemetery, it was able to build its long-anticipated office, located just to the side of the new entrance. Gothic revival in style, it was built of Weymouth seam face granite and Indiana limestone. The cemetery added a chapel to the building in 1932 and enlarged the chapel and crematorium wing in 1947 and again in 2002. A new crematory building was added near the office in 1991, and it and the various buildings maintain a harmonious coexistence. In 2006, the cemetery added a chapel and columbarium with a mausoleum at the southwestern end of the cemetery, a building capable of seating a hundred people. Subsequent additions have added to the services available.

With the office building finally completed as well as the avenue and entrance, the board reported in 1913 in *Park and Cemetery* that it had consulted with "Olmsted Brothers, Landscape Architects as to the layout of the land between Swan Point Road and the Boulevard." They anticipated that Olmsted Brothers would "probably recommend the removal of all the dwellings, stables, greenhouses, stone-crushers, etc., to some new location to the west of the Boulevard. The intention is to obtain a comprehensive plan that may be worked toward in the most convenient and economical manner."

The cemetery used some of the land cut off by the new road in the late 1800s for several years before ultimately deciding to dispose of it. The land was essentially unused for two decades, and then in 1917, with an eye to its ongoing cemetery beautification needs, the cemetery erected a greenhouse on the land. In 1923, it added a superintendent's house nearby, followed by a few service buildings in 1932. However, despite these additions, the cemetery soon decided to part with some sections cut off by Blackstone Avenue, which, as the years passed, became a busy thoroughfare. The roadway, although it provided the needed access, was otherwise proving a handicap.

In 1933, the cemetery deeded the City of Providence two parcels of land west of Blackstone Boulevard. Part of this land was used for local road extensions, but a public park was built on one piece and was called the Alexander Farnham Lippitt Memorial Park. Other parcels of land were subsequently disposed of. The superintendent's home was sold in 1959, and the remaining six acres were also sold soon thereafter. New service buildings were built on land east of the road before the final western parcels were sold.

Whereas Mount Hope had added new land when a road extension cut a portion of its property off, with less property in question, Swan Point gave its isolated land, or most of it, to the city. However, the city also returned some property to the cemetery after it discontinued the Old Neck Road as a public road in 1933. Swan Point and Butler Hospital had previously owned the land, and the land reverted to them. The hospital subsequently conveyed its interest in the roadway to the cemetery.

Its various land transactions did not leave the cemetery bereft of sufficient and suitable land. Its remaining 200 acres served the cemetery well. Moreover, the cemetery is still—as it always has been—irregular in shape, bounded by the river at its widest stretch and by public roads and a neighboring cemetery. Interments and construction had continued at Swan Point throughout the decades, even as modernity had reached the cemetery.

During the nineteenth century, while the laying out of the grounds had continued, other improvements had also taken place, especially the planting of various species of trees, which continues to the present time. There is currently a 200-year-old sassafras tree on the grounds that predates the cemetery's establishment, as well as innumerable other ornamental trees and shrubs.

The cemetery also added a small pond to its landscape in the late nineteenth century. Called Rock Pond and created circa 1885, it offers a tranquil resting place for the visitor, complete with seating. It features a small fountain "sprouting" from a large boulder. In the early years of the twentieth century, the area near the pond became a favored location for private family mausoleums.

Another small resting place was created at the "dell" circa 1880. A small pool was created but then replaced after city water became too expensive to justify the expense. It was eventually redone, and it now has a small fountain in a rock-lined pool supplied by well water.

In 1885, a rustic gazebo was built near Benjamin Anthony's burial site. Being constructed primarily of wood, the structure deteriorated over time, and the cemetery razed it in 1975 after it became unsafe. In 2005, Swan Point built a replica of the gazebo, adding a cremation garden nearby, with twenty steps leading up to and around the gazebo. Some older style markers were also added to memorialize people interred earlier at Stranger's Rest, the name of the current location.

The Forty Steps were also added to enhance the beauty of the natural landscape and make portions of it more accessible, much like the One Hundred Steps at Mount Hope Cemetery. The steps are located near the river, rising from Forest Avenue up the hillside to Ridge Way and blend well into its surroundings. Rhododendron bushes flank the natural stone stairway. At the top are ornamental maple and oak trees. A shorter, wide flight of stairs was also added at another location near the river.

A brownstone receiving or holding tomb was eventually built at the cemetery. Tefft designed the vault to fit the curvature of the land, and it was built with a rounded arch doorway, in the "Lombard Romanesque" style, which the architect favored, according to cemetery documents.

Another major tomb at Swan Point, and perhaps the most intriguing of all, is located close to and overlooking the river. The Marsden Perry tomb was built into the side of a hill, and essentially, it is contiguous to an intriguing lot in its own right, the Aldrich lot.

The entrance to the Perry tomb was built to duplicate, full-scale, the entrance to the local John Brown House, where Perry, a man who had risen to great wealth through banking, utilities, railroads, and other concerns, had lived from 1902 until his death in 1935. The impressive tomb features a brick face and a porch or portico with granite columns, and it is not readily visible until one approaches the nearby river landing and looks to the side or backward.

In 1961, the Rhode Island Historical Association gave Swan Point Marsden Perry's marble fountain, which Perry had much earlier imported from Italy. The fountain had stood at the historic John Brown House, where Perry had lived. The historical association had acquired the fountain in 1941 and, twenty years later, they presented it to the cemetery. The fountain is about ten feet in diameter, with four lions' heads carved into the rim of the bowl of the fountain, dividing the basin into quadrants. The white marble fountain stands near the office and chapel buildings, giving the entrance to the cemetery grounds a visual grace tied to antiquity.

Marsden Perry's fountain came to grace the grounds of Swan Point in the 1900s. So, too, did other gifts arrive and sometimes disappear. The "Boy and Girl Fountain," was installed in the cemetery in the 1870s but also was to have a 1970s component. The small fountain of a boy and girl sharing an umbrella was stolen in 1968. It was replaced in 1974, the cemetery having commissioned a replica of the original, but was erected in the courtyard of the by then "Historic Chapel" near the office.

Another theft of an historic monument occurred a decade later. In 1978, *Little Sarah* was stolen from the Wilkinson family plot. The statue of the child, carved in marble, had stood there for more than one hundred years. After the 1978 theft, the cemetery had a replacement statue carved by an Italian sculptor, using photographs as a guide, and installed the new Sarah in the inner office/chapel courtyard not far from the Boy and Girl Fountain, with a ledger stone plaque placed at the original location.

These monuments or child memorials are not necessarily the most impressive of those at the cemetery, although Sarah, in particular, is compelling. Other child statues or monuments in the cemetery are just as intriguing. Near some of the most impressive lots in the cemetery can be found a small monument, a carving of a baby in a crib. Marked simply with her name, she is still quite visible. She will be discussed later, as will others.

A number of people who died in their teens or early twenties are also commemorated at Swan Point, often with the symbolism common to the mid to late 1800s. For example, the Dyer lot contains several monument styles popular in their day, most of them made of white marble, including ones for those who died young.

The Dyer lot contains two of the "ledger" memorials seen from Maine to New York in garden cemeteries, as well as in New Haven, which is the forerunner of the movement. The tabletop or ledger-top memorial is a table of sorts formed with columns, often with a book or ledger on the top of the "table," also known as the "ledger-on-column marker" and generally used for adults.

The two ledger-top memorials on the Dyer lot are complete with scrolls, and they were erected to honor the progenitors of the family: Frances Dyer and Governor of Rhode Island Elisha Dyer, who died in the 1870s and 1850s respectively. Next to these two is a "broken-column monument," a column seemingly cut off halfway or so up and symbolizing a life cut off too soon, memorializing their son, George, who died in 1833 at about age twenty. "Eternal ivy" vines entwine the column, which sits on a tiered square base. Also on the family site is another symbol of early death: a broken vase, toppled onto its side, memorializes George Rathbone, who died in 1851 at approximately seventeen years of age. Along with these are a few other monuments, including that of another governor, Elisha Dyer Jr., who died in 1906. His marker is a trefoil-cusped cross. Curbing sets off most of the family lot.

The edge of the Dyer lot, facing away from the lot and toward the river, features an Egyptian-revival-style tomb. It was designed by Russell Warren and was originally built at the Beneficent Congregational Society Burial Ground in 1839. It was removed to Swan Point in 1863. Made of brownstone, it is similar in some ways to the gates at the New Haven Burial Grounds and, perhaps more closely, to a few other mausoleums found in New England's garden cemeteries (as well as one at New Haven). It features an overhanging cornice, underneath which is carved a detailed orb with a wings symbol above the family name. Columns with detailed capitals flank the doorway, and wing walls set off the tomb.

One of the cemetery's most haunting memorials to those who died young is found at the Sprague family lot, and it is a large, circular one. At the center of the site is a massive, circular, Greek-inspired granite monument (based on a fourth-century BC monument in Athens). The family gave rise to two Rhode Island governors, an uncle and his nephew, who were both named William Sprague (III and IV) and served during 1838–1839 and 1860–1863 respectively. The first, the uncle, was buried on this family lot, but his nephew was not. White marble is a feature of the lot, although not all gravestones and memorials are made of it.

The two children whose memorial draws so much attention are Mary Comstock Sprague (1850–1860) and her brother, William Comstock Sprague (1857–1860). Charles Hemenway carved them in marble in the 1860s, and their sculpture rests atop a large sarcophagus. When the author first visited, someone had added small toy figures of the sleeping children and placed a white teddy bear between them. On their next visit, there were the remains of a flower, and the third time, there was a votive candle on the memorial. The statues are haunting, and they, as well as others, may cause the viewer to reflect on the short life of many children in the nineteenth century.

The Sprague family also has a commanding lot in another compelling location at Swan Point. William Sprague—the second governor in the family—had built as his memorial what remains the largest tomb in the cemetery. Sprague lived from 1830 until 1915, served as governor of the state during the Civil War, and fought in the war while governor. His large circular tomb is based on those of the Etruscans and Romans, according to cemetery literature. He married Kate Chase, daughter of Salmon P. Chase, Abraham Lincoln's first secretary of the treasury, and the two reportedly led a glamorous life in Washington, DC. The burial lot features a large tomb, a granite wall with much decorative curbing, a double flight of steps leading up to the tomb entrance, and two separate flights of steps on the opposite side. Decorative urns flank the stairways.

Not all Rhode Island politicians chose elaborate memorials, however. A more modest memorial was erected for Henry Bowen Anthony, a newspaperman who became Rhode Island's twenty-first governor, serving 1849–1851, and was also a four-term US senator. Anthony has just a bronze plaque on a stone to mark his resting place.

Another example of a large family lot with a child's memorial has two such memorials, one placed alongside the other. The memorials are in the crib style that was then popular, markers with space left in the middle for plants. The memorials are for Nannie Nyle Sayles and Louise Marsh Sayles. Nannie has a vine-covered harp to ornament her crib, while Louise has a lamb on hers.

These two children are not the only people buried at the immense Sayles family lot who died young, however. The Sayles commissioned noted sculptor Henry Baerer to create a monument for William Clark Sayles, who died while studying at Brown University in 1876. The cemetery considers the resulting pensive artwork, cast in bronze, as "undoubtedly the most sublime of those to the many young women and men who died too young."

A small, classic temple memorial on a tiered base built for Frederic Clark Sayles and his family graces the opposite end of the large oval lot, located at a key intersection of cemetery avenues, with low but substantial granite walls enclosing it and stone curbing beyond that. Steps flanked by urns lead up to the lot. The lot holds memorials for numerous family members and includes other types of markers besides those already mentioned, including flat, bronze-topped ledger markers.

Another child's marker, a tiny one with an infant sculpture—that of a baby in her bed—is located nearby, but it is to the side and rear of the large Sayles lot. Simple but compelling, the child's name, Harriet Virginia Sayles, is inscribed on her memorial. Her memorial is rather isolated, although there are other graves not too far away.

Not too distant from these markers but a little closer to the river is one that memorializes both children and their mother, one with a simple yet beautiful angel sculpture. Created for the Jenks family, the delicacy of the female angel's wings sets her apart from some others. Similar to statues elsewhere, the Jenks's angel is somewhat larger than life. Like others seen elsewhere, too, she stands in front of a cross much larger than she is, but her pose is different since she looks downward and to one side and stands a step below the cross.

Bronze angel monuments are also to be found at Swan Point. Two noted ones near the river include the Lownes monument and the Nightingale memorial. The bronze sculpture by Viennese-born Isidore Konti at the Lownes' burial lot is of an angel sitting on an expansive white exedra-style bench with steps leading up to the angel, located just in front of the cemetery's boulder boundary wall. The sculptor was well known, and his commissioners were both wealthy and connected to the art community. Edgar John L. Lownes, who died in 1924, was a textile manufacturer, and his wife, who died in 1970, was a suffragist and an accomplished musician. Although an angel, there is something about this angel—his pose and facial expression—that might make a person wonder if it is the fallen angel who sits there on this bench.

And then once one learns a bit of background, that peculiar and intriguing face and pose are perhaps explained. Lownes, whose name had been Lowenstein prior to World War I, made his fortune and became something of a philanthropist. He volunteered not just at Brown University but also at the Rhode Island School of Design. In his will, he requested that a casting of Konti's *Genius of Immortality* be placed over his grave. (One of the six castings of the sculpture is on display at the Metropolitan Museum of Art and was acquired in 1916, before Lownes's death.)

Lownes' wife requested than Konti—who had moved to the United States in the 1890s—add wings to this particular version of the pensive young man, as well as two plaques of angels. Konti did so, and the winged genius was placed upon his white marble bench. Angel, genius, or some combination of the worldly with the otherworldly, Lownes's is a unique statue and memorial, on all counts.

Not too far distant is the monument commissioned by Samuel A. Nightingale. Artist A. Roland cast the bronze sculpture, which features a female angel bearing a baby aloft in her arms. The angel stands on an oval, decorated plinth or base with her free arm raised to the heavens, a classic pose in funerary art of the era. Nightingale commissioned the sculpture after the death of his first child, Nina, in 1875, and that of his wife, also named Nina, the following year. In his grief, Nightingale then, according to cemetery literature, left the family home and thereafter lived in a downtown Providence hotel.

The Wilkinson memorial features one of the cemetery's stone angels, a female one who wears a crown, carries flowers, and rests one hand upon a trellis-covered tree trunk or other feature. The memorial was erected for Jessie Wilkinson, who has her first name inscribed inside a wreath near the top of the base. Her husband, William, also buried at the lot, had the statue erected for his wife, who died in 1885, followed many years later by himself, in 1919.

The Young family lot has another compelling stone statue, one including an angel, but this is an angel bearing aloft, it seems, a young woman. Such statues have been interpreted as representing the soul carried aloft while still trapped in human form. Both figures were exquisitely carved and are supported by a "cloud" of white stone. The angel, perhaps Gabriel, carries a trumpet and has his other hand raised upward, with his fist closed as though in victory.

Another memorial featuring an angel and human is at the William O. and Emily L. Briggs lot. In this instance, a male angel rests one hand lightly upon the young person or soul, who rests against him, as they seem about to depart for another world. The Briggs died in the late 1800s.

And, of course, other winged creatures reside in or about the cemetery: birds. There are swans, turkeys, ducks, blue herons, small songbirds, and other avian species. The river attracts the larger waterfowl, while the pond and the landscaped grounds with its shrubs and flowers attract all sort of birds, as well as some four-footed animals.

Swan Point has some magnificent figural sculptures on its grounds, including those already mentioned. Overall, however, Swan Point—like most of the garden cemeteries—has more architectural and other monuments than figural ones, as well as some wonderful Celtic crosses, but its sculptures are still, overall, fantastic, as are its other features.

Located between the Nightingale and Lownes lots at Swan Point, overlooking the Seekonk River and essentially atop the Marsden Perry Tomb, is a tremendously well-landscaped lot featuring granite walls, stone walkways, and stairs leading to interments on several levels. The family of Abby Pierce and Nelson W. Aldrich owns the lot.

Nelson Aldrich (1845–1917), in addition to being a Civil War veteran, businessman, and Speaker of the Rhode Island House of Representation, was elected to fill the seat in the US Senate left vacant by Ambrose Burnside, another "resident" of Swan Point, after Burnside died in office in 1881. ("Iron" Burnside had been a Union general during the Civil War, was elected Rhode Island's governor soon thereafter, and then entered the US Senate.) Architect William T. Aldrich, one of Nelson's sons, is buried on this river-view site also, as is his other son—a diplomat, state senator, and US representative, Richard Steere Aldrich—and daughter Lucy

Truman Aldrich, a noted Orientalia collector. Nelson Aldrich's grandson, Nelson Aldrich Rockefeller, would become a US vice president, but he was not buried on the Aldrich family lot.

The Aldrich family was a large one, and its several members buried at the site have a variety of markers. The cemetery, however, not the family, undertook to terrace the lot in the 1970s, hiring the work out to a prestigious firm. The stonecutters used dry-laid, flat-cut granite in the terrace walls. The flat-cut walls are distinctive, but they also echo the natural granite walls seen elsewhere in the cemetery.

Various other memorials may be of interest to the visitor for their history, their associated people, and their beauty. Several impressive sarcophagi exist at the cemetery. Besides those already mentioned, those of the Sharpe family—founders of the Brown & Sharpe precision tool company—designed in the Italian Renaissance style—are worth visiting. The memorial to Joseph Brown of Brown & Sharpe is also at Swan Point, and his lot features a small pyramid.

Perhaps one of the more visited sarcophagi is that of Colonel John S. Slocum. His memorial is granite and reflects his military career. President James Polk commissioned him a lieutenant in the US Army in 1847, during the Mexican-American War. In early 1861, and early in the Civil War, Rhode Island governor William Sprague, one of the governors buried at Swan Point, granted Slocum the colonelcy of the 2nd Rhode Island Regiment. Slocum led his regiment in the Battle of Bull Run in Virginia, where he was killed on July 21, 1861. His memorial is inscribed with the name of his battles in both wars, and lying atop his sarcophagus, carved in the stone, is a military cape, cap, epaulets, and sword. His lot overlooks the river. A very similar marker is found at Cedar Hill for another decorated veteran of the war.

Another often visited monument at Swan Point is one of its simplest. Howard P. Lovecraft, a Providence native who lived from 1890 to 1937, achieved little fame during his lifetime. He died in poverty, but after his death, he became something of a worldwide cult figure for his works of horror and other fiction, and some of his works were made into movies. His popularity has only risen in the last few decades, but those who go seeking an elaborate gravesite will be disappointed, as Lovecraft has only a simple, small granite stone marking his name, years, and the words he penned after a brief and purportedly unhappy trip to New York: "I am Providence." The stone was placed at his burial site thirty years after his death. Fans regularly adorn his grave with trinkets, and some meet there yearly, near the date of his birthday.

Lovecraft's memorial is simple, as are many at Swan Point. Many crosses are seen on the grounds, as are a few zinkies (zinc memorials). Family lots feature a variety of memorials, including ones with draped and undraped urns. Some family memorials are simple; others, including some already described, are not.

One of the more distinctive monuments at Swan Point is that for Jerothmul B. Barnaby. A towering obelisk—topped with a statue of a female figure holding a wreath, the female figure of this classical type is considered a standard symbol or allegorical figure of grief, while a wreath symbolized mourning, remembrance, and everlasting life—overlooks the surrounding grounds, which were different, in terms of their extent, when the memorial was erected. The figure faces east, and it is situated on what was then the western edge of the property, according to cemetery records. Hence, it would have overlooked essentially the entire cemetery. This type of towering, statue-topped obelisk memorial would be seen in a few other rural cemeteries, yet each remains unique and impressive.

The Barnaby memorial marks the burial sites of Barnaby—who was a wealthy dry goods merchant—and his immediate family, as well as one of his descendants who would become a president of Brown University in Providence, Barnaby Keeney. The plinth of the obelisk is girdled with columns, Romanesque ones, and has ornate friezes as further embellishments.

Other female figures of mourning are also represented at Swan Point, in an impressive array. The F. A. Abell mausoleum, dated 1882, features a stunning sculpture of a female figure rising high above the blue Westerly granite edifice. She holds a large cross with a wreath of flowers in one hand, her other arm upturned, a finger pointed toward the heavens, in a pose classic in Victorian funerary art. Ferdinand Augustus Abell was a businessman and one of the founders of what became the Brooklyn Dodgers. He died of Bright's disease in 1913, but he ordered his mausoleum for $8,000 in February 1882 from the Smith Granite Company. It was delivered that September, according to the records of the Babcock–Smith House Museum.

Other compelling examples of statuary include the Arnold–Bullock, Weaver, Robert Abell, and Smith and Austin memorials. A simpler memorial than the F. A. Abell mausoleum, the Austin memorial also draws the eye. It has a statue of a woman with her eyes cast down, her hair mostly shrouded, standing over a broken column and holding a garland of flowers, likely for Alice Austin, who died at age twenty-one.

The Rose memorial features a seated woman, her hair done up, clutching one rose to her heart, while in her other hand she holds a bouquet of roses. The use of roses is perhaps both symbolic and, in the case of the Rose marker, meant to reflect the family name.

The Smith memorial has one of the mourning-woman-with-a-wreath figures seen elsewhere, but this one has variations. The figure has her hair tied back, holds a closed wreath of flowers, and wears shoes and simple attire. A somewhat similar but less ornate statue is located on the Weaver lot. Here, the standing figure holds flowers—lilies, it seems—against her chest with one hand, and the other is held aloft to the sky. Her face is strong, as are those of so many statues of funerary art.

The Robert Abell memorial, however, features a much different version, with its female figure standing, holding a flower garland, her hair down, and standing atop a rather tall and ornate base, decorated with a large palm leaf and other embellishments. Flowers are at her feet, too, but she has a more haunting quality in her home beneath the bowers than do some such memorials.

Other intriguing statues and memorials ornament the grounds at Swan Point and pay homage to the families and others who commissioned them. Only a sampling of them have been covered here; to experience these more fully, and to view others, one must visit the cemetery.

However, like the other garden cemeteries of New England, Swan Point is more than its markers and memorials. It is a place full of mysticism, symbolism, and natural beauty. It is a microcosm of social history and a place to learn of art and architecture, of turkeys and herons and swans.

In 1977, Swan Point Cemetery was listed on the National Register of Historic Places. Similar to the others discussed herein, Swan Point is well deserving of the honor.

Swan Point has a wonderful visitors' booklet called Swan Point Cemetery, An Historical Walking Tour, *which is highly recommended. It contains a map and historical information on some of the sites discussed here, as well as others.* Yesterday and Tomorrow, Swan Point Cemetery, *is also recommended.* Providence Business News *and the* Providence Daily Journal *have included articles over the years, and* Park and Cemetery *also included several articles about Swan Point in the late 1800s and early 1900s, as indicated, and these are also well worth looking at, as is the cemetery's application for inclusion on the National Register of Historic Places.*

8

The Forgotten Gem of the Garden Cemeteries

Brookside Cemetery, Watertown, New York

In far northern New York, just an hour away from the Saint Law-rence River and Canada, is located one of the perhaps forgotten gems of the rural or garden cemetery movement. Purportedly designed by Frederick Law Olmsted himself, which is actually an error or a mis-understanding, Brookside Cemetery is blessed with one of the finest configurations of water bodies of the garden cemeteries of New Eng-land. Moreover, Brookside has an approach or "foreground" that rivals that of the more famous, and somewhat younger, Cedar Hill of Hartford, Connecticut, as well as that of any other cemetery discussed herein, some of which were indeed designed by Olmsted associates. Visit Brookside and wind your way around the brooks and pond and roads to reach the older sections farther back; you will not be disap-pointed, and you will see the work of a talented landscape architect.

BROOKSIDE CEMETERY'S LAYOUT AND ATTRIBUTES DO INDEED ENCOM-pass several of Frederick Olmsted and his associate Joseph Weidenman or Charles Elliot's design ideals. It could well have been Olmsted—who is perhaps best known as the co-designer of Central Park in New York City, completed a few years after Brookside Cemetery opened—who designed Brookside, as many local residents believe, but it was not. It was Howard

Daniels, a native of Pennsylvania, who designed Brookside, established in 1853, as well as a few other cemeteries of note in New York and other states. Howard Daniels was a noted landscape architect in his own right, and Watertown leaders chose wisely when they chose Daniels to design their garden cemetery. However, for those who still wish to see an Olmsted connection, Daniels was one of the runners-up in the competition to design New York's Central Park. Daniels and Olmsted were likely acquainted.

Brookside Cemetery has rolling hills, water in abundance, lovely trees, and several other advantages. Its location was well selected. One of the differences that would develop over time at Brookside Cemetery, as opposed to many of the other cemeteries discussed, was that as the decades passed, and really after the twenty-first century, for the most part, newer graves would be placed closer to the front of the cemetery, in front of the older sections, as opposed to behind the earlier ones or off to the side as seen in many garden cemeteries. If you are looking for the older and overall more ornate monuments, go to the back of the cemetery, to the more hilled areas, and you will be well rewarded for your efforts.

Located at the edge of Watertown, New York, and incorporated on April 27, 1853, Brookside Cemetery was designed to encompass an older burial ground, one with its first known burial being in 1805. Including an earlier burial ground, as opposed to having reinterments create a link with the past, is unique to the cemeteries included here, although another one would later, well after it was established, absorb an older burial ground.

Brookside was located in a community that still had sufficient burial sites near some of its burial grounds; the important thing at the time was to ensure that land for burials continued to exist and to incorporate some of the newer ideas about burials and cemetery design. The burial ground incorporated into Brookside Cemetery had been called Sawyer or Burrville Cemetery—Burrville being a town contiguous to Watertown.

To discuss a possible new and large cemetery for the area, the Watertown Cemetery Association (later renamed the Brookside Cemetery Association), met at the local Perkins Hotel on April 27, 1853. The community already had a number of small burial grounds, but the association believed there was a need for a newer, larger site.

Watertown's newest cemetery would be organized at a time when other new entities were also being formed or built in the town or village that would soon become a city. The year 1849 had seen a major fire rip through the streets, destroying numerous structures, including some in the downtown area near what is known as the Public Square, an open area around which streets flowed and some of the more commercial businesses and "blocks" as they were then called were built.

The years leading to the establishment of the cemetery at Brookside saw the construction of some of the buildings for which the city would be most noted for the next hundred-plus years, including the Woodruff Hotel—torn down in the late 1900s—and the Paddock Building or Arcade, which would feature an arcade running through it that survives to this day and is considered the oldest continuously in operation, enclosed mall in the nation. Both the Paddock and Woodruff families would purchase family sites at the new cemetery.

The Woodruff family lot at Brookside would feature a tall obelisk mounted on a substantial base, along with several smaller markers. The Paddock family memorial features a tall base upon which stands a classical female figure, her hair down and flowing and holding in her hands a large cross. Brookside Cemetery would have a plethora of obelisks of different varieties by the turn of the century but would have proportionally many fewer statues.

Most of the land on which Brookside would be established was sold to the Watertown Cemetery Association, but a small portion of it was donated. The properties had been farmland, and one of the clauses in the first land purchases reflected that situation; the sellers would allow some manipulation of the water on the property, but they would not allow any post-purchase changes that might seriously impact their own water supply, as they would continue to farm their adjacent property. A brook, Mill Creek, ran through the land tract, as well as through other portions of the seller's property.

Agreeing to the terms of the sellers, the Watertown Cemetery Association made its initial land acquisition for the new cemetery. The association met in September 1853 to discuss the land purchase and for organizational purposes. Composed of some of the leading members of the local community, according to surviving cemetery records, the association elected an executive committee as well as a committee to establish bylaws and a grounds committee. They also entered into a contract that month to purchase land from Alonzo M. and Antoinette Rogers and Joseph and Elizabeth Rogers. In July 1854, the Rogers deeded the cemetery association 55.41 acres for the sum of $2,548.86.

The purchase deed granted the cemetery the right to dam the brook to create ponds, with the provision that the water levels, in general, would not be raised more than two feet from their current levels. The brook would indeed be dammed in following years, especially as the cemetery gained more land, and from it was created a series of ponds and waterways, with at least four distinct ponds. Small waterfalls link the more westerly ponds. Another, separate small pond also exits near the brook on the eastern side of the cemetery now, near where the brook was allowed to continue on its natural course.

The association hired thirty-eight-year-old Howard Daniels of New York City as its lead engineer to design their new cemetery, with George R. Parsons designated as a project engineer. The two men created a plan map for the cemetery, dated 1854 and entitled simply "Plan of Brookside Cemetery." Brookside was not Daniels's first major cemetery design, however, and he was more diverse than what some people might now consider an "engineer" to be. The terms "engineer" and "designer" were still in flux, and Daniels's background embraced a number of career designations, including that of "architect."

Daniels had worked primarily out of Ohio as an architect during the late 1840s, and he designed a few cemeteries there and elsewhere before he undertook Brookside Cemetery in Watertown.

Daniels had designed Riverside Cemetery in Waterbury, Connecticut, in 1853, on a then thirty-one-acre site. Daniels's design was greatly appreciated, the cemetery was deemed a lovely one, and according to a contemporaneous article, "great credit is due to Howard Daniels, Esq. of New York, the civil engineer, as well as to the superintendent, Mr. John North. It is unusual to find such perfect harmony in landscape gardening; all the available natural beauties of the spot seem to have struck the quick eye of Mr. Daniels, and he has developed them to the best possible advantage."

The citizens of Watertown would seemingly feel the same way about the work Daniels had done for them when Brookside opened the following year. The projects in Waterbury and Watertown perhaps overlapped a bit. Indeed, Daniels seems to have had three major cemetery projects going in 1853–1854. In addition to Brookside and Riverside, he also designed Spring Forest in Binghamton, New York, in 1853. Before this, he had designed Dale Cemetery in 1851 and the Poughkeepsie Rural Cemetery in 1852. Both of these cemeteries are also in New York State and are garden cemeteries.

After finishing all of these projects, Daniels would go on to design at least three other New York rural cemeteries: Laurel Grove in Port Jarvis in 1856, Woodlawn Cemetery in Elmira in 1858—the same year his design for Central Park came in fourth place—and Oakwood Cemetery in Syracuse in 1859. Daniels was a critical figure in the rural cemetery movement in the Northeast. Some of his designs were for smaller cemeteries, some of them for quite large ones.

Daniels had studied in England and in the United States. He was considered a landscape gardener as well as an architect. In 1855, in the *Horticulturalist*, he advertised his services as being those of one who could design "Plans for Parks, Cemeteries, Country Seats, Villas, Farms, Orchards, Gardens &c., also designs in all styles for Mansions, Villas, Cottages, Conservatories, Greenhouses, Rustic Statuary, &c." As his advertisement indicated, Howard Daniels was a multitalented designer, and his work included several well-known buildings.

Daniels, like Charles Elliot, whom Springfield Cemetery had consulted, would publish various pieces during his lifetime, including letters of correspondence in the *Magazine of Horticulture*, articles in the *Horticulturalist* on his design elements, and a report on a public park he designed for the city of Baltimore in the *Baltimore Parks Commission Annual Report for 1860*. Daniels designed Baltimore's Druid Hill Park, one of America's largest public parks at 745 acres, compared to Central Park's 843 acres. Like Central Park, it was one of the nation's earliest landscaped public parks, opening in 1860, just two years after Central Park. Daniels would die in Baltimore in 1863 and be buried at Green Lawn Cemetery in Columbus, Ohio, a cemetery he had designed in 1848.

The plan submitted by Daniels and Parsons for Watertown or Brook-side Cemetery showed the winding roads typical in the era of the new garden cemetery, as well as the ponds at least partially man-made at the cemetery and the natural brook. One who knows the grounds can easily discern the overall design. Some of the sections were laid out as true circles; others are in a more oval pattern. The actual layout of the grounds, however, including the location of the surrounding roads and ponds, may have varied from the original plan, although the overall design would hold true.

The association held a dedication cemetery on June 20, 1854, shortly before another garden cemetery opened in Mystic, Connecticut. Both of cemeteries were in the less-populated areas of their states, and each would have some unique features, especially when it came to water: one would have a delightful series of ponds or miniature lakes and waterways, and the other would be situated on a major river.

Watertown's cemetery association made a major event out of its dedication that June—as would Mystic's shortly thereafter—starting the celebration out at the Public Square before having the procession travel along town streets for more than three miles to reach the new cemetery. Reverend E. H. Chapin of New York presided, as well as poet R. Johnson. Several members of the clergy from different denominations spoke, and the Watertown Six Horn Band played. The dedication was not made in the name of the Brookside Cemetery, however, but rather in the name of what the cemetery was first called, the Watertown Cemetery.

The procession was essentially a parade. General A. Baker served as the parade marshal, according to a poster or flyer printed for the event. The general led the procession, followed by the band, the trustees of the cemetery association, the clergy, and the "citizens and strangers."

Once the cemetery grounds were reached, the band played, the trustees delivered a report, and the Watertown Six Horn Band performed again. Following this, Reverend George Morgan Hills read from the Scriptures, and then a choir sang. Next, Reverend P. Snyder led those assembled in prayer, Reverend J. Bouchard did another reading from the Bible, and then there was a "Reading of the Ode" by Reverend J. B. Foote.

It is uncertain who the author of the poem was that Foote read, but it may well have been the poet R. Johnson, as he is not otherwise listed in the event schedule. He may, however, have spoken at the Public Square. Although the poem or ode is quite religious and Christian in its tone and content, it also includes the more secular or trans-religious aspects of the garden cemetery movement, of the search for beauty for one's final resting place.

Excerpts from the ode read:

Here we'll bring the fir and yew tree,
Here we'll consecrate the pine,
While with flowers of rarest beauty,
Our affections we'll entwine.

Oft we'll come when Spring is blooming,
And our vesper vigils keep,
New affections still entombing
Where our loved ones sweetly sleep.

Eight stanzas or verses made up the poem. After the reading of the poem, another reverend spoke, the band played, the dedication prayer was read, the choir sang, and Reverend J. Erwin delivered the benediction. It was a full day.

A few burials and reinterments took place before winter set in that year. These early interments occurred, it seems, without a superintendent, as extant cemetery records (most records of the cemetery's historical records purportedly disappeared with a former employee) list the first superintendent, Milton Minter, as having started work in 1856. Over its first 165-plus years, ten superintendents would serve, four of them—in succession—being members of the Donahue family (from whom some of the cemetery land was purchased), including Patrick Donahue, the family serving altogether from 1866 to 1955. By the mid to late 1900s, the cemetery would encompass some 168 acres.

In October 1860, the cemetery purchased additional property, this time from a member of the Cook family. Then, in November 1865, it purchased land from Robert Sherman, followed by land purchases from Margaret and Philip Hanlon in 1898, 1904, and 1905, and from Patrick and Catherine Donahue in 1906. In 1912, the association purchased additional land from Catherine Donahue after Patrick's death.

In the meantime, the cemetery may have hired a landscape architect to design the cemetery further, and this would seem to be when Olmsted might have come into the picture. However, there is no proof that an Olmsted or an Olmsted associate ever had anything to do with Brookside, and the idea that another landscape designer came in after Daniels may simply have been an error, as most cemetery documents have disappeared.

Olmsted has also been credited with designing Watertown's Thompson Park, which is arguably one of the three great entities of this small city, the other two being Brookside Cemetery and the R. P. Flower Memorial Library. That the three are connected in history is not surprising, yet the attribution of Thompson Park to Frederick Law Olmsted, like the belief that he designed Brookside, is also an error: it was not *the* Frederick Law Olmsted who designed the park.

Local businessman John C. Thompson donated land to the city for a park in 1899. As the story goes, he knew of Central Park and Olmsted from his visits to New York City. He purportedly wrote to Olmsted in 1899 and engaged him to design the park. However, Olmsted was in failing health by 1899; indeed he was hospitalized with dementia and had been suffering from it for many years. The brilliant landscape architect, conservationist, antislavery writer, and journalist was no longer in a position to design a large park.

More likely, if an Olmsted designed Thompson Park, which now exceeds 350 acres (originally, it contained about 200 acres) and overlooks the city and surrounding countryside, it was one or both of his "sons": Frederick Law Olmsted Jr. and Olmsted's nephew and adopted son, John C. Olmsted, who were carrying on his business as Olmsted Brothers. They, according to more reliable sources, designed at least the top portion of the park, completing their design circa 1899, with the park—as it was at the time—finished by 1904–1905. The confusion may have started from Frederick Law Olmsted Jr. having dropped the "Jr." from his name soon after his father died.

In the meantime, while Watertown gained a beautifully landscaped cemetery and land acquisitions continued, cemetery beautification also continued. Mountain ash trees were planted, and in the 2000s, a magnificent row of poplars would flank the long drive into the burial portion of the cemetery. Into the mid-twentieth century, in addition to the ducks and Canada geese, herons, and other waterbirds, the cemetery had swans, beautiful white ones. The swans, unfortunately, have not been regular visitors for some time and have also largely disappeared from some other garden cemeteries over the years.

Initially, lots at Brookside sold for 6 cents per square foot in open areas and 8 cents per square foot in wooded sections. These rates would increase to 10 and 15 cents, respectively, after a few years and even further as the decades passed.

By 1876, when the Watertown Manufacturers Aid Association published a history of the city to date—Watertown having incorporated as a city in 1869—the cemetery association had changed its name to the Brookside Cemetery Association, the cemetery name also having been changed. Brookside then consisted of seventy acres of land, and a book, entitled *Watertown, A History of Its Settlement and Progress, with a Description of Its Commercial Advantages*, clearly sought to promote the community as a fine place to do business. It included a short description of the cemetery and praised it quite highly.

"Brookside Cemetery is a quiet and beautiful spot," the tome stated. "It is located in a valley, and seems an especially appropriate place for the purposes for which it is used." The cemetery, according to the history, "abounds in hills and vales and romantic ravines. Much of it remains with its natural growth of trees, and is crossed by a handsome stream." There was no mention of the ponds being developed at that time.

The cemetery site was "beautiful in itself by nature, in situation and surroundings." However, the work of twenty years had improved it, such that "the laying out of walks and drives has added greatly to its natural beauty. Its avenues are tastefully planned, and great care is bestowed upon the proper improvement of the spot." The cemetery association may well have provided the description, but either way, with other records being scare, the history does show that much had been done by way of "improvements" in Watertown and elsewhere.

The description concluded that Brookside "contains a large number of fine monuments, many of them of more than ordinary beauty and excellence." Brookside would indeed hold a large number of fine monuments by the late 1800s, and although the 1876 description was highly positive, there is no reason to believe that it was not accurate.

Iron gates were added at the turn of the century at the main entrance, ornate ones with "Brookside Cemetery" mounted at the crest of their arch. The cemetery also added ornate iron fencing along the perimeter, some of which would later be replaced by more utilitarian fencing. A pedestrian gateway was built next to the main vehicle entrance, with a short stone wall flanking the gateway.

The cemetery had hired Anchor Post Iron Works of New York to construct an impressive gateway for Brookside. Known originally as the Flower Memorial Gateway for a leading local family, the company used an image of the gateway in a 1906 advertisement in *Park and Cemetery*, identifying it specifically as Brookside Cemetery. A man in a hat was pictured next to the pillar supporting the vehicle entrance, showing just how tall the main gate and the urn-topped pillars were—towering as they did above the man at about three and a half times his height. The old farmhouse is visible through the ornamental iron bars behind and off to the left of the left pedestrian gateway, seemingly a white, large, two-story homestead, which the cemetery would use for some time. A small stand of evergreens now fills the space where the house had been. Another building, also white, is just visible beyond the right gateway. The gateway itself is essentially unchanged from the early 1900s, except for the addition of some signage.

The advertisement included a sketch of an anvil and other tools used by an ironworker or blacksmith, and below the photograph of Brookside was written, in bold font "The Entrance to Your Cemetery," followed by "Should be dignified, beautiful—and appropriate." The company, it noted, made specialty gates for cemeteries, parks, and so on, as well as ornamental iron fences. The company could design and manufacture these, or it could work with one's own architect.

Beyond the gateway, at the turn of the century and now, the cemetery approach is about a quarter-mile long before one reaches the first large pond and the brook, with the graves situated yet farther back from the main entrance.

Although there may not be as many architecturally significant buildings and memorials at Brookside as at some of the larger garden cemeteries, Brookside has its share of notable ones.

Perhaps the most impressive structure at the cemetery is a mausoleum that can compete with any mausoleum found in New England's garden cemeteries regarding style and simple beauty. The Henry Keep mausoleum was built in the 1870s in honor of Henry Keep and his family. Emma Woodruff Keep Schley had it constructed after the death of her first husband, Henry Keep. A large, Greek-style mausoleum made of white granite with a white granite walkway, the mausoleum holds the remains of Keep, his wife Emma, and his daughter, Emma Gertrude Keep Halsey. Inside also are a bust of Henry Keep and two marble statues, one of his wife and the other of his daughter. Stained glass windows add to the tableau, the whole seemingly built with a Greek cross footprint with decorated pilasters flanking each equal-size arm of the cross: two framing the arched double doorway, the others flanking arched windows.

According to cemetery records, the remains of William Schley (second husband of Emma) and Frederick Halsey (Emma Gertrude Keep Halsey's husband) are interred in the basement of the mausoleum. It is Henry Keep and his nuclear family who are on the main floor, seemingly because it was Henry Keep who made the ornate mausoleum possible.

Keep rose from poverty to become one of the regions most noted philanthropists. Born in 1918 in nearby Adams, Keep would enter the county poorhouse as a youth, and his father apparently died there. Young Keep would stay at the poorhouse for some time with his mother and siblings, but he was eventually hired out to work for a farmer who reportedly physically abused the boy. Keep ran away, found a job working on the Erie Canal as a teamster, and later drove a hack in Rochester, New York.

During the 1837 financial panic, Keep started buying depreciated banknotes in western New York, and he then resold them for a profit. He did something similar with New York State banknotes, and he then started trading in Canadian notes. So successful was Keep with his banknote activities that he was able to open his own bank in Watertown in 1852, the Frontier Bank; he then opened a branch in Fulton, New York, two years later. He also opened the Mechanic's Bank in Watertown in 1851 and invested in yet another bank soon thereafter.

Keep soon took his investing and banking skills to New York City, and in 1850, he opened offices on Wall Street. Keep invested in railroads on the eve of the Civil War, and some sources rank him as one of the greatest stock market speculators of his day. He also became a successful stock pool manager on the New York Stock Exchange. He refused to discuss his investment schemes with anyone, and thus, he earned the nickname "Silent Henry." In one of his financial schemes, Keep manipulated stock of the Michigan Southern and Northern Indiana Railroads such that he essentially gained control of them, financially destroying the person who had previously controlled the majority of its stock.

According to the *New York Times* obituary and funeral notices of Henry Keep, Keep next turned his focus to gaining control of the New York Central Railroad. In this, he came into conflict with Cornelius Vanderbilt, but Keep formed alliances with Le Grand Lockwood (with whom Keep formed a partnership but who had also been a longtime ally of Vanderbilt), and William Fargo, founder of Wells Fargo and American Express. The power struggle that ensued between the railroads cut off New York City from rail traffic that year, at a time when railroads were crucial to American cities. Keep eventually lost this particular battle, retired from the Central Railroad, and turned his attention to gaining control of the Chicago and North Western Railroads with Rufus Hatch. The two men succeeded at this, and Keep also became involved with a few other railroads, the sum of all his investments making him an extremely wealthy man.

In 1847, Keep had married Emma Woodruff of Watertown's Woodruff family, her father being Norris M. Woodruff, a real estate developer and founder of the Woodruff Hotel on the Public Square. The couple had one child, Emma Gertrude Keep. In early 1869, soon after Keep had offered $1.5 million to anyone who would establish a National Academy of Art, he became ill. He died that June. His funeral was held at his home on Fifth Avenue in New York. His widow had his mausoleum built at Brookside. In 1973, vandals broke into Keep's mausoleum and disturbed his remains, perhaps looking for jewelry or other valuables.

After the death of her husband, Emma Keep built the Henry Keep Home for the widowed, infirm, and elderly on Washington Street in Watertown. The large Victorian building was razed in 1977. A new building was constructed later and, known as the Samaritan Keep House, continues to provide community services. The site is located across from the Good Samaritan Hospital. Emma Keep had established a foundation to support the Henry Keep Home, and the foundation continues to own several apartment houses and other buildings in the city.

Before his death, Keep had asked Roswell Pettibone Flower to help his wife, Emma, manage his estate. Flower was married to Emma Keep's sister. Flower was also a local leader and eventually a state governor, and he, too, would be buried at Brookside Cemetery, as would his brother, Colonial George W. Flowers, Watertown's first mayor.

Roswell P. Flower was born in 1835 in Theresa, New York, not far from Watertown, and died in 1899. He was one of nine children, and after he graduated from high school, he taught in a local schoolhouse before working in Philadelphia, New York, as a clerk for a short time. In 1853, he became the deputy postmaster of Watertown. He saved up his money, purchased a jewelry store with a partner, and then bought out his partner two years later. He married Sarah M. Woodruff in 1859, daughter of Norris M. Woodruff. They had three children. When Henry Keep asked Flower to help manage his estate, he moved to New York City, and besides helping manage the estate, he opened a banking house called R. P. Flower & Co.

Flower soon entered politics as a Democrat, and he was elected in 1881 to the US Congress to fill a vacant seat. He served there until 1883 and was later elected to Congress in 1888 and in 1890. In September 1891, he resigned to run for governor of New York State. Flower won the election, and he served as New York's thirtieth governor during 1892–1894, the last person to fill a three-year term. He reportedly liked good cigars and kept several boxes of them while in office to hand out. He did not smoke in the office, however, and did not permit anyone else to do so either. Two of his most notable actions as governor, according to state records, was to sign into law the creation of the Adirondack Park and the City of Niagara Falls.

In 1899, while planning another economic move, this time into steel, Flower died of a heart attack at a country club in Eastport, New York. Even before his death, Flower had given money to charitable causes, and he had served as president of the board of trustees of Cornell University. Of the Henry Keep Home, he had said, according to an 1884 history of the county, "What better use could be made of the money of Henry Keep, whose father died in a poorhouse, than to erect, with some of it, a home for aged men and women." Keep and Flower donations and endowments would also go to numerous institutions in New York City.

Flower was interred at a family lot at Brookside, in a large sarcophagus with a top carved with flowers serving as the main marker. Flower also has a small individual marker. However, it is not Flower's small marker that would prove significant to the people of the region; instead, it would be a marvelous institution built for books that would influence future generations.

Flower had continued to maintain a home in Watertown during his years working elsewhere, and in later years, he had created quite a home library, one that included congressional papers, including, supposedly, copies of every message sent to Congress by a US president since George Washington's administration.

After Flower's death, reflecting his love of books and education, his daughter erected the Roswell P. Flower Memorial Library. Emma Flower Taylor, the only child to survive her father, presented the library to the city on November 10, 1904. She also donated the land upon which the library is located.

The library, described as being "in the Grecian style with some Roman features," is as "massive and dignified, and characteristic of the man in whose memory it is built." The library is indeed both massive and dignified with its white stone exterior, rotunda featuring bronze zodiac symbols inlaid in a white marble floor, and a large dome. A bust of Flower and a marble statue of a young girl grace the entryway. Reading rooms feature artwork, large windows, and fireplaces. For a small city, the library is a tremendous memorial, and it is one accessible to all.

High above the rotunda floor, the visitor can look up to see marvelous paintings and portraits of historical, scientific, religious, and mythical figures. Homer, Dante, Darwin, Newton, Milton, Virgil, Shakespeare, Molière, Herodotus, Gibbon, La Fontaine, St. John, Moses, Scott, and Dumas were all painted under the dome by Frederick S. Lamb. Above them soars a stained glass skylight or oculus, containing the same color scheme as the paintings.

Outside the library are two stone lions flanking the entrance, lions known to perhaps every child of the city, as well as two graceful, marble water fountains. A white stone walkway leads to the library, and a white stone fence surrounds it. Noted architects, artists, and designers created the Roswell P. Flower Memorial Library, and with this and their other gifts, the Flowers were indeed generous to their communities, in Watertown and elsewhere.

The Keep, Flower, and other families helped strengthen and beautify the city and the cemetery. In 1881, at Brookside Cemetery, land holdings were greatly augmented and improved through funding provided by Roswell P. Flower. Other improvements would be made possible in later years, including road paving, through the Flower Fund.

John A. Sherman, another leading local citizen, one who would donate a building for a city YMCA and also be interred at Brookside, oversaw the cemetery improvements of the late 1800s. Sherman would have a wonderful mausoleum with a curbed yard for individual memorials constructed at Brookside. Constructed with two small side wings and, it seems, in the Greek cross style, a Celtic cross is mounted at the front of the peaked roofline, and pilasters flank the arched doorway.

Besides his original stone at Brookside, the granddaughters of Norris M. Woodruff erected a stone chapel in honor of Colonel George W. Flower, a Civil War captain and brother of Roswell P. Flower. Born in 1830, George Flower started his career as a merchant and became involved in railroads. His chapel, centrally located in Brookside, was dedicated on April 26, 1884, and it was erected primarily for funeral services. Anna and Nellie Cadwell gave it to the cemetery on the condition that it never be used as a receiving tomb. Along with the Keep mausoleum, the seam-faced Victorian Gothic chapel with its front tower and arched doorways and stained glass windows is probably the most remarked upon structure in the cemetery.

Other local and state dignitaries chose to be buried at Brookside as the decades passed. George Augustus Bagley died in 1915 after a lifetime in business, owning an ironworks and legal practice, and he served in the US Congress from 1876 to 1879. Before this, he had been the president and then town supervisor of Watertown. A plain, white stone cross with a highly decorated base of carved flowers, lilies, and other flowers serves as Bagley's memorial.

Numerous state and federal congressmen were interred at Brookside in addition to Bagley. Ambrose William Clark, Charles Ezra Clarke, William Ives, Joseph Mullin, Albert Duane Shaw, Charles Rufus Skinner, Micah Sterling, Egbert Ten Eyck, and Frederick Lansing also served. Watertown streets are named for these men, and some of them have rather substantial memorials, while others are quite simple.

One of the more interesting memorials of congressional members was erected for Orville Hungerford, who was born in 1790 and died in 1851, which is before Brookside opened. He served in the US House of Representatives during 1843–1847, and he was the first president of the Watertown & Rome Railroad. Several years after his death, he was interred in a rather interesting little house—a mausoleum—a multistone one with a tall conical roof, small side buttresses, an arched doorway, and several embellishments along its double roofline, in the small windows, and on the door. Steps lead up to the Hungerford vault, which is inscribed with the year 1860. Other family members, including Hungerford's wife, are also interred in the vault, and smaller markers are also present.

Besides the politicians already mentioned, Watertown native and attorney Robert Lansing served as the US secretary of state from June 1915 to February 1920 under President Woodrow Wilson. His predecessor had been William Jennings Bryan. Lansing had already enjoyed a long career before this appointment.

Lansing was born in 1864 to Maria Lay (Dodge) Lansing and John Lansing. His grandfather was Robert Lansing, a New York state senator.

After attending Amherst College, he studied law and was admitted to the bar in 1889. In 1890, Lansing married Eleanor Foster—daughter of Secretary of State John W. Foster. He served as an attorney for Lansing & Lansing in Watertown. He then became an international law specialist and entered federal service as an associate counsel to work on the Bering Sea Arbitration in 1892. He became the counsel in the United States Bering Sea Claims Commission in 1896–1897, the Alaskan Boundary Tribunal in 1903, and the 1909–1910 North Atlantic Fisheries arbitration at The Hague. He helped establish the American Society of International Law in 1906, the *American Journal of International Law* the following year, and then served as an agent of the federal government for American and British Arbitration during 1912–1914. Lansing also—before World War I—worked with the federal government as a legal advisor or "Counselor of the US Department of State" from April 1914 to June 1915.

As events unfolded during the war, and after the German forces sank the USS *Lusitania* in May 1915, Lansing advocated that the United States enter the war. William Jennings Bryan had resigned as secretary of state following one of President Wilson's letters to the German government, which Bryan had found too aggressive or belligerent, and Wilson appointed Lansing in his place. Lansing had advocated before the war for the rights of neutral nations and the freedom of the oceans.

As secretary of state, Lansing is credited with establishing the Diplomatic Security Service, according to federal records, and hiring the agency's first special agents during World War I. He attended the Paris Peace Conference held at Versailles, France, at the close of World War I, as one of the United States's five delegates. However, Lansing did not consider the League of Nations as essential, and the League of Nations was essentially President Wilson's beloved child. This caused some rift, and then, after President Wilson fell ill, Lansing convened the cabinet a number of times. He also suggested that the vice president assume the presidency. This brought him into further disfavor, and Edith Wilson requested that he resign as secretary of state. Lansing did so and resumed working in international law as an attorney in Washington, DC.

An author and coauthor also, Lansing penned several articles and books on international law and the Paris Peace Treaty negotiations. He died in New York City in 1928. He is buried at Brookside in a large family lot. A distinguished lot suitable for a distinguished man, it features a tall obelisk with a detailed base and low stone and iron fencing.

Alexander Copley, who had owned vast timber holdings in the region, especially around Antwerp and Chaumont, was also interred at Brookside, with a large shaft of Chaumont limestone marking his grave. The capped obelisk on an architectural base towers above surrounding stones, and tall curbing surrounds the lot. Numerous other local businesspeople were likewise buried at the cemetery in the 1800s and early 1900s.

George Massey, another of Watertown's most renowned citizens, had a large, "cloth"-draped sarcophagus memorial erected in his honor, located not far from the Hungerford mausoleum and the Bagley cross. The white marble marker features finely shaped sides, Massey's name carved in bas-relief, and other flourishes.

Massey's family was among the earliest Caucasians in the region. According to a 1905 source, written when Massey was still alive, "No name in the annals of Watertown holds a more conspicuous or more honored place than Massey. The family has been represented there since the earliest settlement of the town, and has been a virile element in its development and growth." The Masseys had come via England, New Hampshire, and Vermont. Family members had served in the Revolutionary War, helped defend Canada in the early 1800s, and had served in the War of 1812 as well as in other capacities before Massey's birth in 1836.

Massey started work early in a pharmacy, one that he would eventually control. He would later serve as vice president of the city's well-known—and still ongoing—New York Air Brake Company. He would also serve as president of the local Jefferson County National Bank and run a prestigious carriage company and serve as a director of the Watertown Street Railway Company, the Watertown Steam Engine Company, and the Davis Sewing Machine Company. He was a founding member of the ongoing Jefferson County Historical Society—housed with its museum just across the street from the Roswell P. Flower Memorial

The Marsden Perry fountain at Swan Point Cemetery greets cemetery visitors after they pass the indigenous stone entranceway and the cemetery office and chapel. Imported from Italy by Perry, the fountain was later donated to the cemetery. Four lion faces mark the bowl of the fountain. Nearby, another fountain is located in a courtyard.

The Marsden Perry tomb is built into the hillside overlooking the Seekonk River. Its façade was built to replicate the entrance of his Providence home, where he had installed the fountain from Italy that the local historical society later acquired and donated in 1961 to Swan Point Cemetery.

The towering Barnaby memorial at Swan Point, like one or two at Cedar Hill
Cemetery, features a female figure atop a massive obelisk. She holds a wreath of
mourning or remembrance.

The Young family memorial features a male angel bearing aloft a young woman, a type of marker interpreted as a soul being carried into the afterlife while still encased in the human body.

The Sprague family lot at Swan Point Cemetery features a variety of markers. The two most noted ones are the sarcophagus marker for a brother and sister who died in 1860, as children, with a marble sculpture resting atop it, and the central, circular Greek inspired granite memorial. Like the other massive, circular, family lot at Swan Point, this one olds a Governor of Rhode Island, William Sprague III.

The Briggs statue at Swan Point rests atop a substantial base, not seen here in order, as with a few other photographs of statues, to give a different perspective to the funerary art. Like the Young statue, a male angel supports a human or soul, as they prepare to leave, it seems, for the next world.

The highly lauded Lownes bronze angel with his exedra bench is located near the rear water landing, just up from the Perry tomb. Behind the memorial is seen part of the boulder wall that surrounds Swan Point Cemetery.

The Henry Keep Greek style mausoleum at Brookside Cemetery is one of the more stunning and ornate of all the New England mausoleums. Inside are statues as well as a sarcophagus. Stained glass windows are located around the edifice, and a stone walkway with steps leads to the main door.

An especially ornate version of a tree trunk memorial, often used to symbolize a life cut short, the Kemp marker at Brookside includes vines growing the tree trunk, and, resting atop it, an owl.

The Rosa mausoleum nestled in the poplars is one of the more intriguing mausoleums at Brookside. Seen to the left side of the statue through the trees is the large Parker family memorial with a classic female, or a seated woman-in-mourning-with-wreath sculpture. Another, virtually identical, such figure is located nearby for the Cook and Granger memorial, as are similar ones at other garden cemeteries.

The George Flower Chapel at Brookside was dedicated in 1884 and overlooks a good portion of the cemetery. Like many cemetery chapels, it features stained glass and ornate stonework.

The gates at Elm Grove Cemetery feature Westerly granite walls that are 6 feet thick, 54 feet wide, and 32 feet tall at the center. Pedestrian gateways flank the larger vehicle entrance and the walls are inscribed.

The Mallory family lot at Elm Grove features a number of classic monuments including the haunting baby or child memorial seen here to the front, the flaming urn main family marker to the rear, and the female statue holding a large anchor with her hair arranged in a classic mourning style, her clothing draped, and one arm crossed over her chest as seen to the left. Behind her, the Mystic River opens.

The Packer tomb at Elm Grove is one of two facing a small valley in the cemetery. Built in the 1860s, it is considered a Greek temple style one, and includes vases on its peak and along its walkway.

The chapel at Elm Grove is constructed largely of marble and brick, with a squared off front with a porch, and a circular back portion. It sits above one of the curves in the Mystic River.

The Benjamin Hoxie memorial is one of the most noted at Elm Grove, and commemorates the life of a community leader and his family. The memorial is 16 feet tall and made of blue Westerly granite. It features a Classic female figure holding a floral wreath, a standard figure in funerary art generally representing sorrow.

A combined office and holding tomb serves as the gateway to Green Mount Cemetery in Montpelier, Vermont.

A staircase carved into the ledge serves as a memorial to William Stowell. This "tomb" at Green Mount Cemetery, with the John Erastus Hubbard memorial, is one of the most visited and remarked upon markers at Green Mount Cemetery. It was carved out of a single granite ledge, and fronts Route 2.

In this relatively small and humble garden cemetery, Green Mount, in Vermont is one of the grandest pieces of funerary art found in New England. The John Erastus Hubbard memorial features a seated bronze figure surrounded by a gray granite exedra wall with his head thrown back in agony. Steps and a large flat marker lead up to the figure, while to the side and rear can be seen a popular angel style statue erected on his family's lot. The angel stands on steps in front of a large rough hewn cross. This is a particularly fine version or interpretation. A draped urn memorial is seen to the right above the Hubbard memorial and slightly further up the slope is an open-cathedral style architectural memorial.

Viewed closer, the bronze John Erastus Hubbard memorial shows the grief for which it is called *Thanatos*, or death.

WILBUR F. BRAMAN
JULY 18, 1826   DEC. 1, 1903
FANNY CABOT BRAMAN
FEB. 18, 1818 MARCH 19, 1904
WEALTHY CABOT CLARK
APRIL 28, 1815   DEC. 19, 1899.

BRAMAN

The Braman family lion sculpture rests atop a large architectural base near the crest of the hill at Green Mount Cemetery. Lions are considered guardians of both the living and the dead. Behind the lion, further up the slope can be seen two seated women-in-morning-with-wreath memorials, situated almost back to back to one another although separated by some distance.

The Gerrish woman in morning is a classical version found on three separate family memorials at Evergreen. A different version, a unique bronze one, is also found atop the Wescott mausoleum. The Gerrish statue rests atop a large base, as do the Kimball and True ones, and is located near the Baxter family memorial.

The Chisholm Mausoleum in Evergreen is one of the most celebrated in the cemetery, and indeed in the region. The mausoleum was built to be an exact replica of the *Maison Caree* in France, a Roman temple.

The Valley of Kings of Evergreen features a wide variety of tombs and mausoleums. See here are the F.O. Smith Egyptian style tomb along with portions of others on the hillside and much of the long fortress like tomb that holds large separate chambers and entranceways for five families and looks directly over the pond area.

The Baxter family memorial is one of the finest at Evergreen and features a central temple edifice on a square tiered base. Smaller stones mark the resting places of family members, including that of Governor Percival P. Baxter, located on the other side. To left rear one can see just the top rear view of the Lunt memorial, which features a woman with an anchor, and further back is an identical female figure on the Cummings and Rand memorial to that on the Abell mausoleum at Swan Point with one hand raised to the sky, the other holding a cross and wreath. To the right in the background is the rear view of the Gerrish memorial.

The J.P. Morgan family lot at Cedar Point Cemetery embraced the basic principles of the Weidenman plan. Smaller markers surround the massive central, Scottish granite, marker for the Morgan family, known as the Ark of the Covenant, for individual family members. Financier John Pierpont Morgan is buried to the far side of the Ark.

The Jewett memorial at Cedar Hill Cemetery towers above the cemetery at the top of the hillside. The bronze statue that stands upon the massive granite Corinthian column represents the figure of *Hope*. The memorial is located near the similarly towering memorial erected by the family of Samuel Colt.

"I Awaken to Glory" is one of three detailed bronze bas-relief panels on the sides of the Dr. Horace Wells and family lot marker at Cedar Hill Cemetery. The opposite side reads, "I Sleep to Awaken," while the front and larger panel features an angel bringing medicine to a suffering person and is inscribed, "There Shall Be No Pain." Wells is considered the father of modern anesthesia.

The Howard Pyramid/Mausoleum at Cedar Hill is unique among the garden cemeteries. Build of pink granite, the pyramid is about 18 feet tall and female angel standing in the doorway is life-size. The entrance and stairs include butterflies, often considered symbols of rebirth.

The Pike statue at Cedar Hill features one of most moving versions of a woman comforting a younger person of those found in the New England cemeteries. The massive sculpture rests atop a tall and ornate architectural base.

Although cemetery beautification would not have proceeded as it did without the hundreds of stonecutters who came to America, or received their training here, the stonecutters often paid the price, the price being their lives. The Louis Brusa memorial at Hope Cemetery in Vermont was carved by Brusa as he was dying of silicosis caused by his many years as a stonecutter, from breathing in fine particles of stone.

The Governor William Sprague IV tomb at Swan Point is one of the largest ones in New England and the second large lot for the family. Three sets of steps lead up to the ornate structure. Two stairways not seen here are located on the opposite side.

Library. He had married Sarah H. Thompson, but she died soon thereafter, and they had no children.

Massey's brother, Albert Parson Massey, spent some time away from the city, but he would later return and bring his mechanical and engineering "brilliance" to the air brake. He essentially saved the company by developing the Massey air brake and a new valve as well as having defended the company in a major lawsuit with a competitor. Albert Massey, however, died in 1898 and was buried at sea. He had been on a journey to try to regain his health in Europe. He had had five children with his wife, Phoebe Scott Griffith, four of whom survived him.

Another leading local family, the Holcombs, would have a large sarcophagus-style memorial serving as its main marker. An interesting marble work, it also resembles a table ledger in some ways. The top is draped, and on it rests an open book, and on that sits a floral bouquet. Time and weather have taken their toll, but it remains a compelling memorial.

The Cooper family was another well-known Watertown family during the late 1800s. At Brookside, the family erected a wonderful Egyptian-revival-style mausoleum. It has an architectural depth greater than many seen elsewhere, with wings to either side of the main entrance, or, perhaps, the entrance is the projecting "wing." The weathered iron door holds a variety of symbols, including reversed torches, a garland, and a woman in prayer or grief. The entrance to the mausoleum does not hold the customary columns flanking the door, but rather the shape of the entranceway itself serves as flanking columns. The mausoleum has an overhanging cornice with a winged orb at the front and the family name carved above the doorway. The doorway is in some ways reminiscent of the center section of the Mount Auburn gateway.

Cooper Street would be an important one in Watertown, as would Holcomb, Massey, Lansing, and Flower Streets. Schools were also named after many of the leading families buried at Brookside.

One of the other most intriguing mausoleums at the cemetery would be the Rosa mausoleum. It resembles a small chapel with its peaked roof, tall, slender copula, small spires, and Celtic cross, and it is seemingly designed in the Greek cross style with four equal arms or sides projecting from the center. Built for Maus Van Vranken Rosa (Roosa), his son Dr. William Van Vranken Rosa, and daughter-in-law Cornelia Elizabeth Rosa, who died in 1871 (at age ninety-one), 1882, and 1893, respectively, the mausoleum has small side buttresses and small columns with ornate capitals flanking the arched doorway. The front of the structure is heavy with symbolic carvings and the like, and it has a short run of steps and a walkway leading to the bronze doorway as well as urns to hold plants.

Not far under the poplar trees from the Rosa mausoleum is the Parker family monument. It features a seated female figure holding a wreath, one of her bare feet projecting just over the ornate architectural base bellow, the base girdled with columns. Not far away, an essentially identical woman-in-mourning-with-wreath figure tops the Cook and Granger family monument.

A classical figure also tops the memorial for the Buck and Sanger family lot. Surrounded by high-curved walling with a few steps leading up to the lot, a number of individual markers are also on the lot. The female figure holds a small anchor in her left hand, while her right hand is held across her chest.

The Jess family memorial also features a large female figure standing above an architectural-style base. Similar to the Buck and Sanger memorial, the figure also holds a small anchor in her left hand and holds her right hand across her chest.

Brookside Cemetery would also have a stone figure "sitting" on a long, curved bench or exedra memorial, although one more specifically Christian in symbolism than some others. It features a woman, her back toward the front of the memorial, as she turns to embrace a large cross. Located downhill from the chapel, she has a rather prominent site. Inscribed on it are the words "Simply To Thy Cross Do I Cling," and the phrase is split on either side of the woman.

Brookside, like the other New England garden cemeteries, has several war veterans as "residents," some of them already discussed. It also has a large memorial to local firefighters, the Watertown Fire Department, established in 1891. In some ways, the memorial resembles some of the Civil War monuments at various cemeteries, with a mustached male figure standing on a large pedestal base equipped with a hose instead of a weapon and wearing his fire hat instead of a military cap. A hook and ladder, a rope, and a hatchet are carved on the sides of the base with flowering branches carved behind them.

Another type of memorial seen at the Watertown cemetery, erected for John Edwin and Caroline Kemp, who died in 1896 and 1867, respectively, is a version of the tree trunk or stump variety. However, this one is definitely of the trunk variety, as it is one of the tallest encountered in the New England rural cemeteries. It is also one of the more realistic examples, with vines climbing up the bole and an owl perched on top, naturally so, with part of its body hidden. The Kemps's names are carved into the tree trunk as though someone had shaved off some of the bark to create a clean surface to cut into the wood.

Brookside includes pretty much the entire range of nineteenth-century markers in its historic section, from various architectural forms to small stone markers to broken columns to obelisks of all varieties to a tree trunk memorial to zinc markers (or zinkies). There is also the angel in front of a large cross built for the Weston family, a statue that differs from several similar ones in that the ornate stone angel points upward and carries a scroll in the other hand, and there is also the neoclassical sarcophagus memorializing Carson Peck and the polished orb-topped memorial inscribed for Watertown Mayor John Nill. Brookside has the stunning Keep mausoleum and the intriguing Rosa and Hungerford mausoleums, as well as others. A bronze memorial has recently been added to memorialize the youngest of children. A gazebo adorns the landscape and offers a place for a visitor to sit and reflect.

However, it is perhaps, overall, the rolling hills and the waterway that winds from one side of the cemetery to the other along small passages and ponds and the brook, with their ever-present birds, that the visitor to the cemetery will remember—those and the long graceful approach among the poplars. Similar to other cemeteries, Brookside has adapted to new burial practices, yet the core of a beautiful garden cemetery remains waiting to be discovered.

Daniel Burnham, contemporary of Frederick Law Olmsted, who received numerous accolades during and after his lifetime, said of him, "He paints with lakes and wooded slopes; with lawns and banks and forest covered hills; with mountainsides and ocean views." Although some locals have credited Olmsted with "painting" the landscape at Brookside Cemetery, it was Howard Daniels who actually did so—and Watertown leaders made a wise decision when they commissioned his services. Brookside is a garden cemetery no to be missed.

Unfortunately, a former employee purportedly absconded with the cemetery's historical documents, so invaluable records have been lost. You may want to read the New York Times *obituary or articles about Henry Keep: "The Late Henry Keep," September 14, 1869; "Death of Henry Keep," July 31, 1869; and "Funeral of Henry Keep," August 2, 1869. Other sources include Dave Shampine's* Colorful Characters of Northern New York: Northern Lights *(Charleston, SC: History Press) and John Haddock's* The Growth of a Century: As Illustrated in the History of Jefferson County, New York, from 1793 to 1894. *(Philadelphia: Sherman & Company), also known as* The Centennial History of Jefferson County, New York, 1894, *also includes relevant information. And see Flower's obituary in the* Watertown Daily Times, *May 13, 1899. A biography of him was written in 1930 by his daughter, Emma Flower Taylor, entitled* The Life of Roswell Pettibone Flower *(Watertown, NY: The Hungerford-Holbrook Company, 1930). Another source for local figures and families is the* Genealogical and Family History of the County of Jefferson, New York, *compiled by R. A. Oakes, 1905.*

9

The Mystical Garden

Elm Grove Cemetery, Mystic, Connecticut

Located on the Mystic River, Elm Grove Cemetery offers the visitor a delightful and impressive entranceway, a competitor for an as yet unestablished category of "largest rhododendron ever seen," several beautiful "ancient trees," a number of intriguing memorials, a truly unique chapel, and a fine view of the river—a view full of geese young and old in the spring and other waterfowl as the seasons progress. Although one of the smaller garden cemeteries, Elm Grove—with its solid shipbuilding historical connection—is well worth seeing.

JUST AS BROOKSIDE CEMETERY WAS OPENING ITS GATES, IN MYSTIC, Connecticut, another garden cemetery was about to open its own. Indeed, the two were founded within months of one another, and only a few details of timing determined which one opened first. The cemetery movement was well underway in the Northeast, and in the early 1850s, some Mystic citizens decided it was time to establish their own.

With the idea of establishing a rural cemetery, a group of residents met on January 17, 1853, at the office of Joseph Cottrell to discuss the matter and take action. They adopted a set of bylaws, established a board of trustees, and decided to meet annually in April and allow anyone who purchased a lot of 320 or more square feet to vote at meetings.

The men planned to establish a cemetery that would serve as a "burying ground or place of sepulchers," one they would "enclose with walls, fences, and gates, and grade and layout . . . into suitable lots, squares, alleys, [and] walks." They would ornament the grounds with "shrubbery, trees, and plants." As decided at that first meeting, the trustees were to purchase a plot of land, one containing between twelve and twenty-five acres, at a price not exceeding $4,000.

The trustees first considered a tract of land on White Hill Farm, but finding that beyond their designated price range, they located another one south of White Hall owned by Hezekiah Williams that they could afford. They agreed to pay Williams $3,800 for the land. The transaction soon completed, the association became the owners of twenty-two acres, which were soon to become a cemetery. The original association members put up much of the purchase money as stockholders, with another nine individuals joining them. The fifteen original stockholders then sought a way to recover their funds.

To pay for the land it had purchased, the association, as had others before them, raised the money by subscription. They divided interest in the association into forty shares, with 75 percent of each lot sale earmarked to repay the original stockholders their principal, plus 6 percent interest. The remaining 25 percent was to be used to improve and maintain the property as well as to pay for the services of a superintendent. Once the stockholders were fully reimbursed, money from subsequent sales would go into a trust fund, and any amounts more than $300 would then be invested for the association.

Lots were to sell for 60 cents per square foot for sites fronting a road; those reached by footpath were to sell for 5 cents per square foot. Of course, prices would increase over time. A special section was set aside for families, an idea first seen in nearby New Haven in the 1790s. Elm Grove, named for the many elms already on the property, was to be open from dawn to dusk, and the board could determine lot ornamentation. As it worked out, obelisks and architectural markers would predominate the cemetery's funerary art, some with Grecian-style urns and vases topping them, while others were simpler, although a few mausoleums and a number of statues also existed. As seen in some other garden cemeteries, to maintain a park-like feel, the cemetery banned fencing within the grounds (with one exception), but it did allow lot owners to install stone curbing to set off their individual lots.

As soon as they could, the association hired a landscape architect, Niles Bierregaard (N. B.) Schubarth, then of Providence, to lay out the grounds. Schubarth had previously been a partner in Atwater and Schubarth, which had designed Swan Point Cemetery in nearby Rhode Island, and he came to Mystic with much experience.

Schubarth designed the new cemetery in the shape of an elm tree. Elm Avenue served as the main road—or the bole of the tree—being "rooted" at the cemetery entrance—with the road then winding around the grounds, forming the crown of the tree, and returning to the gate. The roads overall were gently curving ones. Elm Avenue was to be twenty feet wide and other avenues were eighteen feet wide, with the exception of two roads, which measured sixteen and ten feet, respectively. Paths were to be six feet wide. For the most part, these original plans held true over time.

Interestingly, a few sources yield a "blueprint" of Schubarth's, one that seemingly showcases his design for Elm Grove. The drawing depicted the skeleton as it were of a tree-shaped cemetery, with roads and paths included and lot borders drawn in. The header for the print was "N.B. SCHUBARTH'S New Method of LAYING OUT RURAL CEMETERIES." Beneath the plans—which designers of the era sometimes sold both for the money they received as compensation and to inspire others—were the words: "Combining the Geometrical with THE NATURAL STYLE." To the left of the plan was sketched a man with a top hat and a surveyor's transit and tripod; to the right of the plan was drawn a three-story building with a sidewalk approach and a tree. The whole was contained within an oval, with vines drawn along the two sides with the sketches. Two ponds were included in the cemetery grounds, with small streams linking them with a larger body of water indicated simply by waves, which would seem to represent the Mystic River Harbor. Along the right side, just outside the oval, is lettered, "Thompson[,] PROV. R.I."

Schubarth (1818–1889) had emigrated from Norway in 1840. He worked on the Erie Canal in New York State and would later work as an engineer and an architect. Schubarth's cemetery design work in Providence proved instrumental in his securing commissions for other cemeteries, including Elm Grove, along with ones in Connecticut, Rhode Island, and Massachusetts. Seemingly the only cemetery Schubarth designed after Elm Grove, however, was Juniper Hill in North Attleborough, Massachusetts, in 1859.

Kurt Culbertson, in "The Contribution of Scandinavian-Americans to the Development of Landscape Architecture in America," states that Schubarth's design for Elm Grove had been included in the *Providence Directory* for 1860 but noted that Schubarth did not secure any additional cemetery design work after the 1850s. He did continue other design work, however.

Their subscription drive generally successful and their design plan underway, on July 11, 1854, the Elm Grove Cemetery board held a dedication service. As seen elsewhere, local clergymen spoke, and the Mystic Cornet Band performed.

Lots, which were of various shapes and sizes, sold briskly, and beautification continued over the decades. Winter and inclement weather being a problem throughout New England, Elm Grove constructed a receiving or holding tomb in 1875, one built by the Smith Quarry Company of Rhode Island for $3,655, according to cemetery sources.

The 1895 letter of the association published in *Park and Cemetery* noted that Elm Grove's receiving tomb was in one of the most "beautiful portions of the grounds, and is surrounded by monuments of choice and finished work, both in material and art." Flower beds were soon planted near the gateway.

The year 1875 was also the first year that perpetual care for lots was received: a sum of $300 from the Greenman family for the care of their lot. More than one Greenman was instrumental in establishing the cemetery—George, Clark, and Thomas were each board members in 1853. A simple central memorial—a square, capped obelisk—serves as the family marker, while smaller markers of various types surround it in a circular fashion. Curbing encloses the central memorial in a circle. The lot now features a majestic weeping copper beech tree imported from Holland. (Weeping beech and birch trees would become the stars of the cemetery's tree offerings.) After the Greenman family started the process, other families and individuals signed up for perpetual care for their lots during subsequent years until it became the standard practice. Meanwhile, the Greenmans would continue a long association with the cemetery, and they eventually sponsored a major building project.

A decade or so before the cemetery had built its holding tomb, the S. R. Packer vault was built at Elm Grove in the early 1860s. The mausoleum is a modified Greek temple style, with a Grecian vase on the roof peak and two others flanking a short walk to the tomb. Four Corinthian columns are carved in heavy relief below a Roman arch. A small wing or retaining wall is to either side of the structure, built partially as it is into a small hillside.

Built beside the Packer tomb, the Burdick vault or mausoleum is less ornate than its neighbor, yet it is still a graceful structure, with its decorated pilasters flanking the doorway with its Roman-style archway, granite face, and bench for visitors. Both tombs are close to the water, and both are largely aboveground and are generally referred to as mausoleums. Flowers hung on the doorways of both the Packer and Burdick tombs change with the season.

Across from these two is the Williams–Haley tomb. A much simpler but still dignified structure, it was built into the small slope on which it is located. All three tombs open onto a small valley with an avenue running through it.

In the 1930s, across the cemetery, the Cobb mausoleum was constructed of Vermont white granite. It features four Doric columns beneath a Roman arch, and it has a bronze double door.

One of the more ornate monuments in Elm Grove can be found at the Cottrell lot. The towering 1865 monument is topped with a child angel leaning partially on a vase, and it is flanked by short pedestals that hold draped urns. The main base or obelisk is detailed and capped with children's or cherubs' faces peeking out from each side of the ornate, architectural cap. Granite curbing one foot high surrounds the lot, as does one surround the neighboring Griswold lot. The Cottrells, like the Greenmans, were long involved with the cemetery as well as the local economy, and Joseph Cottrell served on the 1853 cemetery board.

Next to the Cottrell child angel, a figure of an adult female stands in front of a large rough-hewn cross in an arrangement seen in other garden cemeteries and even in another monument at Elm Grove. The Griswold figure wears classically draped clothing with a loose cloak flowing down her back. She holds one hand across her chest, and in the other, she holds a rose. Across the cemetery, an almost identical memorial marks the Treakle family lot, although the faces on the two women are clearly different. They both closely resemble angel memorials found in a similar pose in a few of the other garden cemeteries. The Griswold statue was made of blue Westerly granite and was sculpted and installed in 1900.

Next to the Griswold lot is a family plot with perhaps the greatest diversity in grave markers of any in the cemetery, and more than most seen elsewhere. The plot is a basically circular one, in terms of the arrangement of the memorials, is located nearer the water, and features a large central memorial on a square tiered base with bas-relief carvings on each side, including those of a wreath and a woman with an infant on her back, the two, perhaps, heaven-bound. The marker has an embellished cap and a large "Aladdin-style" urn, seemingly a lit one symbolizing eternal life. Inverted torches, symbols of life extinguished, are carved on the four beveled "corners" of the base.

However, the central memorial—the one erected for Charles Mallory as well as his family and inscribed specifically as: "For the Family of Charles Mallory" in a way most family markers are not—is not necessarily the most intriguing marker on the lot. Born in 1796, Charles Mallory became a local shipping magnate, as many of the locals in the town were involved in the shipping business at the seaport, as well as in a few mills and other industries. Mallory was a sailmaker first, then a whaling agent, and then a shipbuilder, according to his biography in the 1898 tome, *Men of Progress*.

According to a Mystic repository of the family papers, Mallory leased the boatyard of Joseph Williams in about 1850, by which time his sons had joined him in business. They launched a number of ships from Mystic, and they eventually owned steamships as well as large sailing ships. They founded the Mallory Line, under which name a number of their shipping interests would be grouped informally if not formally. Charles Mallory & Co. would, for a time, be the main family company. Mallory would also become a bank president; he was the president of two banks, actually, one of which he purchased and then bought all of its capital stock. His sons would also join him in his banking concerns. He had married Eliza Rodgers in 1818, with whom he had five children, the first of them, Charles Henry Mallory, being born that same year.

During the Civil War, Charles Henry Mallory—the son—teamed up with Elihu Spicer, a long-time family acquaintance and associate, to form the New York & Texas Steamship Company. Other family members soon joined them, and they built many ships for the US Navy. With various sales and purchases, the family would be involved in the shipping business well into the twentieth century, and one of their vessels would be the first to transport American soldiers to Europe at the outset of World War I.

The family would produce many children, but unfortunately, the Mallory children did not all survive. Two haunting memorials at the cemetery were built for them; a marble infant sculpture on an oval plinth, and a six-sided "baby" memorial, with the carved faces of young children or cherubs with wings under their chins on each face of the ornate marker. The six sides also have the dates and names for the deceased children.

Charles and Eliza Mallory also had individual markers on the lot, and they were identical Gothic-style ones. Another marker, one inscribed for Anne Mallory, features a classical barefoot female figure, her hair arranged in a mourning style, holding a large anchor to her side and standing atop a square base. The infant sculpture is just in front of her memorial, and the child seems to have lived only one day, if that.

The Mallory lot contains several other markers. These include a significant ledger or table tomb marker with eight supporting, detailed columns and made of blue Westerly granite, a favored stone at the cemetery, which was installed in 1920; a large number of upright stone markers for numerous family members; and a plot right on the river that holds a memorial bench and small flat markers for another generation of the family. The largest and most impressive memorial to the Mallorys, however, would not be any single grave marker or lot but instead a gateway.

By the early 1890s, a desire was felt by many to have Elm Grove set off by a suitable entrance and fencing. The opportunity to do so arose when Eunice Mallory, the widow of Charles Henry Mallory, and the couple's children donated the money to erect a granite entranceway to the cemetery.

As part of the project, work first began on a rock wall along the eastern boundary of Elm Grove in 1892. G. W. Allen built the stone wall, which went fine until he announced plans to remove two old and massive elm trees that flanked the current entranceway to allow construction of a larger gateway. Many Mystic residents and lot owners expressed outrage at the plan, and the local paper, the *Mystic Press*, published an article entitled "Woodman, Spare that Tree." The paper stated, "The erection of any work of man's hands, however artistic, would poorly atone for the undoing of half a century or more of Nature's grand handiwork." And the cemetery was, as it were, approaching its fiftieth anniversary.

The trees did come down, and the gateway construction was soon underway. The Westerly Granite Company, according to their records, brought in several stonecutters from Italy to work on the Mallory Memorial Arch, built of Westerly granite, which was a popular stone at Elm Grove as elsewhere during the late 1800s. (Italian stonecutters were extremely popular at the time, and they had crafted uncountable garden cemetery monuments as well as several gateways.)

The entire gateway at Elm Grove when completed measured fifty-four feet in length and thirty-two feet in height. The flanking walls of stone spanned some 900 feet altogether. The edifice remains the main cemetery entrance in the twenty-first century. As seen with the Brookside Cemetery entrance and other rural cemetery gateways, the memorial gateway at Elm Grove consists of a vehicle entrance with pedestrian gates flanking either side. In its massiveness, however, if not its style, it is more reminiscent of the gateway at nearby Grove Street Cemetery in New Haven.

The walls of the Elm Grove gateway are six feet thick. The gateway has three large arches, each of them with a double, wrought-iron gate. The vehicle entrance of the main arch measures twenty-two feet in height and twenty feet in width. The pedestrian arches are each ten feet high by six feet wide. Chiseled above the main arch and just below the capstone are the words, "I am the Resurrection and the Light." To the sides of the main entrance, the pedestrian arches are inscribed with the Greek letters for alpha and omega. Crosses and pillars grace the upper portions, above the pedestrian entrances, as do other ornamental details. On the inside of the gateway, above the arch, are the words, "He Giveth His Beloved Sleep." Iron gates can be opened or closed to visitors.

In 1895, *Park and Cemetery* ran a two-page article about Elm Grove Cemetery. It included a photograph showing the newly constructed gateway and the dirt road leading into the cemetery. Beyond the gates, a tree-lined approach welcomed the visitor, and the visible grave monuments were seemingly set back much farther than is true now. Details are hard to distinguish in the background of the 1890s photograph, but both Brookside and Elm Grove Cemeteries would add gravesites in front of the oldest ones.

The article may well have been submitted by the Elm Grove Cemetery Association, but even so, it does show much of the state of the cemetery at that time. The author of the article called the gateway "one of marked and massive grandeur" and "one of affection, alike to the living and the dead." It stated that the gift was from the children of Charles and Eunice Mallory "to perpetuate the love and devotion to honored parents, and is in itself a tribute of nobility to the tender memories and generous hearts of the children of such parents."

The cemetery held a dedication for the new gateway on August 7, 1895. It was held at a local Methodist church instead of at the cemetery due to inclement weather. Reverend O. O. Sherman wrote an ode to the gateway, sung to the tune of "America the Beautiful," which attendees seemingly enjoyed.

Closely affiliated with the Mallory family was Captain Elihu Spicer. As noted, Spicer, born in 1825, had gone into the shipping business with the Mallorys in 1861. Their company would be especially successful in the New York, Florida, and Texas trade. Before that, Spicer had sailed the seas himself from age nine, rising through the ranks to become a shipmaster or captain. By age twenty-two, he had charge of the clipper ship *Fanny*.

One of the cemetery's classic female figures is the focus of Captain Spicer's lot. His family lot also features ornate, tall curbing. Several small individual gravestones are on the site, which has a water view. The female figure of the central memorial wears draped clothing and stands atop a square architectural base clutching a small cross to her chest with both arms. Her eyes gaze at the skies. The statue and polished stone base are made of blue Westerly granite from the New England Granite Works.

Like the Flower family in Watertown, New York, however, Spicer and his family's legacy to the community would be far greater than his work with his local garden cemetery; Spicer built the Mystic & Noank Library. The library was established in 1892, looked medieval in some ways when compared to its contemporaries, and, as noted in the 1899 *Connecticut Magazine*, Spicer's sister brought ivy from Ireland, from Blarney Castle, to transplant to the library walls. The library has also been described as Neo-Romanesque.

Spicer announced his plans to build the library in 1891 and chose to locate the library across from his home on Elm Street. He had his own architect, William Higginson, oversee construction, with William B. Bigelow of New York drawing up the plans. Spicer had the building constructed of Connecticut granite, Massachusetts sandstone, Roman brick, Numidia marble from Africa, and Vermont and Tennessee marble. The library has some Italian mosaic floors (others are oak) and stained glass windows. It initially had a Roman tile roof. In some ways, it is English Gothic in style. An addition was made in the early 1990s along with other renovations.

Groundwork on the library was broken in the summer of 1892. However, Spicer died in February 1893, just months before completion of the project. In January 1894, the library held a dedication ceremony, which more than 400 people attended, according to its library records. The library remains a community treasure, and the Spicer House, too, donated later by the family, attracts its share of visitors.

Other seafarers and shipbuilders, be they captain or crew, owners or laborers, are also interred at Elm Grove. Captain Pierre Rowland and his family had a substantial memorial commissioned for their lot. Atop a large architectural base stands the figure of a male in a flowing garment with a trumpet, seemingly Gabriel, but like some other male figures meant to represent angels, he has no visible wings. Born in France in 1791, Captain Rowland died in 1836, and his wife Abby followed him to the grave four years later. His family subsequently built the memorial and seemingly reinterred the remains of Rowland and Abby. Other family members are also buried at the lot, including Captain Pierre E. Rowland (1818–1890) whose years of life are exactly those of shipbuilder Charles Henry Mallory. The Rowland lot is on the water, but it is not on the same stretch as are the Spicer and Mallory lots; the river takes a couple of turns along the edge of the cemetery, such that much of the grounds has frontage along the Mystic River.

Another classic female form tops the monument for Benjamin Franklin Hoxie, and it is perhaps one of the best-known memorials in the cemetery. Hoxie was one of the original cemetery board members, as well as a well-known businessman. A number of stonecutters and carvers of the Smith Granite Company worked on the Hoxie memorial, made of blue Westerly granite and measuring more than sixteen feet in height. The base accounts for more than five feet of it, according to the Babcock-Smith House Museum. The round base or pedestal has a polished finish. The female figure wears classical clothing with detailed draping in the back and holds a floral wreath with both hands.

Other statues of women, who generally represent mourning, appear elsewhere at Elm Grove Cemetery. One particular monument, however, has a variation of a woman comforting or embracing a younger person, in this case, a young boy.

According to the Babcock-Smith House Museum, John Francis sculpted the blue Westerly granite memorial for the Cheesebro family at Elm Grove. The statue is a unique one as it features a woman and a boy in marvelous detail. The boy rests against the seated woman, sitting on a cushion, with an open book on his lap. The two figures wear Victorian clothing. The woman has one arm around the youth, perhaps her son. The large base features symbolic carvings on each side, including a laurel wreath.

The main memorial is surrounded by several "scroll-top" individual markers. Those directly in front of the statue are labeled "Mother" and "Father" on the front, with further details provided on the scroll tops.

The Morgan family memorial offers another example of a female figure, this one holding a small anchor in her left hand, her right crossed above her chest as though taking an oath, her eyes cast upward. The woman, dressed in classical garb, stands atop an ornate circular plinth capping another circular section, which in turn rests upon a square tiered base.

Ebenezer Morgan, one of the people buried on the lot, was born in Mystic in 1831 and lived until 1903. He had labored in a few workshops as a carpenter, including the Greenman and Mallory yards, eventually becoming a superintendent at the Mallory yard. He then served in the Lighthouse Department of the East Coast, including serving as a district engineer. He would marry twice and have a number of children.

Several other interesting memorials are located on the grounds, including the Smith obelisk along the river, the zinc Edmondson marker, the tall Watrous family obelisk, and the Leeds marble obelisk atop its large embellished base. In front of the Leeds monument is an open book memorial. The cemetery has numerous other distinguished markers.

By the early 1880s, according to a 1981 cemetery article by Marilyn Comrie, the cemetery had close to 2,000 interments and needed further space. To that end, the trustees were empowered to purchase additional land. In 1894, they procured land from the heirs of John Greenman for $810 and land from John Babcock for $1,100. This expanded the boundaries of the cemetery to the north and to the south, and according to an 1895 article, these purchases brought the total cemetery acreage to fifty acres. Addition acreage to the north was purchased in the 1930s.

Regarding the grounds themselves, the association stated in its 1895 article in *Park and Cemetery* that the cemetery was situated on "the banks of the beautiful Mystic River, whose waters shimmer in the light, like waves of liquid silver; the cemetery slopes toward the setting sun, 'beautiful for situation.'" Moreover, the cemetery had "choice trees, luxuriant maples and spreading elms" that "stand in chosen spots like faithful sentinels, to guard this quiet resting place of the absent—the dead." The authors noted that they had visited "many of the larger and more pretentious cemeteries of our great cities," and though each had its own place, they found Elm Grove to be a restful and welcoming haven.

Much of the praise for the fine condition of Elm Grove was due to the efforts of its superintendent, Henry Schroder, who at that point had been at his duties for some twenty-eight years. His long-term devotion was a great advantage to the cemetery, the association noted.

Schroder would continue as superintendent for some time, serving faithfully until his death in 1923. He was highly praised over the years and was responsible for planting the cemetery's ornamental weeping copper beeches and weeping white birches as well as other rare ornamental trees and shrubs. A 1938 hurricane destroyed some of his plantings, although others survived into the twenty-first century. In 1891, the trustees granted him a lot where he and his family would later be interred. The lot overlooks Lily Pond, and it has a four-tiered fountain built in 1909 from funds donated by a former Mystic resident, J. D. Crary. In 1917, the superintendent was too sick to attend the association's annual meeting, so the board brought $100 in gold to his house. The year before, they had presented him with an ebony cane for his fifty years of service—which would ultimately extend to fifty-six years.

Soon after the building of the gateway, in 1897, the cemetery built a landing along the western side of the grounds for visitors arriving by boat. The cemetery had marble benches set along the river and inland, to allow visitors to take their time touring the grounds and contemplating all they saw.

The next major project at Elm Grove was the 1911 construction of the mortuary chapel, set on the northwestern part of the grounds. The chapel was a gift from Mr. and Mrs. Edward S. Harkness, in memory of her parents, Charlotte Rogers and Thomas Stillman Greenman, the Greenman family having been involved with the cemetery since its establishment. Built largely of brick, the cemetery used marble from Greece for architectural accents, marble supplied by James MacLaren's Sons of Brooklyn, New York, according to Marilyn J. Comrie. The marble was remnants from stone purchased for a bank building in New York City. John Thatcher and Son, of Brooklyn, served as architects for the chapel, along with James Gamble Rogers.

The cornerstone of the chapel was laid in September 1911. Members of the Greenman family sealed a box inside the cornerstone, which contained memorabilia, including a $5 gold piece, plus silver and various other denominations of coins and some paper money. US stamps were also included, as were photographs and other items related to the cemetery. In 2008, the cemetery renovated the chapel, which seats fifty and remains available for services.

Another building was constructed at Elm Grove in 1979, an administrative building. The cemetery dedicated the grounds to J. B. Stinson, who had served as the association's treasurer for more than sixty years, having retired the same year the building was constructed.

Like the other cemeteries discussed thus far, with the exception of New Hampshire's Valley Cemetery, Elm Grove remains a working cemetery. However, interment space has become scarce. To combat this shortage, similar to other cemeteries, Elm Grove has established columbarium space, located on a spot just above the Mystic River, and has designated spaces for cremated remains, including two cremation interment gardens, one on the northern portion of the grounds and the other in the center of the most historic burial section and close to the river.

However, almost wherever one goes in this small garden cemetery, the river is close by. Some of the lots farther from the river are near one or other of the two ponds (in one place they are close to both pond and river), while others are closer to the Mallory gateway. The layout, in its tree shape with the crown portions along the river, is unique, and like the others, this cemetery is well worth visiting.

For further reading and for some source information, see the 1895 article in Park and Cemetery, *later known as* Modern Cemetery, *as well as the cemetery's website and its* History of Elm Grove Cemetery, *written by Marilyn J. Comrie in 1981. See also the records of the Babcock-Smith House Museum, local records collections including that of the library, the 1898* Men of Progress, *and the* Connecticut Journal *from the late 1800s. The local press has also carried articles over the years about the cemetery, including recent developments. Plans for the cemetery can be found on the website agincourtiowa.com as well as in other places.*

10

Cemetery on a Hill

Green Mount Cemetery and a Brief View of Lakeview Cemetery, Montpelier, Vermont, and Burlington, Vermont

Green Mount is another of the smaller cemeteries established in New England in the mid-nineteenth century. However, it is rather far away in style from the coastal ones such as Elm Grove at Mystic, Connecticut. It is situated in Vermont, and in some ways, it contains the elements many people associate with pastoral yet mountainous Vermont: a steep hill, trees that turn golden in autumn, and a winding body of water in the Winooski River. It has less glamour, in some ways, with regard to man-made elements than some of the larger and more financially secure private garden cemeteries, yet it, too, is interesting and worth seeing. Moreover, there are a few monuments there that just might take your breath away. Its gateway alone, with its almost Spanish feel, and the amazing view of the sharp incline you encounter directly in front of you when you go through the large entrance archway is enough to let you know that this, too, is a place worth exploring. And then you can just drive down the road a mile or so and explore the state capital.

You can also travel another thirty miles west and visit Lakeview Cemetery on Lake Champlain, and the water view alone will make you glad you came. Look across the lake at the New York Adirondack Mountains and you will understand why even the smaller garden cemeteries of New England can pull you in, especially when you look down and see a long line of small stones marking the graves of orphan children. Municipal garden cemeteries often do not fare as well financially as the larger private ones, but they also fill a crucial role in American culture: they are open to all, and not just in specified circumstances. Like the private Mount Hope in Maine, Lakeview has been generous to all.

VERMONT, LIKE NEW HAMPSHIRE, GENERALLY EXPERIENCED LESS OVERcrowding in its burial locations in the early 1800s than did states like Massachusetts and Connecticut with their larger population bases. However, Vermont also had issues that needed addressing. Moreover, with large open spaces still available outside of its cities, which were relatively small, Vermonters understood the lure of the rural or pastoral cemetery and had beautiful locations in which they could be placed.

Two crucial communities in the state, Montpelier and Burlington, heeded the call for the new style of cemetery. Also, Barre, a nearby stonecutting center, would later create something quite different that would echo the basic elements of garden cemeteries but add a few features that would make it, like New Haven, something different, something transitional. However, the garden cemetery movement came first to Montpelier, and it came uniquely. And it is here that the weight of this chapter will rest.

In part, Montpelier owes its garden cemetery to one specific person. In September 1853, Calvin Jay Keith, Esq., died in Montpelier. In his will, the local attorney instructed his executors to spend $1,000 to find a "suitable place for a burial ground in Montpelier, and in enclosing and planting trees in the same." His executors, Elisha P. Jewett and George Howes, along with Constant W. Storrs, were to serve as trustees of the new cemetery "and lay out the ground into lots, and dispose of the same at a reasonable price, reserving a portion to be given gratuitously to the poor." Proceeds from the sales were to go toward improving the grounds "and planting the same thickly with trees." Besides the money bequeathed for the cemetery in general, the executors were to spend an additional $500 to enclose a suitable lot on the chosen grounds and erect a memorial there for Keith.

The town responded in kind, knowing that it needed a new cemetery, its older burial grounds having reached capacity. Thus, at the town's annual meeting in March 1854, it voted that three other local men would work with the three appointed by Keith to find and purchase a tract of land for the cemetery and use any necessary funding from the town to acquire a suitable location.

According to a surviving document from the 1850s, one of the commissioners reported that they had almost despaired of finding a suitable location before they found the land that would soon be called Green Mount, in the Green Mountains, overlooking the capital, with a small river, the Winooski River, flowing at its edge. The hill itself, which makes up the majority of the land acquired, would be the focal point of the cemetery, and from it, one can still see for miles.

The committee purchased this plot of land from Isaiah Silver, the lot containing roughly forty acres, at the cost of $2,210. In autumn 1854, the deed was transferred to the town, "and the work of grading and enclosing was commenced."

In October 1854, the Vermont legislature passed an act establishing the cemetery at Montpelier and placing it under the "care, superintendence, and management" of "a board of five Commissioners, to be selected by the Town, and with the authority to convey Lots for the burial of the dead."

The town accepted the legislative act at their March 1855 meeting. A sum of $5,000 was placed "at the disposal of the Commissioners to defray the expenses of the Cemetery." A board of five commissioners, one of them being Jewett, was appointed, and the liberal endowment by the town and the other funding, the cemetery later reported, "enables the Commissioners to furnish a retreat for the dead, which will remain sacredly devoted to that object forever." Protection from "molestation or encroachment" would be provided "by Law."

Work had already commenced on the property, and it continued through summer 1855. The first "engineer," as the commission later referred to him, the term *landscape architect* still not in use at the time, had been Daniel Brims of Roxbury, Massachusetts, to whom "the design and arrangement" of the grounds was "wholly attributable." Patrick Farrelly succeeded Brims as cemetery engineer, and the commission later stated that it was to him that "the graceful finish and symmetry, displayed in the execution of the original design" was attributable. The commissioners, in a rare move, also thanked the work of "the laborers" who had worked on the cemetery for a year with "persevering industry, temperance, civility, and good moral deportment" by the time of the cemetery's dedication. By the end of that first year, the property had been largely enclosed, paths and drives laid out, and ornamental flora planted.

In autumn 1855, on September 15, the cemetery held a well-attended dedication ceremony. The Union Choir Association sang, and several clergymen spoke, as did a member of the commission, who formally presented the deed of the cemetery to the town. Aside from the regular religious commentary about death and the fleetingness of temporal life, a few telling remarks were made about the condition of Green Mount, why garden cemeteries, in general, had value in a religious context, and even about how those assembled might best view reinterments. These present a different contemporary insight than those seen thus far.

The Reverend F. W. Shelton observed to those assembled that:

> We stand upon a hillside, which, almost yesterday, lay un-reclaimed in its original wilderness, and now already it begins to look like an embellished garden. Art has redeemed it from its rude estate, with an almost magic transformation. It has winding walks, and will have shady avenues. It is the most choice position in this valley, and its natural surface presents the charm of variety. There is no stretch of landscape, in this neighborhood, around the abodes of the living, which can vie in beauty with this Paradise.

They were there to dedicate the cemetery "as the resting place of your beloved." Following years would make the site even lovelier, "when affection shall have beautified its every nook, and watered its flowers with tears."

The reverend made a few comments about how various peoples had buried their dead and then discussed what a garden cemetery might do. The "charm" of such places as Green Mount could not deprive death "of its sting," but, he said, "It is not that the darkness of the grave can be mitigated, because the outside of it is beautiful like a garden, nor that the sleeper will rest more softly on a bed which is perfumed with violets." Indeed, he said, "It will be as cold and hard and dark beneath the clod, as if no garlands were above it.

"It is because of the effect which they will have upon ourselves, and not for any good which they will do the silent sleepers," that such places had value, according to Shelton. Looking at death in this context helps a person to gain strength for his or her own death and to reflect on the memories of those whom they had lost.

"It is from the past . . . that we gather all our wisdom, and live a thousand years in a day," Shelton opined. It arises from "a refined motive" that places such as Green Mount are created because adorning such places, "is to cherish the memory of those who have gone before us, and to show that Love is not an empty name." The care we bestow upon the graves of those we love shows that we have not forgotten them.

The reverend went on to address the issue of reinterments. He noted that the community already had a cemetery but that it was reaching its limits concerning future burials. The older Montpelier burial grounds held memories for those still alive and, he wondered, "How many tears have fallen onto its hitherto untroubled and quiet graves?" For those who had buried their dead there, "there, truly, are deposited the richest treasures which you had on earth." However, he continued:

> *If in love and tenderness you shall disturb those ashes, to bring them here, it will only be as when one shall rearrange a couch, that they may rest more sweetly and securely and quietly forever. Here you will come afterward to smoothe [sic] their narrow bed, to recall their virtues, to renew your vows of constancy, and to say—"My Father! My Mother! My Brother! My Sister! My Child! Forget thee? Never!"*

Shelton anticipated further cemetery beautification in future years: "But if no sculpture memorialized the dead, these glorious hills would be a monument. Yon silver stream shall chant a constant requiem." He continued, "There is an Echo here which mocks the ear, but wakes up sympathies within the heart. . . . It is Death alone which dies." And with the last statement, he returned to more scriptural messaging to complete his address.

Tombs were discouraged in the new cemetery's bylaws, but they were not forbidden, as long as they were constructed "wholly underground." Lot owners could erect monuments and enclose their lots, as well as plant trees, shrubs, and flowers. Any enclosures, however, were not to be "solid walls or fences," as it was "desired that the prospect through and over lots should be interrupted as little as possible." The cemetery had the right to remove any objects deemed "improper or detrimental to the cemetery or any adjoining lot," as long as deemed so by the entire commission.

Its land acquired and dedicated, its basic regulations in place, and its initial layout plans underway, the cemetery opened. As Reverend Shelton, the board, and others anticipated, the cemetery would indeed prove popular in subsequent years.

In 1893, a town history stated that the cemetery was "the great glory" of Montpelier, "both for what it contains, its beauty of situation, and the perfection of its maintenance. Most of the chief actors in its history are buried there." To learn almost the entire history of the town, one need only take "an old man, in whom memory abides," to Green Mount and "walk with him beneath the trees of this peaceful grove, read, with his aid, the writings in stone there, and you will have almost the perfect story of the town."

Several interesting memorials are located at Green Mount. If one just wanders in and drives up the hill, one will encounter a few of them, from some small animal statues that might make one wonder if this was one of America's original pet cemeteries, to a classic lion memorial, to a Grecian set of columns overlooking the gateway and the river, to one of most striking angels of the garden cemeteries.

Look a little closer, and you will find a set of more than twenty stone steps dug into a ledge on the hillside for one specific memorial, a breathtaking bronze statue that is rumored to be cursed, and a celebrated statue of a little girl leaning against a stone fence. Two of these are part of cemetery lore, one tale claiming that a little girl is wandering the grounds seeking her mother and the other asserting that sitting on one specific memorial might lead to one's destruction.

The celebrated child statue is a memorial to Margaret Pitkin, who died in 1900 at the age of seven. Her monument is reminiscent somehow of *The Wizard of Oz*, if one thinks of the original Dorothy in the Baum books leaning against a fence in a pastoral setting. More commonly, it has been said to embody the Victorian ideal of childhood. According to cemetery lore, Margaret's family commissioned a sculptor to create the statue, but they were then dismayed to discover that Margaret in her statue form had a button missing on one of her shoes. The sculptor then purportedly showed her parents the photograph they had given him to use as a guide, and it showed that the girl had indeed been missing a button on one of her shoes. The life-size statue remains popular among cemetery visitors.

The John Dieter grave is also frequently discussed by cemetery visitors. It is topped by a figure of Jesus, tended in his death by his mother. Both figures are life-size, and Jesus is shown gaunt, hollow-eyed, and with his wounds obvious, which seems to be part of what draws people to the monument. Various versions of the pietà are seen in many of the garden cemeteries, some of them artistic masterpieces as are some of the other figures of mourning.

The most talked-about monument at Green Mount, however, is undoubtedly the monument built for John Erastus Hubbard. Hubbard died in 1899 and left a generous bequest—$25,000—that allowed the cemetery to build a combined chapel, holding vault, and gateway a few years later. He also left $10,000 for a personal monument.

Hubbard left it up to the executors of his will to handle the details of his memorial, and Vermont governor William Dillingham, one of the executors, helped engage Karl Bitter of Vienna, who had had a studio in New Jersey for many years, to create a memorial with a bronze figure for Hubbard—and what a memorial it would be. It would feature one of the most compelling statues found in any of the garden cemeteries; it is simply stunning.

The bronze statue of a seated figure that Bitter created portrays a person in great sorrow, his head thrown back and sideways in agony. Shrouded, the male figure is called *Thanatos*, the Greek word for "death." However, the Green Mount statue is more commonly known as "Black

Agnes," in part a reflection of the fact that many people see the statue as being female, and in part an association with another cemetery tale.

Hubbard has been condemned for not being generous enough with his inheritance while alive and for deflecting a large inheritance that, according to the will of his aunt, Fanny Hubbard Kellogg, who died in 1890 in New York City, was to have gone directly to the town. Because of this, some stories go, those who sit on Black Agnes's lap will be cursed.

However, Hubbard did contribute significantly to his community after his death if not as much as he might have before it. Hubbard left funds not only to the cemetery for a building and gates and for a monument for himself but also to the town for the creation of a public park and to support a public library he had established and built shortly before his death, the Kellogg-Hubbard Library in Montpelier. The terms of the previous Kellogg will, which Fanny had signed just after the death of her husband, Martin M. Kellogg, had allotted funds for such a public library, as well as for a chapel and gates at Green Mount. Hubbard, who has been blamed for using devious means to funnel the Kelloggs' money to himself, would eventually take care of these matters as well as leave his and his parents' land for a public park, the Hubbard Park.

However, in response to an outcry about the will and Hubbard's role in creating the library and adding his own name to it, an alternative library had been set up before Hubbard's death, and artist Thomas Waterman Wood, a painter of national acclaim, president of the American Watercolor Society, and vice president of the National Academy of Design, donated numerous oil painting to the alternate library, one that initially did better in terms of book holdings and popularity, set up in the local YMCA building. (Wood would also be buried at Green Mount, as would his wife, Minerva Robinson Wood, both of them with bronze bas-relief busts on their shared memorial.) Therefore, although Hubbard would redeem himself, a shadow was cast over his legacy.

On the gray granite wall behind the seated figure Bitter cast for Hubbard, known as an exedra wall or bench, are inscribed verses from William Cullen Bryant's poem "Thanatopsis," or "Thoughts on Death." It was a poem well-known to the educated American in the nineteen century, and it reads as follows:

Thou go not like the
Quarry slave at night
Scourged to his dungeon,
But sustained and soothed
By an unfaltering trust.

Approach thy grave
Like one who wraps
The Drapery of his couch
About him and lies down
To pleasant dream.

The mysterious statue of Thanatos at Green Mount, however, was not the only one Bitter created, and other cemeteries have other versions of it. In addition, a famed bronze memorial to the wife of Henry Adams in Washington, DC, had earlier been created by American sculptor Augustus Saint-Gaudens—who also created statuary for Springfield Cemetery—and is considered by some people to be quite similar to the one Bitter cast for Green Mount. According to Cynthia Mills's 1996 doctoral dissertation, bronze sculpture was an association with Europe that the American elite would seek to emulate, and the very inward mystery created by the Adams monument, commonly known as *Grief*, became extremely influential in following funerary art. (Mills also suggested, based on other sources, that both statues may have been influenced by the *Dying Slave* sculpture by Michelangelo, but this would stretch the similarities even further.)

Moreover, the legend that surrounds "Black Agnes" originated, according to Mills, not with the Bitter monument at Green Mount, or one of his elsewhere, but with a statue created to honor a war veteran that copied the original Saint-Gaudens memorial, causing much anger on the part of some people, including Saint-Gaudens's son. The haunted stories commenced there, with that statue, created for Felix Agnus and nicknamed "Black Agie" or "Black Agnus." The slight change to "Agnes" would be understandable.

However, Bitter needed to copy no one's artwork: his Green Mount memorial is stupendous. It resembles the more famous Saint-Gaudens work only in that it features a mysterious, seated bronze figure wrapped or draped in mourning cloth. The two resemble each other in this, but beyond this similarity, it is as if the Hubbard bronze figure's face changes in features and expression, the position of the torso changes, the hood or shroud is thrown back from the face and upper torso, and the arms are thrown out and head thrown back and in grief. In other words, the Hubbard statue of grief conveys just that, and it does not resemble the seated figure in Washington.

The Adams memorial may be considered androgynous; the Hubbard one is perhaps more hermaphroditic, there is more mystery about it, even though more of the face and head and the upper torso are visible. Bitter truly captured a universal representation of sorrow. Steps lead up to the Hubbard bronze figure; a massive (more than ten feet by six feet wide), semi-flat carved and inscribed marker is above Hubbard's remains, and the lot includes decorative curbing. The exedra alone is about fifteen feet long and, in addition, the stele behind the five-foot figure, who, of course, would be correspondingly taller if he "stood up," is six feet wide. Bitter would later display a plaster cast of the Hubbard figure. The enigma of Hubbard's statue perhaps reflects the enigma of who Hubbard was and who he became.

Adjacent or to the side of the more famous John Erastus Hubbard memorial is another memorial for the Hubbard family as a whole: a female angel standing in front of a rough-hewn rock or "rock-face" cross. This basic arrangement is seen elsewhere. However, the Hubbard angel is a bit more intricate in the carving of her face and features than some others are. Her wings are delightfully detailed, and instead of a rose, seen in many such memorials, she seems to carry lilies, with another flower dropped at her feet. Her expression is reflective and quite serious. Her eyes are cast downward. The hill rises up behind her, and nearby, one can see a variety of marker styles, including a heavily draped urn and a brownstone memorial. Smaller individual family markers are located near the granite angel, which is inscribed only with the family name.

Erastus Hubbard—John Erastus Hubbard's father—purchased a number of lots in 1864 and seemingly had a few family members reinterred there. Erastus Hubbard lived until 1890 and was in many ways a community leader. Over time, the Hubbards had developed vast real estate holdings, so John Hubbard had more than one source of funding for his various endeavors and donations.

The hillside at Green Mount is filled with funerary art. Some of it is fairly simple; some is not. In general, the memorials are located on spacious lots or are simply well spaced from one another. Another angel of interest, and a unique one, is that of the Fifield memorial, located uphill from the Hubbard memorials.

The Fifield angel does not stand upright, as so many garden cemetery angels do. Instead, she sits on an elevated base, perhaps on a cushion, with her head bowed and her legs tucked up under her. Her wings form almost a crescent moon around her, and she leans slightly to one side, onto an inverted torch, whose flame still burns strong. Her eyes are half-lidded and seem to be looking inward. Her expression is a relaxed one. The large sarcophagus-style base of the memorial is finely sloped and decorated with vines and leaves as well as inscribed with family information.

A third angel marker of interest is the Lane-Barron and Brophy memorial. In this instance, the angel stands, but her long, delicate wings are similar to those on the Fifield stone. In one hand she holds a garland. The other hand has been broken and fallen away.

Angels are part of more than one religious culture, and neither the Lane-Barron nor the Fifield angel holds or stands with a cross. Both are considerably different from the Hubbard angel, and they have a bit of an art deco feel to them. The not-too-distant Bennett memorial does, however, feature a woman holding a garland around a large "wooden" cross, her eyes cast downward with her hair partially covered.

Other memorials at Green Mount also feature statues. Most, but not all, are female. Near the top of the hill, one can find the Kellogg memorial, created for the Kellogg family, from whom John Hubbard inherited much of the funding he donated to Montpelier and the cemetery. Martin M. and Fanny have their names and dates inscribed on the front panel of the towering memorial—the base alone stands close to ten feet in height—which features a substantial granite architectural base and sculpture. The sculpture is of an older woman comforting—or instructing—a younger woman. The older woman wears classical clothing with her hair partially covered. She has a very Grecian look to her. Both figures sit, with the young girl sitting at the woman's feet, the two almost smiling at one another. The woman holds an open book on her lap, and she rests one arm lightly around the girl's shoulder. The front of the memorial also features a wreath and palm leaves and the family name. Martin M. Kellogg's parents' names and a sister's name are inscribed on the back panel.

Not too far down the hill from the Kellogg memorial, at the Bailey memorial, is one of the cemetery's versions of the woman-in-mourning-with-wreath figures. She looks more Roman than do some of the other figures in this style, and she appears contemplative. The Bailey figure is kneeling on the ground, not sitting, as are many such figures, and she is holding a wreath in one hand. The base is a large architectural one, complete with four small Corinthian-style columns or pilasters.

The city of Montpelier erected the Joel Foster memorial in 1904 to honor Foster's long-time work for the city. His is one of the few "portrait" statues in the cemetery, and indeed, they are generally scarce in New England garden cemeteries. Foster lived between 1825 and 1903, and after his death, the city built his large monument, complete with a life-size—if not larger—statue. The city recognized Foster's more than fifty years of service, especially in engineering and developing Montpelier's water system. His statue has one hand resting on a water fountain or hydrant in the style of his day, and in the other hand, he holds his hat. The base of the memorial is a high pedestal one, complete with carvings of a laurel wreath and a dedication plaque.

As noted, pets did have a place in this cemetery. Several markers for dogs are found at Green Mount. Some may be there for the benefit of their people who have died, while others mark the graves of animals themselves, it seems. Lambs and dogs can be found near the top of the hill, the words on the memorials largely washed away with time. One example is that of a dog statue near the markers for Lucy and Harry Boutwell; another is a lamb sculpture with the name Habry carved in bas-relief.

The cemetery also has a lion, a large one lying on a substantial base. The lion appears to be a friendly one, perched upon one of the steepest parts of the hillside, just below the Bailey memorial, in the section overlooking the state capital. Carved for the Braman family, the lion seems to smile, but it could easily switch into the fierce protective mode, at least if it were real. Lions are often considered to be guardians. Symbols akin in some ways to angels, they guard the living and the dead.

A more modern memorial for a dog, made from Vermont granite, is that for Nick, a beloved service dog, at the far edge of the cemetery, perhaps to answer the concerns of any humans who worried that he might be buried among the humans.

Like many New England garden cemeteries, especially the municipal ones, Green Mount has a Soldier's Lot, this one administered by the US Department of Veteran Affairs. The lot is a relatively small and simple one, yet it still bears testament to those who fought to try to hold the Union together. In 1865, the town and cemetery donated a 450-square-foot lot to the US government to be used as a burial site for Union soldiers. Eight soldiers were eventually buried at the site, according to the National Park Service. The lot is located near the flatter, southwestern border of the cemetery.

A number of interesting memorials went up at Green Mount in the later 1800s that speak both to the local community and to the growth of the cemetery. Memorials came to cover much of the hill, both on its "front" side and its side slopes. The Stone memorial, a small temple marker, would come to rest at the edge of the hill about halfway up where its visitors could come to enjoy a view of the river. Short steps behind it inscribed for the Volholm family, as well as the road that winds up the hillside, sometimes quite steeply, lead to markers such as the Whittier column, with a large urn on top, and several tall obelisks and architectural monuments, including the Redfield sarcophagus-style one.

Almost at the peak of the hill, above the Bailey memorial and next to the Kellogg memorial with its woman and girl figures, the Langdon family memorial features a "house"-style central marker with several small individual markers nearby. Moving toward the other side of the hill, to the west, one encounters the massive Lucius D. Taft sarcophagus and, down the slope a bit on the front side, one begins to encounter some of the animal memorials and the upper-level angels.

One of the era's most noted memorials, however, is located off to the far eastern side of the cemetery at the base of the hill just off Route 2. The cemetery saw the construction of the Stowell memorial in 1897–1898, not long before the death of John E. Hubbard, who would have the stunning *Thanatos* statue. Both memorials attract much visitor attention.

The William Stowell "tomb" was cut into a single granite ledge or boulder as one stairway but with the sides of the stairway also exposed as part of the memorial, which is essentially a massive sculpture. People often climb the steps, well over twenty of them, even though a smaller stone stairway exists just a few feet away and provides the pedestrian easier access into the cemetery from the road. The public access stairway is a short one, but it features two curved stone benches for sitting.

With the Stowell and Hubbard memorials complete, the cemetery saw its next major project underway, the construction of its main building. In 1905, the cemetery used its bequest from John Erastus Hubbard, as well as some of its general fund, to construct a combined chapel and vault. Although it has been described as Gothic, the combined building, designed by Cleveland & Godfrey, is a lengthy one that has a rather Spanish air to it. A wide archway between the two sections serves as the main vehicle entrance for the cemetery. Known simply as the Chapel-Vault Building, the vault section can hold up to sixty entombments or caskets, and the chapel side can seat sixty people, according to cemetery publications. The side of the building dedicated as a chapel also currently provides office space.

The entire arrangement provides a striking entranceway for Green Mount, one that continues to attract visitors today. After one passes through the gateway, heading straight ahead, one soon reaches a division of the roads; go toward the right, and the road winds uphill toward the Braman lion and the peak. Go left, and the road winds past the Hubbard memorials and to the peak. Other roads provide different journeys with various memorials along the way.

Meanwhile, while Green Mount was becoming a well-established rural cemetery, just thirty miles away, another garden cemetery opened in the 1870s, and it, too, would be a municipal one. Established on the shore of Lake Champlain in 1871, Lakeview Cemetery originally held just twenty-three acres. The cemetery purchased another seven acres the following year. Still, to the present day, Lakeview remains one of the smallest rural cemeteries discussed herein. Burlington's Parks and Recreation Department currently manages it, one of three so managed, and Lakeview is the only one of them still offering burial lots.

Lakeview overlooks Lake Champlain and the Adirondack Mountains of New York. The view from the cemetery across the lake is excellent. While it retains its lake-view qualities, the cemetery did grant a strip of land just off the shoreline that connects with other sections and currently serves as a bike path and pedestrian way, one widely used by the public. A gated fence separates the path from the grounds proper.

Lakeview is in downtown Burlington, Vermont, much as Valley Cemetery is in downtown Manchester, New Hampshire. However, perhaps because of its location on a major lake, the press of the city seems less. Also, the cemetery has its entryways on the top of a hill, slopes downward and then flattens out, so that the vehicle traffic seems far removed from much of the burial section of Lakeview.

In addition to its wealth of natural water, the cemetery once held three fountains for the enjoyment of visitors. It also has a noted gazebo, one built in the "Adirondack rustic" style, and families frequently picnicked there in the late 1800s.

The cemetery built a large Victorian Gothic revival chapel in 1882. Capable of seating eighty people on its wooden pews, the Louisa Howard Chapel is situated on the hill, or ridge, overlooking the rest of the cemetery and the lake. It boasts some lovely stained glass windows and an ornate painted ceiling. The seam-faced building has buttressed sides as well as dormers jutting out from its steep roofline, a small spire with a bell tower section, and, above that, a cross is mounted on its peak.

Louisa Howard donated funds for the chapel, while her brother, John Purple Howard, donated the cemetery's fountains. The chapel was used for its intended purposes of memorial services for some time, but it was eventually converted to storage space. Both Louisa Howard and her brother are buried at Lakeview, as are their families, with a tall obelisk near the center of the grounds marking their lot. One can drive around either side of the chapel and then down the hill, or descend a long stairway on foot, to reach the burial grounds proper.

Driving to the left side of the chapel to reach the valley, one will soon encounter the cemetery's receiving tomb, built into the hill behind and a bit to the side of the chapel, which faces the road. The tomb faces the lake.

Just down the hill from the tomb is a well-populated veterans' lot. It is maintained largely by the American Legion, Burlington Post 2. The stones in the section are primarily small ones. Closer to the lake, however, are the graves of other veterans. Some of them have large makers; others do not.

Most celebrated of the individual veterans' graves, it seems, is that of General George Jerrison Stannard, a Civil War veteran. Stannard led his troops into victory at the Battle of Gettysburg on July 3, 1863. He later lost an arm leading the attack on Fort Harrison, and that is how he is depicted by the statue at his grave: in military uniform, one sleeve tied up where his arm had been amputated at the elbow, with his sword at his side. The bronze statue stands atop a large, mostly polished stone base.

A more modest—at only a foot in height—memorial marks the grave of L. W. Freeman, a black Union soldier who fought in the Civil War. His stone is located on the southern side of Lakeview. Freeman fought with the North as part of the 54th Regiment, the troop depicted in the 1989 award-winning film *Glory*. Freeman is one of five known African-American Civil War veterans buried in the cemetery, according to James Fuller's 2001 book *Men of Color, To Arms!*

Also located in Lakeview are stones denoting two soldiers who led men of color in the war. Henry Powell's monument—three feet wide by six feet long and "waist high"—is a block of granite that marks his resting place, and he is located a few hundred feet from Freeman's grave. Powell commanded the 10th US Colored Troops in the war and served as a lieutenant colonel.

More centrally located in the cemetery is a small memorial to Major General Oliver Otis Howard. Howard died in 1909 after serving in the Civil War—winning a Medal of Honor for his actions—and then serving as a commissioner of the Freedman's Bureau, which sought to aid former slaves after the war. Howard also helped establish the traditionally black college, Howard University, in Washington, DC, and the university is named for him.

If one were to follow the road down the hill from the right side of the chapel, one would see the superintendent's house near the top of the hill, and then, winding down the avenue, one would soon come to another burial section with small white markers, one that is larger than the veteran's section. The markers are stunning—or unsettling, depending on one's perspective. Rows and rows of hundreds of poor people's graves mark the cemetery lawn. They each have a number instead of a name. In the midst of them is one larger marker, a white one for Isaac Prince, who served in the 54th Massachusetts Volunteers.

And if one were to skip over the rest of the cemetery, to almost the shore of the lake, one would find another row of little white markers, most of them slanted in one direction as if leaning away from the winds that blow across Lake Champlain. They are markers for the graves of children who died while under the care of Burlington's Home for Destitute Children. More than fifty of the little markers stand today, along with a larger marker, one erected by Louisa H. Howard—the same woman who built the cemetery's chapel—dated 1884. The architectural base is topped by a cross, and it is dedicated to all of the children who died at the home.

Lakeview has several interesting memorials of a variety of types. Most are not dedicated to destitute children or adults or to veterans but instead to general members of the community. Besides Stannard's memorial with its figure, there are a few other statues in the cemetery. They include the Converse memorial, which features a female angel carrying a lily, and the Barnes female figure, holding a cross and standing on a tall ornate architectural base, complete with four small pillars. Both the Converse and the Barnes memorials are part of family lots.

Obelisks, small colonnades, Celtic crosses, markers for children who died in the general community, and other types of funerary art are also to be found at Lakeview. Several mausoleums also exist. Two of the more interesting mausoleums are the Allen mausoleum, which is a small church-like structure near the center of the grounds, and the

Thompson-Stone-Patrick mausoleum overlooking Champlain, which is reminiscent of an Italian villa.

Lakeview declined in appearance—in terms of the upkeep of some its memorials and structures—over the years, but in recent decades, it has benefited from an increase in popularity once again. In particular, a preservation committee, the Friends of Lakeview Cemetery, has undertaken restoring the former grandeur of the grounds. The group initiated their work at the chapel, replacing the roof, installing radiant-floor heating, and making other repairs and additions. The chapel is currently in fine repair and serves as a visual focal point for cemetery visitors, as well as being open to the community for various uses. The gates at the cemetery are quite simple, and it is the chapel that first grabs the visitor's attention.

Lakeview is a small cemetery but one worth visiting. It offers a fully restored Gothic chapel on one side and a great lake (in fact, Champlain was initially up for inclusion as one of the Great Lakes) on the other. The municipal cemetery, like others elsewhere, has been quite generous with community lots for the poor, for children, and for veterans. Just a half hour away from Green Mount makes this a welcome side trip—if not a main one—or one could look at it the other way around. Both cemeteries have a distinct New England and Vermont feel to them.

There are a number of short, online sources for both cemeteries and some of the people buried in them, but the amount of publicly available historical documentation is relatively small. Cynthia Mills, in her 1996 dissertation, discussed the statues as noted, and her "Dying Well in Montpelier; The Story of the Hubbard Memorial," in Vermont History, *provides further information on the Hubbard story. Barre writer Paul Heller has also written about the statue at Montpelier for the* Times Argus *of Barre/Montpelier. Touring the cemeteries and studying the inscriptions and talking to Superintendent Patrick Healy of Green Mount and Burlington staff members and Friends of Lakeview good ways to learn more about these two local institutions and their "residents," as is reading surviving town records.*

11

By the Valley of the Kings

Evergreen Cemetery, Portland, Maine

When one walks into Evergreen Cemetery, one soon begins to leave behind the feel of a city. Yet one is never quite away from the City of Portland, which is Maine's largest city, though it is far from the largest city in New England. What a person may well feel in Evergreen Cemetery is the sense of peace and wonder that most garden cemeteries instill, but there is also a sense of coexistence, a sense of city and garden and cemetery coming together in a harmonious whole. Evergreen Cemetery is very widely used by the general public for bird-watching, walking, bicycling, cross-country skiing, monument viewing, contemplation, and, of course—as with most of the cemeteries discussed herein—for ongoing burials.

WHEN THE CITY OF PORTLAND BEGAN TO TRULY FEEL A DEMAND FOR A new burial location in the 1850s—the pressure for one having been building for years, if not decades—it had the examples of other New England cemeteries of recent years, including the one just two hours north in Maine, Mount Hope Cemetery of Bangor, for how to lay out one of the newer garden cemeteries—and plenty of evidence as to why creating such an oasis in the city might be preferable to just creating some sort of humdrum burial grounds. Portland made use of these examples and this knowledge in a wise way. It created a municipal garden cemetery that continues to attract a large number of people yearly, monthly, and daily. Winter to autumn, Evergreen Cemetery is a popular place for local residents and for visitors to the region. Moreover, because of its beauty, a large number of Maine politicians, Portland mayors, industrial leaders, and war veterans have been interred at Evergreen.

In the early 1850s, Portland turned to its city engineer, Charles H. Howe, for guidance in establishing a burial ground. New England had surged forward with the garden cemetery movement in the past two decades, with recent additions to the growing list being Brookside Cemetery in Watertown, New York, and the smaller Elm Grove Cemetery in Mystic, Connecticut. The publicly owned Evergreen Cemetery would be one of the larger garden cemeteries, eventually reaching 239 acres, making it the second-largest open space in Portland. About one hundred acres at Evergreen remain undeveloped woods, complete with hiking paths. Old growth pine and oak trees are common in the wooded areas, while these and various ornamental trees are found throughout the developed sections.

Surviving city records of the cemetery from the 1850s and the next few decades are somewhat scarce, but they do provide some precise information about Evergreen's establishment. The municipal report for 1853 simply stated that "in consequence of the fact that the two Cemeteries within the City were nearly full, a purchase was made, under the authority of the last City Council, of a track of land in Westbrook, containing about fifty-five acres, for a public Cemetery." A later report would specify that the land was purchased on February 8, 1852, and was in two lots. One purchase for 28.33 acres was made from O. Buckley for $3,333 and the other from William Stevens for 26.21 acres at the cost of $1,966. (The cemetery fronts on what is now Stevens Avenue.) Also, as part of the purchase from Buckley, the cemetery received a small parcel of 0.83 acres as a "passageway." The cemetery would next acquire an even smaller parcel, just 0.02 acres, from H. B. and H. M. Hunt for $1, and then another 0.04 acres from Oliver Buckley in 1866 for $10.

The original fifty-five acres (and then the smaller additions) needed development and improvements to turn them into a garden cemetery. The city proceeded with its plans fairly quickly and noted that, acting on a report by the Joint Standing Committee on Burying-Grounds, "the

City Council directed sundry improvements to be made on the lot, and approved fifteen hundred dollars for that purpose." The largest share of the money went to building a fence around the new cemetery. Some $1,196 went to J. R. Mathews and Peter Bolton for building a fence. Another $158 was paid to Richard Gage and others for labor, seemingly for the other improvements. The rest of the money would most likely be expended in the near future since the $1,500 had been "obtained on loan redeemable in twenty years."

During the following fiscal year, which ended on April 8, 1854, the city expended yet more money on the grounds, close to $2,000, to grade its new avenues and paths, as well as about $100 for design plans. The city purchased two new hearses for $355, seemingly for use at Evergreen and at the other municipal cemeteries. The city also employed a superintendent of burials, who made about $100 per year during the era, with his time shared among the city cemeteries.

During the 1854–1855 fiscal year, the city built a gate at Evergreen. Unfortunately, the report gives no description of the gate, but it does note that with other expenses, including avenue grading, it cost $1,588. Other sources state that the cemetery originally had pyramid-style gates. The cemetery was now bringing in money, however, about $850 for the year, which was a fairly substantial amount. Evergreen was already proving popular, and the following year, the city had to expend just $428 on it.

By April 1857, the City of Portland employed a superintendent for Evergreen for a salary of $150 a year. The new superintendent oversaw the labor expended at the cemetery, which cost just a little more than $50 in 1856–1857, as well as the overall management of Evergreen.

The hiring of the superintendent was part of a shift in cemetery management. The city had passed an ordinance stipulating that all monies received from the sale of lots at Evergreen would be used exclusively for "the purpose of improving and ornamenting said cemetery." It had gone into effect the year before, and by the close of 1856–1857, the fund held $766 after expenses of $1,300. These expenses included planting trees, digging a well, and installing a pump with an "ornamental house" installed over it. A total of 130 lots had been sold over the year for $10 each, bringing in $1,300 total.

The new ordinance was critical for the development of Evergreen Cemetery, as it meant that Evergreen would not be "carrying" the other burial grounds but rather monies brought in would be used to care for and improve the cemetery. The following year, the new well house was painted, as were the fence and gates, more trees were planted, further work was done on the avenues and paths, and a new "tool house" was built. Sales of lots brought in $1,130, and another $30 was made through sales of wood. Several cemeteries made money, especially during their first years, from wood sales. The new cemetery was off to a solid start in its city of about 30,000 people.

A combined tool house and office was added in 1858–1859, but the building was probably fairly small. The superintendent of cemeteries made $200 that year, and the cemetery bought and planted more trees, worked on its plans for the future, and planted a hedge fence. The cemetery brought in some $1,463.

The new decade started out with Evergreen Cemetery being on solid financial footing. City reports show that the cemetery was proving quite popular, bringing in enough revenue to support itself, and it had basic buildings, gates, fencing, paths, avenues, and so forth in place. It seems that the cemetery was also starting to pay someone to "staff" the gates. The cemetery started to purchase stone for "fenders," probably used for ornamental curbing. And, as well as trees, other types of ornamental plants were purchased for cemetery beautification. Lots still sold for $10, and during 1859–1860 brought in $1,220; however, the cemetery also sold one lot for $3, though no reason was given as to why.

In 1860–1861, Evergreen built a "Reception House." The building cost $546, and it no doubt added to the appeal of the cemetery. During during 1861–1862, Evergreen saw further progress. Some basic improvements were made and plans finalized to build another, or a new, gateway. Lot sales brought in $1,870.

Soon, however, the nation went to war. Portland turned its attention to supporting the war effort and those injured or killed in the Civil War as well as their dependents. This was true throughout New England. Municipal and some private cemeteries, with Mount Hope leading the way, would soon see veterans' memorials added to their grounds, and this ushered in a new view of death and burial for much of America. Portland, too, would see new markers at Evergreen, and money would come from city coffers to pay for veterans' burials.

The Civil War cost Mainers heavily regarding lives lost directly and indirectly from the war. Some people never made it back from the war, alive or dead. Instead, their bodies remained unidentified or were left near battlefields. One example is Alonzo M. Whitney, who served with the 18th Maine Regiment of Volunteers and went missing at the 1862 Battle of Fredericksburg. Whitney's memorial is one of the cemetery's more unusual ones, in part simply because of the way the stones are arranged. His is a large, architectural-style memorial with columns, topped by an ornate vase decorated with vines. Alonzo's parents are buried at the same site, with small upright stones to either side of the walk leading to Alonzo's marker.

Thousands of Maine men and women did make it back from the war; however, they were in caskets or died later, and well over 1,000 members of the Maine regiments, including navy members, are buried at Evergreen.

Generals, too, were interred at the cemetery. Brevet Brigadier General Henry Goddard Thomas, a Portland native, is buried at Evergreen with a large marker complete with a bas-relief portrait of Thomas in uniform. Thomas died in 1897, surviving the war and such battles as that at Bull Run, his first battle. Generals Neil Dow, George Shepley, and George Warren West are also buried at Evergreen, as are so many other veterans of different ranks.

In the 1880s, Evergreen Cemetery became the home of a Civil War memorial. Similar in appearance to some others in New England's garden cemeteries, such as those in Springfield and Albany, it was given to Bosworth Post No. 2 of the Grand Army of the Republic. The memorial recognizes the more than 1,000 veterans of the war interred at Evergreen as well as those who served but are interred elsewhere. Brothers Henry and Nathan Cleaves presented the memorial, and the cemetery held a dedication ceremony to mark the occasion.

Surrounding the central marker with its sculpture of a Union color bearer are his fallen comrades, so to speak, although they are actually scattered throughout the cemetery; however, some of them, as noted, are only represented through their stones, since their bodies are absent. Its cannon remains in place.

The war perhaps heightened the need for another facility in Portland. The city constructed a city tomb at Evergreen in 1863 for $3,000. The committee had allocated $2,500 for the project, but it had not anticipated the costs of covering the tomb with sod to make it blend more naturally into the environment or the cost of doing work on adjacent land for the same reason, including changing the pathways. J. T. Emory, Esq., furnished the design for the tomb and contracted to build it. Everyone involved seemed content with the results, according to 1864 city records. It would later be removed, after many decades of service.

The next few years saw ongoing work and a restructuring of cemetery economics. For some time, 100 percent of the income from lot sales and the like had been held for Evergreen Cemetery alone, which remained fairly independent. However, this soon changed.

In 1869, Evergreen acquired sixty-eight acres, doubling its size, and then added another fifty-six acres over the next year and a half. In 1870, the cemetery surveyed and developed plans for a new section, and continued with stonework started in recent years. The cemetery sold 204 lots during the ensuing fiscal year, each of them selling for $20. However, of the $4,080 received, only 25 percent was held by ordinance just for Evergreen. Inflation had come to Evergreen, as had mounting expenses. To help offset this, an appreciable amount of money had come in for the care of lots. But problems continued.

Another seventeen acres were purchased in 1876, and three small parcels acquired in 1880 added another sixteen acres to the cemetery. By 1881, Evergreen encompassed 208 acres and was a sizable rural cemetery. More than seventy acres were developed and held ponds, avenues, and burial lots, according to 1881 records. The cemetery had much room for expansion, and it would gain additional land over the following decades until it reached its current 239 acres. The growth in real estate property between the late 1860s and 1880s would add to some difficulties, however, as would lot sales.

In 1869, when the size of the cemetery doubled, the city created a board of trustees to manage cemetery affairs, but its members apparently did not submit consistent records of meetings, actions, or expenditures. The grounds were seemingly neglected and lots sold without adequate record keeping. The original plans for creating the pastoral cemetery had at many junctures been ignored. Therefore, in 1880, the city appointed a new board. The new board reported that it had to expend a relatively large amount of money to get the grounds and their management back in order. The old superintendent or agent retired, seemingly after an $800 insufficiency was discovered, and a new one was hired.

The amount of money needed to run the growing cemetery seems to have pressed on civic leaders, there may have been some irregularities, and the system of funding the cemetery proved problematic. As the mayor explained in 1881, "Large additions made to Evergreen Cemetery from time to time, without correspondingly improved methods in its management to meet the conditions, led to considerable confusion in its affairs." Therefore, "the ordinances relating to it have been revised and changed to meet present and future needs." Cemetery management changed, the city engineer made new and complete maps, and a long-needed water supply was acquired. The grounds were again looking good, and citizens volunteering their time had helped beautify the grounds. It was hoped that soon the department would be "self-supporting," because the cemetery was still the boon to the city that it had once been.

As part of the new system, the city's annual report contained a report by the Trustees of Evergreen Cemetery. In January 1881, the city passed an ordinance mandating that an annual report on the "general conditions and affairs of the Cemetery" be made to the council through the city treasurer. The report, published in 1881, was the first ever of its kind, was lengthy, and was deemed worthy of publication. However, it would be the only one of its type to be published for some time.

The cemetery had 4,405 plots by early 1881, with 2,811 lot holders. As the cemetery report noted, it was clear that "this Cemetery has become an institution . . . of great importance to the City of Portland." The problem was, at least in retrospect, that cemetery affairs had become too complicated to be managed by a committee of the city council. Thus, a new survey and plan for Evergreen were undertaken, and a resulting map was hung in the cemetery's waiting room. Moreover, new record books were created: one copy for the cemetery and one for the city treasurer.

The new board and superintendent undertook the water supply project, laying pipe to aid the cemetery during the dry months of summer. The cemetery installed an Eclipse windmill to pump water up to a reservoir on the highest point of the grounds, as they were at the time. The reservoir could hold 27,000 gallons of water.

The cemetery also "fit up" a commodious building for use as an office and waiting room near the entrance to the grounds. A ledge beyond the ponds was "opened up," and plans were made to use it to acquire foundation stones for the cemetery. Overgrown trees throughout the cemetery had been pruned over the winter.

However, some issues remained. Only one main line to the water supply had been laid, and at least two more were needed, especially to reach the recently acquired properties. Also, the area at the front of the grounds, near Stevens Avenue, had too much water, and drainage was needed.

Furthermore, Evergreen needed a superintendent to live on the premises, as well as a new entrance. The trustees proposed using one of the newer parcels for building "a small but neat cottage house." A greenhouse could be erected near it. The greenhouse, the report stated, "could be easily managed by the Superintendent during the winter, and the propagation of plants carried on for the use of the cemetery and as well the supply of the lot holders." To the rear of the house and greenhouse, ornamental trees and shrubs could be grown. Farther back in the grounds, the lanes leading to the ponds were prone to being washed out in the spring and needed improvements, and the woods also needed attention.

One last, major issue was the receiving tomb. It was deemed essentially unfit for the purpose for which it was designed. The size of the units was such that only a few caskets inside of boxes could be placed there. It had been proposed that most caskets would be removed from their holding boxes, but this was inconvenient and many people objected to it being done. An extension of the tomb had to be made, and soon, one with only larger cells was needed, leaving the current ones primarily for the use of "small bodies." This would serve the needs of the cemetery for years to come.

The City of Portland had established a large and generally pleasing cemetery. As the 1880s opened, however, more work remained to be undertaken, and much of it would be attended to rather quickly.

The cemetery soon varied the pricing of lots to reflect their location and attributes and to establish perpetual care provisions, the price varying depending on the lot. New ordinances specified that a minimum of three feet would be left for ornamental purposes on the front of lots facing avenues and two feet on fronts facing paths. Those seeking to erect tombs were required to secure permission from the trustees, and all portions aboveground were required to be faced with marble or granite. Any tombs had to be equipped with shelves that allowed for individual interments, with each sealed to prevent the escape of "unpleasant effluvia." Lot owners could erect such "proper memorials" as they saw fitting and cultivate trees and shrubs subject to cemetery regulations. No one could remove trees without permission. The cemetery reserved the right to install brick or stone foundations under monuments, stones, tablets, or ornaments.

In other regulations, wooden fences and headboards were prohibited, horses had to be tied at designated posts only and not left to roam, firearms could not be discharged by visitors nor could visitors throw stones or other "missiles," and the cemetery could deny people the right to bring heavy loads of stone, marble, granite or other goods through the main entrance when the trustees deemed it would be detrimental. Fines would be levied against those who brought their wagons in in violation of this rule. Regulations were set for undertakers, too, including rules governing the disposition of bodies stored in the receiving tomb and forbidding unauthorized people from opening graves.

The trustees were to appoint a secretary and treasurer as well as a president, and the secretary and treasurer would be responsible for receiving payments and bills to Evergreen and be compensated for their work. Trustees could set perpetual care fees. The Evergreen Fund would receive 25 percent of revenue from lot sales, the interest on the fund to be used for improving the cemetery and its upkeep. This was accomplished by early 1885. The new regulations had been approved in April 1882. Lot sales continued to be strong, and reports of the late 1880s on the state of Evergreen Cemetery were positive.

The end of the 1880s would see Evergreen bringing in close to $20,000 in revenue annually, although expenses had risen appreciably over the last few decades. Payroll, for example, now reached more than $14,000, and it was the largest expense at the cemetery. Electric lighting and a telephone had been installed.

Cemetery affairs became more complicated after the turn of the century, as the cemetery adjusted to banking, investment, and labor situations and developments. The tomb remained in use, although in 1910, for example, only ten bodies were received there, whereas forty funeral services were held at the new chapel, 374 people had been buried at the cemetery, and on average, the cemetery had thirty-six employees. Some 346 people were interred in 1920, with twenty-five bodies placed in the receiving tomb. Ordinances changed over the years, including the percentage held in the Evergreen Trust, but meanwhile, Portland continued to have a vibrant and in-demand garden cemetery, which would continue to improve, with a few bumps along the way—as in the past—through the next century and beyond.

In the early 1900s, swans swam in the ponds of Evergreen Cemetery as they did at Brookside Cemetery for much of the twentieth century, just as they continue to swim in the river at Swan Point. People came to enjoy the cemetery daily, but perhaps the thing Evergreen was most proud of at that point was its new building, the Wilde Memorial Chapel.

Built in 1890–1892 through the donation of Mary Ellen Lunt Wilde in memory of her husband, Samuel Wilde, the Gothic granite chapel is similar at first glance to the one at Lakeview in Burlington, Vermont, but it is a bit larger having a crenelated porte cochere in front for the access of horses, and then for automobiles, to the front doors as well as a chancel for services. The chapel, like the one at Lakeview, features fine wooden floors and pews and stained glass windows. The stained glass windows at the Evergreen chapel look out upon the cemetery from all sides and both floors, and feature floral motifs and symbolic designs, including an anchor, which is a symbol of strength and an old Christian symbol as well as one appropriate for a seaside city. Chandeliers hang from the ceiling.

The chapel, designed by Frederick A. Tompson, is available for burial services as one might expect, but also for marriages, classes, and other purposes. Tompson also designed the stone cemetery entry gate at the nearest entryway, as well as the stone walls, both added in 1901 when the entranceway was redesigned. A trolley car waiting room was also installed, according to National Park Service papers, but it was subsequently removed.

One can enter Evergreen Cemetery through one of two major entries located along Stevens Avenue. Entering through the southernmost gate leads around an open expanse to the Wilde Memorial Chapel. The northern entrance leads down a more formal drive, which has a bricked walkway to the cemetery office, built in 1893 of "quarry faced Ashlar masonry"—similar to the seam-faced granite seen in some of the other garden cemetery's buildings, that is, cut to leave the outward facing stone rough. The office would be remodeled after a 1961 fire.

Entering through either cemetery gate, one is soon surrounded by fine monuments, many of them of historical significance, although the route past the office leads more quickly to the more wooded acres of the property, as well as passing by a neighboring cemetery, Pine Grove Cemetery, which was added to Evergreen in the later 1900s. Far to the back, or, more precisely, in the northwestern corner, no matter which route one chooses, one comes to the cemetery's small ponds and brooks or waterways, the most popular site in the cemetery for birdwatchers, exercisers, and photographers. Beyond the ponds lay the woods.

Entering through the soutehrn entrance, one quickly reaches the chapel, which is visible throughout much of the front section of the cemetery. After passing the chapel, one approaches a wonderful section of funerary art in and around one of the cemetery's "circles," each circle situated where several roads come together, with a memorial located in the center. Statues, a temple-style edifice, and other types of markers are located together at this one; the first is for the Cummings and Gerrish families and, inside the circle, for the Baxter family.

Evergreen, moreover, contains not just a few similar ornate memorials as those found elsewhere but more than one of each in the cemetery. For example, the classic mourning-woman-with-wreath statue is found not just here, near the Baxter lot for the Gerrish family, but in another location, a ways farther back in the cemetery, one each for the True and

Kimball families. These three statues are virtually identical. Each of the three, although not one of a kind, is a fine work of artistry. The True and Kimball statues are positioned diagonally across from one another with a handsome mausoleum located between them.

Another statue, a bronze one, of a grieving woman is found at the Wescott family memorial, located near Baxter Circle. Although not truly the same, the statue at the memorial is sometimes included with the other three mourning-woman-with-wreaths statues, but she differs not only in material but also in her clothing and general aspect. Moreover, instead of a fairly simple if ornate base, the Wescott grieving woman sits atop a small mausoleum or vault, one with a little bronze door.

The Baxter family has been one of Maine's most well-known families in terms of its members and their humanitarian, social, and political contributions. The best known of these contributions is perhaps Baxter State Park, as discussed by the author elsewhere, but the family first started gaining influence through its economic endeavors. Family patriarch James Phinney Baxter, along with William G. Davis, founded the Portland Packing Company in Portland in 1863 and developed a new method of uniformly packing fresh corn in tin containers. The tinned corn quickly developed a solid reputation for its flavor, specific weight per tin, and its artistic labels. Business soared, and the new company became the biggest food-packing firm in the world.

Baxter soon started sharing his wealth with his city and state. During his six terms as mayor of Portland, starting in 1893, Baxter convinced the city to acquire most of the 400 acres of public parkland it now owns, including land on Portland's eastern and western promenades and a one-hundred-foot strip of land along the Back Cove Bay widely used for recreation—a tree-lined avenue known as Baxter Boulevard. Baxter hired the Olmsted Brothers of Boston, landscape architects, to design the roadway, for which construction began in 1905. By then, Frederick Law Olmsted himself had died.

Besides establishing parks in Portland, in 1888, Baxter built a new home for the Portland Public Library (incorporated in 1867, with a smaller library existing in the city since the turn of the nineteenth century). Baxter also founded the Portland Society of Art, helped establish

Portland Associated Charities, and made various other donations of his time and money. He lived to age ninety and was buried at Evergreen. He left behind much of the wealth that his son, Percival Proctor Baxter, would use in creating Baxter State Park. In the meantime, the family constructed a marvelous temple-style memorial at Evergreen. Six columns support the roof or canopy, and an elevated vase allows for decorative plantings. Smaller markers identify the graves of individual family members.

As the governor of Maine, Percival Baxter worked relentlessly to establish a park in the Mount Katahdin area. The youngest son of James P. Baxter and his second wife, Mehetable Cummings Proctor, Percy Baxter was born in 1876 and became governor in 1921, three months before his father died. Percival had started lobbying for a Mount Katahdin state park in 1917, and he fought for the park during his tenure as governor, which lasted until 1925. Unsuccessful in his endeavor, between 1930 and 1962 Baxter purchased the land himself and gave it to the people of the State of Maine, deeding it in several parcels. The trust deeds mandated that the park remain forever wild and are regularly consulted to this day.

Baxter was controversial during his time as governor—one often told story is his having ordered flags to be flown at half-mast when his beloved dog, an Irish setter named Garry, died. In addition to Baxter State Park, Baxter donated Mackworth Island, his family home site, to the state in 1943. Mackworth Island is now the home of the Baxter School for the Deaf. Fourteen of Baxter's beloved dogs are buried on the island, and Baxter stipulated that the state maintain their burial site. His own burial site upon his 1969 death was with his family, at Evergreen Cemetery.

Also located near "Baxter Circle," besides the Gerrish family marker, are two other large memorials that feature impressive stone statues. The Cummings and Rand memorial features an immense architectural setting with double columns and a floral wreath with ivy on a tiered base, with a fine version of a classical woman pointing at the heavens and holding a large cross with a garland wrapped around it. The Wilde family marker has another large but less ornate architectural base that also has elements of a sarcophagus memorial, on top of which stands another classical figure: a woman holding a large anchor at her side, with a small cross against her chest. The Wilde lot, like several in that part of the cemetery, has ornamental curbing.

Besides other forms of funerary art, Evergreen has a number of mausoleums and tombs. One of the more unusual mausoleums, regarding its shape and construction, is the Milliken mausoleum, located fairly close to the front of the cemetery and the Baxter memorial. Made of white granite, the mausoleum is an irregular shape.

Down the avenue a ways from the Milliken mausoleum, is the Davis mausoleum, another impressive structure but one that is more simple and classic in design, yet also somewhat late Egyptian. Built for the family of William G. Davis, who had founded the Portland Packing Company in Portland in 1863 with James P. Baxter, the mausoleum has the words "Believeth In" carved in large capital letters well above the bronze double doorway. Above the doorway also is a religious carving, and below that are the words "I am the Resurrection and the life, saith the Lord. He that believeth in me though he were dead, yet shall he live." The mausoleum is situated near a curve in the avenue.

A cluster of six mausoleums and tombs (or ten to twelve depending upon how one counts them) is located closer to the back of the cemetery, centrally located and overlooking a lawn area facing the ponds. The A. W. H. Clapp mausoleum was built for Asa Clapp, a local businessman who served in Congress during the late 1840s. He died in 1891, after serving on the boards of the Portland Public Library and the Maine General Hospital. His mausoleum, built circa 1860 and designed by Francis and Edward Fassett, features a stepped roof façade topped by a cross. Steps lead up to the doorway, flanked by four short columns, which in turn flank the arched doorway. The Clapp mausoleum is located closest to the summit of the hill, is unique in design, and has granite curbing.

Next to the Clapp mausoleum, another odd one is located: the J. B. Carroll tomb or mausoleum. One has to walk down a few steps, past flanking decorative urns, to reach the tomb's tiny door. Several other tombs and mausoleums are located just slightly down the slope. The area as a whole is known as the Valley of the Kings and is noted for the granite used in its structures.

Just slightly down the slope and left of the Clapp and Carroll mausoleums is one of the most remarked-upon tombs in Evergreen, the F. O. Smith Tomb. Francis Ormand Jonathan Smith had the tomb built in 1860 following the death of his daughter Lizzie to hold her remains and those of other family members. Deemed one of the more "sophisticated" examples of Egyptian-revival-style architecture in the region, the tomb, like many, is currently sealed up. Smith served in the US Congress during 1833–1839, after terms in both the Maine House of Representatives and the Maine Senate. The tomb itself was added to the National Register of Historic Places in 1974. On its door are various inscriptions, including the words, "Nature teaches that all flesh must die."

Another two vaults are located fairly close to the Smith tomb, one on either side. Each of them is interesting. However, one of the most intriguing tombs here or elsewhere in New England is the immense tomb built into the hillside overlooking the lawn and ponds.

The long tomb is an impressive structure that is actually divided into five family vaults. Each vault of the quarry-faced structure has its own entrance, with family initials over the doorway. From a distance, the expanse looks like a masonry wall; it is long and well incorporated into the landscape. In some sense, it actually is a wall, a retaining wall for the hillside, and a few monuments are located on the top of the tombs. It has also been fittingly described as "fortress-like."

Constructed in the 1870s according to cemetery records and known then as simply "the five-chamber granite mausoleum," the tomb is about 200 feet long. The Brown, Greely, Hanson, Smith, and Libby families each have one of the individual tombs or family vaults.

Two other vaults are located to the more northern side of the long, combined-family tomb. These are the Tweksbury and Shaw tombs.

What these tombs and mausoleums on the hillside overlook are the small ponds and waterways that attract wildlife and human visitors alike. Frogs, turtles, birds, and other animals make the ponds their home, and fox, deer, moose, and other creatures have been known to visit them also. Squirrels and other small creatures abound in Evergreen, but it is to the waterways that most of the wildlife goes, sooner or later. Snapping turtles and painted turtles have lived in the ponds. Ducks, geese, and other birds live there seasonally. Swans did live at the cemetery in earlier years.

The most celebrated birds at the cemetery now, however, are perhaps the blue and the white herons. Visitors photograph them regularly, and others simply stop to watch the majestic creatures, just as they do farther north at Mount Hope.

There are three distinct ponds at Evergreen, as well as a small section of winding waterway. The largest pond is to the back of the others, and it more than spans their length. In particular, the ducks seem fond of cruising from one end of the waterways to the other, with a blue heron often seen walking and fishing calmly among them.

Unlike some garden cemeteries, like Mount Auburn, and similar to Mount Hope farther north, Evergreen chose not to center large monuments along the ponds. The series of tombs and mausoleums on the hillside do face the water, but they are quite a distance away, and although other, smaller memorials are situated on the lawn, none is located directly on the shorelines.

Besides those already noted, Evergreen has a number of mausoleums—located entirely aboveground—as well as the tombs facing the ponds. However, the most celebrated one at Evergreen Cemetery, and certainly one of its most classically stunning, is located closer to the northeastern side of the cemetery and the office than are the Milliken, Clapp, and others already mentioned: the white granite Chisholm mausoleum. Finished in 1914, it is a small-scale copy of the *Maison Carree* in southern France which is a Roman temple believed to have been built under the auspices of Augustus Caesar circa 16 BCE. The mausoleum at Evergreen was built in the classical Greek proportions of being exactly twice as long as it is wide and resting on a raised podium foundation. It faces south, also a classical design feature. At the time of its completion, the Chisholm mausoleum was one of the most expensive private funeral monuments in the nation.

The Flint Granite Company of New York designed and built the Chisholm mausoleum. It features six Corinthian columns framing a deep portico, a bronze doorway, and stacked vaults inside its entry chamber. Inside, a carved white marble sarcophagus can be seen, as well as a stained glass window believed to have been created by Tiffany, according to Bob Riley in an article published by the Friends of Evergreen Cemetery.

The window and sarcophagus in the mausoleum are located in a square central chamber. The sarcophagus is a replica of one discovered in 1897 which was believed to hold the remains of Alexander the Great. According to Riley, the one at Evergreen was made of three slabs of Vermont marble and carved by Vermont Marble artisans.

The mausoleum was built for Hugh Joseph Chisholm, a man who could clearly afford such an elaborate memorial. His wife, Henrietta Mason Chisholm, commissioned the monument and oversaw its construction. Both are interred at the mausoleum, as are other family members.

Chisholm was deemed the wealthiest or most powerful man of the pulp and paper business at the time of his death in 1912. Chisholm had founded International Paper Company, a vast consortium of paper mills, as well as founding and operating power, iron manufacturing, and publication firms. He invested widely. Born in Canada in 1847, Chisholm is credited with developing the first forest management system used in the United States.

Spring, summer, autumn, and winter, the mausoleum is one of the most striking monuments at Evergreen, its beauty enhanced by the ornamental plantings that surround it. Other members of the Chisholm family are buried near the mausoleum. The Chisholm mausoleum is almost opposite the Milliken mausoleum, with the two nearly facing each other across the center of the grounds.

Turning away from the larger interment structures, one finds many other memorials of note at Evergreen Cemetery. These would include such markers as the life-size granite statue of J. S. Winslow standing atop a large base; the Burroughs colonnade, consisting of six columns with a decorative and functional vase in the middle of the curved structure; and the very detailed "house" markers of the Cleaves family.

However, as seen elsewhere, people of note do not always have ornate markers. Neil Dow, for example, long deemed a colorful character in terms of his personality and actions, has a rather plain but graceful marker in a modified sarcophagus style located close to the chapel entranceway avenue.

Dow, a Portland mayor and state representative, is remembered most for his attempts to enforce temperance in Maine in the 1800s. Maine was involved in rum-running in the 1800s, and that included, and was even centered upon, Portland. However, despite its role in rum-running, or in some ways perhaps because of it, as explained in another work by the author, the temperance movement leading to Prohibition in Maine is often associated with Portland and with Neal Dow. Dow, a Portland native and a descendant of Quakers, became a temperance leader and argued against drinking alcoholic beverages. As Portland's mayor, he pushed a bill through the state legislature in 1851 that effectively banned the sale and manufacture of alcohol in Maine. The 1851 act gave previous legislation more strength, primarily concerning enforcement.

Dow took his message to other parts of the nation, but at home, he made numerous enemies. At one point, a crowd tried to tear down his front door, and a riot ensued. Dow's actions had become suspicious when it appeared—due to an error—that he might be involved in illegal liquor sales. Maine legislation still allowed towns and cities to appoint an agent to distribute alcohol for "medicinal and mechanical purposes," and Dow had ordered such supplies for Portland. The bill of sale listed his name instead of that of the city's designated agent. One person was killed when Dow subsequently ordered the militia to fire on an unarmed crowd of protestors at City Hall. A few years later, however, the so-called Napoleon of Temperance and Father of Prohibition won a seat in the Maine House of Representatives but eventually left due to a financial scandal. He would subsequently serve as a Union general during the Civil War. He was captured and traded, and later, he made an unsuccessful run at the White House.

Born in 1804, Dow died in 1897 and left his Portland home to the Maine Women's Christian Temperance Union, and the Dow House is still a feature of the Portland landscape. Dow has a simple sarcophagus-style marker, and his wife, Maria, was buried at the same location. Other people at the cemetery had neoclassical, nearly identical sarcophagi markers, including Portland's John Deering, George Foster Shepley, and William Brown, who was buried near the Valley of Kings and the Fessenden family.

The Fessenden family is also well represented at Evergreen. William Pitt Fessenden of Portland, son of the antislavery activist Samuel Fessenden, would serve in the US Congress, serving both in the House and in the Senate during 1854–1869, as well as being President Lincoln's secretary of the treasury. After the war and President Lincoln's death, Fessenden served as chairman of the Joint Congressional Committee on Reconstruction, charged with establishing the parameters for bringing rebel states back into the Union. Fessenden was one of only a few Republicans who did not give in to the Radical Republicans in Congress who sought President Andrew Johnson's impeachment, primarily over the president's more lenient Reconstruction policies, policies that more closely approximated the deceased President Lincoln's plans than did their own. The Fessenden family is related to Maine's Baxter family, and theirs is a delightful cathedral-style architectural memorial.

So, too, is the Phinney family closely related to the Baxter family. The Phinneys have a lot next to the Fessendens, one that features curbing, steps leading up to the lot, and a large obelisk.

Near the Fessenden and Phinney lots, the Deake family has a plot that features an angel figure, with one hand broken off over the years. The marble statue has darkened to near black in places. Another angel, across the cemetery, graces the grave of Lena Maitland Warren, the only child of her parents, who lived for less than eleven years. Her angel holds a quill pen poised over an open book, perhaps to add Lena's name to the rolls of heaven or to the list of angels. Both of these angels are unique.

Other memorials exist for people who died young, in a variety of marker styles, including a few zinc memorials. One for Willis M. Knight marks the resting place of a twenty-year-old man. Knight's small zinc marker has a simple but moving inscription: "He was pure and good, and we loved him."

People have lost children, parents, friends, and other loved ones, and some of these have been firefighters and policemen. The "Baxter Circle" holds the remains of some of the wealthier citizens of the region; the "Firefighters and Police Circle" holds the remains of some of those who have risked their lives to save other people.

A smaller lot for just the Portland firefighters existed for a long time, owned by the Relief Association of the Portland Fire Department, founded in 1848 and aimed—as were other such fraternal organizations of the nineteenth century—at providing support to their members in the event of tragedy, in this case severe injuries sustained while on the job. The police section was added much later.

For many years (1902–1987), a large statue of a firefighter sculpted of Maine white granite by Edward Souther Griffin in 1898 stood at the firemen's lot. In 1987, it was moved to Portland's Central Fire Station, and a large fire bell, made in Troy, New York, was moved to the site at Evergreen. Inscribed "Portland Fire Department 1879–1880," the bell hung for a long time on Munjoy Hill, and it was used for fire alarms as well as to call people to church services. The lot—including both the police and fire department sections—has a number of markers, but perhaps the most moving is the bell, for, in the end, the bell tolls for us all.

See "Portland Municipal Reports" for 1852 to 1920 for the early history of the cemetery and later reports for subsequent years, as well as various books by Trudy Irene Scee on Maine history, several of which include the Portland area and Maine as a whole. The Friends of Evergreen have a number of articles available online, in addition to those mentioned, and the National Park Service has published the cemetery's application for inclusion on the National Register of Historic Places that contains an overview of the cemetery's history and layout.

12

A Plan for Everything

Cedar Hill Cemetery, Hartford, Connecticut

All of the cemeteries discussed herein are unique, and each has its own character, yet just approaching the burial grounds at Cedar Hill and looking down the long driveway from the cemetery's historic gateway, chapel, and offices to the first gravesite off in the distance, with woods and water on each side, you know immediately that this is something different, this is something special, and it was planned that way. It was planned to awe and inspire. That long approach was planned; the relationship of buildings and entranceway was planned; the placement of graves was planned; and, barring the changes in modern burial practices, it was all—or almost all—planned right from the beginning.

CEDAR HILL CEMETERY WAS ONE OF THE LATER GARDEN CEMETERIES of the nineteenth-century movement, established, as it was, in 1864, yet it would in no way be the least of them. Building on what had already been learned of cemetery and landscape design, the founders of Cedar Hills planned, quite deliberately, to take cemetery design to a new level. While it would not have such a grand tower as Mount Auburn or as impressive a carved stone stairway as Green Mount in Vermont or the stone staircases of Mount Hope and Swan Point, it would have its own stunning memorials, perhaps most notable of these being its "triangle" and its incredible female statuary.

However, the founders of Cedar Hill Cemetery wanted more than stunning monuments. They wanted something that could compete with any of the other garden cemeteries then in existence. They wanted a planned cemetery. They wanted a detailed design plan, and Joseph Weidenman (also spelled Weidenmann) would provide them with such a plan and more.

Born in 1829 in Switzerland into a family of means, Weidenman would become an influential landscape architect in America. He studied engineering and architecture in his native land, spent some time with visual artists there and studied botany, and then traveled to the Americas before eventually moving to New York City in 1856.

Weidenman became interested in landscape gardening, now more commonly called landscape architecture. According to his biographer, Rudy J. Favretti, sometimes determining which projects should be credited primarily to Weidenman is problematic as some projects credited to Frederick Law Olmsted and William La Baron are also credited to Weidenman, depending on one's sources. Weidenman worked extensively with both men during his career. There is no question, however, that Weidenman deserves the credit for designing Cedar Hill Cemetery, even though the founders may have had some input.

When Weidenman returned to America from a trip abroad in 1856, plans were underway for establishing Central Park in New York, and the design competition would begin the following year. Locally, William Cullen Bryant of the *New York Evening Post* championed the park movement. Bryant quoted horticulturalist Andrew Jackson Downing of the *Horticulturalist*, who argued that the residents of urban America needed public parks in harmony with nature for recreation, their need evidenced in the popularity of the new garden cemeteries. Some of these cemeteries were becoming crowded with the dead, he stated, and many people felt that it was disrespectful to use cemeteries for recreational purposes. Downing died in 1852, however, before Central Park became a reality.

Meanwhile, Weidenman arrived in New York just as the competition was getting underway. He began work as a landscape gardener with the man who would catalog the native plants found on the chosen site and who would later serve as Central Park's head gardener. Weidenman also secured a few commissions of his own.

At the same time, in Connecticut, in the early 1850s, Reverend Horace Bushnell was advocating that Hartford establish a park central to its city. Such a desire had been voiced thirty years earlier, and Bushnell now gave it a new voice. Bushnell located forty acres upon which he wanted to see a city park established, and then he began a campaign to persuade city leaders and ultimately the public to support the project. Bushnell succeeded, and the residents voted a resounding "yes" to his plan in January 1854. A few skirmishes ensued, but eventually, the land was acquired for what would become the first public park in America totally funded with public money.

With the land acquired, the city announced a competition for its design in 1857—the same year New York initiated its competition. The results of the competition proved unsatisfactory, however, and in 1860, the board interviewed Jacob Weidenman for the position. The board may or may not have wanted Olmsted for the job, and/or Olmsted may have recommended Weidenman. Either way, the board promptly hired Weidenman to survey the land, design the park, choose the trees and plant them, and so forth. Weidenman moved to Hartford with his wife and young family, and the park was successfully completed by spring 1870. Subsequently, the Soldiers and Sailors Memorial Arch was built in the park, designed by architect George Keller, in 1884–1886, and the Corning Fountain was added in 1899. The state capitol was built at the edge of the park in the 1870s after some had urged that it be built in the park.

In the meantime, Weidenman had made a name for himself and acquired some crucial contacts, and Hartford continued to make more plans for the city. Nearby Mystic, Connecticut, had a garden cemetery by the early 1860s, and Mount Hope in Maine and Mount Auburn in Massachusetts were already thirty years old by then. With Hartford garnering attention for its new city park, which was later renamed Bushnell Park for its staunchest advocate, some civic leaders—reiterating earlier sentiments—asserted that it was time that Hartford established its own rural cemetery. In 1863, a group of men organized a committee to explore that possibility. Creating a new burial place of some type was becoming critical, since the expansion of the city was bringing the older burial grounds close to the homes of the living and the new "street railway" threatened to hasten that encroachment.

William Collins served as the first secretary of the cemetery association, and Dr. James C. Jackson was its chairman. Jackson had served on the park planning board that had hired Weidenman. The committee asked Weidenman to join them. The group visited a few sites, and then they selected one at the edge of Hartford for the new cemetery. According to a short 1903 corporate history of the cemetery, *Cedar Hills Cemetery, 1863–1903*, the land was not one parcel owned by one person or entity; it was nine properties with various owners. Together, the selected parcels totaled 268 acres. It took a year to acquire all the property, the committee ultimately taking two of the parcels by eminent domain, as approved by the state in 1864. Collins would later be buried at the cemetery with a large architectural memorial topped with a cross marking his family lot.

As the 1903 history of the cemetery stated, the natural lay of the land and its water resources, its cedar trees and other evergreens, its advantageous soil, and the land's ability to meet the city's burial needs for generations to come made it fitting for a rural cemetery. Of course, the land had to be paid for, and to that end, the committee devised a plan to organize a corporation with $50,000 capital stock of 500 shares of $100 each. Funds would be returned with interest at whatever time it became possible. Seventy-six people bought shares in the corporation. As it turned out, in 1895, one half of the par value of the stocks was repaid, with the other half paid in 1897; therefore, the original shares "ceased to exist," and the corporation thereafter became one comprised of the cemetery's lot owners.

The first meeting of the cemetery shareholders convened in June 1865, and the name Cedar Hill Cemetery was officially chosen (some people had preferred the name Cedar Mountain) for the red cedars crowning the western ridge of the cemetery. Some of the burial land sold immediately. On September 11, a committee was authorized to have the grounds of the cemetery laid out, developed, and graded. The work started the next day under "the superintendence of Mr. Jacob Weidenman, who entered the services of the corporation on the 1st of August," the history stated.

The first problem Weidenman faced was that the committee wanted the cemetery entrance to be located in Hartford, but only twenty-eight acres of the combined property was in Hartford. Most of it was in Wethersfield, with a small portion in Newington. Like Mount Auburn, the cemetery would be most associated with one town or city, but it would actually span more than one, and indeed, it had a majority of its land located in the lesser-known municipalities. Unfortunately, the property located in Hartford was largely marshland.

The chosen and acquired property was generally well suited to a garden cemetery. It had natural water supplies and hillsides from which one could see Hartford, the distant Holyoke and Berkshire ranges of Massachusetts, and the Connecticut River—depending on one's vantage point. The only major problem was the situation at the Hartford end, where the committee wanted the gate located.

Before undertaking the project, Weidenman had consulted with his friend, Adolph Strauch, who had designed a foreground for Cincinnati's Spring Grove Cemetery in 1858, an approach that incorporated fountains and ponds and several acres of landscaped grounds, the foreground being what one first encountered when entering the cemetery. Cemetery records state that Strauch visited the grounds and reportedly stated, "I have visited every cemetery of any note, from the St. Lawrence to the Rio Grande, and I have never seen the spot that has so many advantages as this, or so splendid a landscape."

Strauch went to Hartford, and there is no doubt he did view the grounds positively. With or without his direct advice, Weidenman would design a sweeping foreground for Cedar Hill Cemetery. Weidenman had the waters in the marsh area reorganized into ponds—the largest one, to the left as one proceeds along the main road, known as a lake—with a small stone dam and overflow areas included. A bridge some forty feet wide and 120 feet long was soon constructed of stone also, and the avenue would pass over the bridge. The foreground would add greatly to the beauty of the cemetery as well as provide drainage for the burial sections. Weidenman also wanted to have a swan house located on the larger pond or lake, as it is called, which would further enhance the foreground.

Otherwise, he advised that buildings should be avoided in the cemetery, as they might detract from the scenic vistas.

The approach at Cedar Hill as designed by Weidenman encompasses some seventy-three acres, and besides its aesthetic values, it helps "facilitate proper drainage of the slope," as noted in 1903. A long drive, Inway Avenue, leads through the foreground. It runs "between picturesque sheets of water to the hills beyond. On both sides, tall spruce trees flank the approach." The "sheets of water" are pretty much located to the left of the avenue in the twenty-first century, but otherwise, the entranceway and foreground are generally unchanged, as shown or discussed in historical records and images. The layout still "removes the burial lots to a retired distance from the entrance and highway." The approach in some ways resembles that of Brookside Cemetery in Watertown, New York, with the avenue lengths roughly equal and water to be found on both sides.

Weidenman wanted to see an "open lawn" cemetery, such as Strauch had used at Cincinnati's Spring Grove Cemetery, and Spring Grove and Cedar Hill have been identified as the first two such American cemeteries. Cemetery views would be kept open as much as possible, with trees used primarily as accent pieces used to frame specific vistas. One large monument would serve the needs of an entire family or group, thus keeping the views uncluttered. Any individual markers would be placed flush with the ground, as would the corner markers of family lots. Therefore, when a person looked at the cemetery, one would see large artistic monuments dotting the landscape, which was a landscape improved by judicious plantings and the like.

As the 1903 cemetery history described it, praising the cemetery as it was at the time, "Amid flowers, shrubs, and trees, many varieties of which are visible, the countless shapes of stone in pillar, shaft and block, are brought into harmony, and the extensive greensward is the relieving screen upon which their outlines are shown." The newest sections—those added from the mid-twentieth century on—lack some of this distinction despite cemetery efforts, as families and individuals are generally not buying larger lots or memorials, and the usually smaller, rectangular or largely rectangular stones simply do not have the same impact as the large memorials. Horticultural landscaping may relieve some of this, yet an open vista remains the overall desired cemetery trait.

One feature Weidenman promoted in his plans for burial plots was to have the one central family monument surrounded by the individual burials in a perpendicular fashion. He illustrated this in his later book on cemeteries, denoting how the plan could accommodate a large number of burials. One illustration showed the square base of a monument with two graves running out on each side of the square, for a total of eight graves directly at the foot of the monument, and ones farther out spaced almost like spokes, except in the "front" of the monument, where they are arranged in a pyramid formation, the "apex" of the pyramid being closest to the monument. One can see this basic plan used in the older sections of the cemetery.

One example of Weidenman's desire to have one central monument suffice for a family, without individual stones being used, is that of Katherine Gertrude Parry. Although noted on the "back side" as having been erected by William H. Parry on April 1, 1882, it is the inscription for Katherine Gertrude that faces the avenue and is located below the front of the wonderful sculpture of a woman seemingly representing *Hope*, with her left hand holding a book and her right hand held up with one finger pointed at the sky. She wears a demure smile, and her eyes are cast slightly heavenward. Parry, whose nameplate is on the front side of the memorial, is noted as having been born on March 23, 1840, and she died on September 17, 1926. She seems to have survived her entire family.

Parry's body is apparently buried to the front of the memorial, and her daughter, Ida Gertrude, is to one side. Ida Gertrude died at age six years, six months in October 1876. Buried next to her is her brother, Charles Phillip Parry, who died at age two years, five months, in April 1883. To Parry's other side is buried her son, Oscar Leon Parry, who died in 1885 at age eleven years, eleven months. On his side of the monument is inscribed the words, seemingly meant for all three children, "Gone in their Childish purity, over the silent way." No date or individual inscription is included for William Parry. The family lot is in the shade of a large cedar.

A larger version of the central monument with surrounding interments being placed perpendicular to it is found at the John Pierpont Morgan family lot. The lot may not have reached such a size as to require the "spokes" arrangement, but the Morgan lot did have four small stones on each side of the memorial, so sixteen interment spaces were created there in the Weidenman plan. Morgan's central and immense modified, sarcophagus-style monument purportedly reflects what Morgan perceived the biblical Ark of the Covenant to have looked like, but the overall design was undertaken by George Keller, who also designed the cemetery's chapel and gateway. The large marker is made of Scottish red granite, with detailed stonework on each side, and it rests on a tiered base. Morgan's personal marker is away from the avenue side of the memorial.

Hartford's native son John Pierpont Morgan could afford the lavish arrangement because he was *the* J. P. Morgan of financial fame and acumen. He started with the business of his father, Junius Spencer Morgan, which was J. S. Morgan & Co., and Morgan gained control of it after his father's death in 1890. Morgan came to specialize in investment banking.

Morgan spread his business interests into various fields, including railroads, the Edison Electric Company (which he merged with another firm to create General Electric), and steel—taking over the Andrew Carnegie company as well as other steel companies and forming the United States Steel Corporation. His combined company became the nation's largest steel producer. He also helped establish International Harvester and American Telephone and Telegraph (AT&T). He amassed such a fortune that he was able to back the US government in a few instances. He has been deemed the leading financier of the Progressive Era.

An avid art collector, Morgan's collection was distributed to a number of art museums, and his son, John Pierpont Morgan Jr., would help establish the Morgan Library and Museum, starting it off with the remainder of his father's collections, both books and artwork, and his mansion.

Morgan died at age seventy-five in 1913 in Rome, Italy. His wife, Amelia Sturges Morgan, died in 1862, and his second wife, Frances Louise Tracy Morgan, died in 1865.

Other guidelines besides the one family marker would be followed at Cedar Hill. Mausoleums would be allowed, under the cemetery's plan, but in Weidenman's illustration of the planned cemetery, they were shown grouped together in the distance. In general, they remain fairly close together in one area, spread over a lovely hillside.

At the top of the slope, the Edwin Denison Morgan mausoleum marks the burial site of a local businessman and politician who would later serve as New York's governor, during 1859–1862. President Abraham Lincoln appointed Morgan a major general of volunteers during the Civil War, in 1861, to complement his responsibilities as governor. In 1863, no longer governor, Morgan resigned his assignment to serve as a US senator. He lived until 1883 and was interred at the large family vault built at about the same time according to the cemetery's application for inclusion on the National Register of Historic Places. Made of granite ashlar, buttress-like supports were built at the edges of the building, and others, topped by small columns, flank the doorway. Morgan's son of the same name, as well as other family members, would have small arched markers around the structure.

Many more classic mausoleums are also located on the hillside, including the Porter-Valentine mausoleum, the La Penta mausoleum, and the Turner-Hooker mausoleum. Mingled in with them are several fine markers.

The most visited and photographed mausoleum at Cedar Hill, however, is no doubt the Howard mausoleum. The eighteen-foot pink—or "westerly red"—granite pyramid-shaped mausoleum has attracted cemetery visitors since its construction. Built to honor Mark Howard—local citizen, president of the National Fire Insurance Company, and organizer of the Republican Party in Connecticut with a subsequent appointment by President Lincoln—who died in 1887, the memorial features a life-size female angel standing in the doorway, which is flanked by Howard's name and inverted torches, in bas-relief, with butterflies, symbols of rebirth, carved on the steps leading up to the doorway.

True to the Weidenman model, or more precisely a modified model, individual small markers surround much of the Howard Egyptian-based pyramid, but the lot is without curbing or fencing. Cedar Hill may not have started the central-marker-with-no-surrounding-enclosure model, but it did manage to have many family lots that adhere to the model.

Overall, the cemetery stuck to the original plans for the grounds as much as possible, adding additional plants and trees over the years as well as developing new burial sections. It may be noted that if Elm Grove

Cemetery in nearby Mystic resembles an elm tree in its design or layout, Cedar Hill Cemetery rather resembles a tulip.

The cemetery corporation spent $50,000 on its initial improvements after the plans and maps were drawn. Besides those already mentioned, a receiving tomb was built near the entrance of the cemetery, one that would later be repurposed. Sufficient work had been completed between mid-1865 and the summer of 1886 that lots were offered for sale on July 16. On July 17, 1866, the first interment took place. Successive bouts of inclement weather delayed the consecration ceremony for Cedar Hill until June 24, 1868. On that day, the corporation president presided, clergy and others spoke, hymns were sung, and a choir performed.

Things went pretty well for the first year or so, but it was not all smooth sailing. One problem that arose soon after the cemetery opened involved what had been identified as the best location in the cemetery: the hilltop area where the Colt stone monument currently stands. The Colt memorial might have been one of the types of monuments most favored by the cemetery in the late 1800s: a fifty-foot-tall, slender column of Scottish granite with an acanthus leaf capital on top of a white-gray granite base, with a bronze sculpture of the Angel of Resurrection or Gabriel atop the column, the figure seemingly overlooked the entire cemetery grounds, or, at least, in the direction in which his face is turned. A bronze family coat of arms and a bronze plate of the winged orb with snakes decorated the front of the base.

Elizabeth Colt had commissioned James Batterson soon after the cemetery opened to create a memorial for her husband, Samuel Colt—the famed gun inventor and manufacturer. Colt was one of the first businessmen to use the new methods of mass production, manufacturing guns for the Mexican-American War and the American Civil War. Colt's patented revolver enjoyed a monopoly until 1857. Eli Whitney Blake of New Haven, an inventor and nephew of inventor Eli Whitney, who was already in the arms business, made guns for Colt during the Mexican-American War: Colt Walker revolvers. Samuel Walker of the Texas Rangers had ordered the guns after stipulating certain changes. Colt used the money he made from the Colt Walker to purchase Blake's machinery and tooling and built the Colt's Patent Firearms Manufacturing Company at

Hartford. Colt continued to make various improvements to his guns, and they became part of America's westward expansion.

Colt would enter litigation to protect and extend his various patents, sue a rival or two, and fire one of his men for suggesting an improvement to his revolver. The former employee, Rollin White, took his plans to Colt's rivals, Smith & Wesson. Colt, Smith, and Blake would all be buried in New England garden cemeteries. Colt's memorial would be the most spectacular, perhaps, but the other men and their families would have impressive obelisks on their own family lots.

James Batterson, commissioned by Elizabeth Colt to create a family memorial, was a founding member of the Cedar Hill board, and he owned a granite company. Sculptor Randolph Rogers designed the statue of Gabriel, according to cemetery sources, and the base is classified as Egyptian revival. Rogers exhibited the statue across the nation before installing it on the memorial. The memorial was erected in 1867, but no one was interred there until 1894, when the Colts' only surviving son died. At that point, Elizabeth Colt had him buried at the site, and she had her husband, Samuel, and their four other children—who had been interred elsewhere—moved to the family lot.

Not too distant from the Colt memorial, another towering column, a detailed one, supports another bronze figure: the Jewell monument. Representing *Hope,* the female figure with dressed hair holds an anchor at her side and stands atop a granite Corinthian column with an acanthus capital. This sculpture, too, was created at James Batterson's New England Granite Works and carved by Carl Conrads, house sculptor for the company during 1866–1903, according to cemetery records.

The Jewell memorial was created for Marshall Jewell and his family. Jewell was a prominent businessman who entered politics, joining the new Republican Party and successfully running for the office of Connecticut governor in 1869, serving two terms as the forty-fourth and later the forty-sixth governor. He served for a short time as minister to Russia under President Ulysses S. Grant and then for a longer period as postmaster general. Jewell was a vice presidential candidate and then chairman of the Republican National Committee. He died in New Haven in 1883 at age fifty-seven.

Several expensive monuments in the favored sections had already been erected and were "awaiting" burials when the time should come, and a few interments nearby had taken place nearby while other lots had been sold in the highly desirable locations. When the cemetery discovered, within a couple years of opening, that much of the area had a slate ledge that projected up to within three and a half feet in some spots and covered more than a quarter of an acre of prime land.

Pressed with this problem, the cemetery considered its options. With winter approaching, according to Joseph Weidenman in a later publication, the board decided to hold off all burials until the next year. It would also not allow any additional monuments to be erected. The board decided not to advertise the problem but rather quietly fix it, with any bodies awaiting burial to be kept in the new receiving tomb located just south of the cemetery entrance.

The cemetery had every lot in the affected region examined to a depth of at least six feet, and it was discovered that more than 36,000 cubic feet of slate ledge had to be removed from eighteen different family lots. That winter, the cemetery excavated each of the lots individually and then filled the excavated portions with good quality soil. They restored the surfaces of the lots with sod and redid plantings in the spring. Lot owners were not informed of these activities, at least not at the time.

Weidenman included this story in a late 1880s discussion of general guidelines to follow when establishing a rural cemetery, including the hiring of a "cemetery engineer" to avoid such problems. Good advice for the future, but most of the noted New England garden or rural cemeteries had already been established by 1889, when his essay of the year before was issued as a small book, *An Essay on the Improvement and Proper Management of Rural Cemeteries*. Previous to 1889, Weidenman had published *Beautifying Country Homes* and *American Garden Architecture.*

Cedar Hill Cemetery, meanwhile, laid out burial sections as close to the original plans as possible, with Weidenman serving as its first superintendent. The first twelve cemetery sections, now known as the "historical sections," were laid out in the 1800s. Each section had an avenue surrounding it. The lots were designed within the original concept of the cemetery, with fences, hedges, and other enclosures around individual lots prohibited.

The cemetery retained a broad strip around each avenue and section for horticultural and other purposes, as well as a strip around each individual plot for a grass walkway or open space or for cemetery plantings. Lots 1 and 2 were laid on the first hill or ridge of the cemetery, which was the main hill, lots from which much of the cemetery, if not all of it, could be seen. (This is also the area in which the slate ledge had been a problem.) The other ten historic sections spread out from these two. Some ninety-three acres had been laid out for burial purposes by 1903. Later sections would be laid out behind the older ones. With no new sections laid out closer to the foreground than were the original sections, the view into the cemetery remains much the same as it was in the late 1800s.

In the interim, while the cemetery continued to see increased numbers of interments and as the population of the Hartford area continued to grow, the well-situated Cedar Cemetery did not feel modernity's impact too harshly. In the late 1870s, a new capitol building was built on the edges of Bushnell Park, and it was visible from the entrance of the cemetery before other towering buildings started to block the distant view.

Trolley cars started to bring visitors to the cemetery in the late 1800s, arriving at the gate every twenty minutes from city hall. By this time, the city had established Goodwin Park just across the avenue from Cedar Hill, creating another destination from downtown, as well as creating a buffer for the cemetery as urban sprawl continued. The new park in the early 1900s also presented a pleasing view from the cemetery entrance, just as the avenue into the cemetery provided an aesthetic vista in the opposite direction. The city had acquired the land for the park decades after the cemetery was established.

Soon after the capitol building was constructed, Weidenman left the cemetery and, for the most part, Hartford. In 1870, Weidenman had taken his leave from his posts as superintendent at both Cedar Hill Cemetery and City Park. He returned to his homeland for a year, and when he came back to Hartford, neither position was open to him. Facing a few other problems, he left for New York City for a time, returned, and then moved to New York City again, where he would work with Frederick Olmsted on and off for the rest of his life, although he would also secure individual commissions. He drew the plans for the 240-acre

Mount Hope Cemetery of Chicago, but problems involving the board modifying his plans led to his being replaced, which in turn led to a court case that Weidenman ultimately won.

Weidenman would start a few new projects in Hartford but would die in January 1893 of kidney failure before completing them. His body was held in New York and then transported to Connecticut for burial at Cedar Hill. His stone is a simple one, located near the main avenue and his planned foreground. True to his plan, one memorial would suffice for them all; his wife and daughters names and dates are inscribed below his own on the marker.

Other changes would meet the cemetery in following years. Before and after numerous facility changes were made, several wonderful examples of funerary art were installed at Cedar Hill to honor some of the region's citizens. Some, like J. P. Morgan and Samuel Colt, were well known throughout the nation. Others, such as Mark Howard, were known more locally, primarily in the Hartford area or in Connecticut and New England.

One of the more noted memorials in the cemetery shows much of Weidenman's design plans. Dr. Horace Wells is credited with being the father of modern anesthesia. His memorial has some unique artwork, created by Louis Potter. The front features a large bronze bas-relief of an angelic female figure bringing mists of medicine or deliverance to a suffering male figure, under which is inscribed, "There shall be no pain." The sides feature two other bronze casts: one side has a woman with her head slightly thrown back in sleep, her eyes closed, and the words "I Sleep to Awaken." The opposite side has the woman with light beams pouring down on her head, her eyes open, and the words, "I Awaken to Glory" inscribed below her flower-decorated bust. The side panels were stolen at one point and later replaced. Wells and his wife were actually reinterred at the site, having originally been buried at Hartford's Old North Cemetery, but their son, Charles, later had them removed to Cedar Hill, and he was the one who commissioned the family memorial.

Three small stones, one for Wells, are in front of the monument. Wells himself was born in January 1815 and died in January 1848. Buried next to him with their own small stones are his wife, who died in 1889, and their son, who died in 1909.

Moreover, there are some well-known people with almost hidden markers. A very simple memorial with small, flat, individual stones marks the burial site of one of America's most distinguished actresses and her family: Katharine Hepburn. Upon her death in 2003, Hepburn chose to be buried with her mother and father at their modest family lot, with a plaque on a stone serving as the central family marker. This type of marker is found for a number of noted individuals at the cemetery.

Like Wells, Hepburn's father, Thomas Hepburn, was a physician, and like herself, her mother, Katharine Martha Houghton Hepburn, was an active feminist. Proclaimed America's greatest film star in history by the American Film Institute in 1999, Katharine Hepburn also starred on Broadway and directed several productions as well as appearing in more than fifty films. She won four Best Actress Oscars with a total of twelve nominations.

Moreover, there is simply some stunning funerary art featuring stone carvings of women, allegorical ones, at Cedar Hill. One of the most striking of them is the sculpture of two female figures atop the massive Pike architectural marker. The sculpture is in the woman-comforting-a-younger-person theme, in this case, as in most, a young girl. The woman holds an open book on her lap and rests one hand on the girl's shoulder and hair. The girl rests against the woman's legs. Both figures wear flowing clothing, and their faces are sublime. The woman bears an uncanny resemblance to actress Drew Barrymore.

Another memorial at the cemetery, one for the Newton Case family, likewise features two female figures. In this one, the female also holds a book but pays it little heed, gazing heavenward instead. She has her hand almost touching the young girl who kneels at her side, seemingly sobbing in grief. The sculpture rests upon a large architectural base, one girdled with four small columns. A touching sculpture, it not only has a place in Victorian funerary art as a type but it is also seemingly identical to one at the Albany Rural Cemetery for the Godfrey family, although its base is quite different. By the time the memorial at Cedar Hill was constructed, as well as the one at Albany Rural, the granite industry was a huge business in the Northeast, and more than one statue would have duplicates in America's garden cemeteries.

In addition, a third memorial at Cedar Hill features similar imagery, with another woman with a book comforting a young girl. This time, the woman looks downward at the girl and rests her hand upon the girl's hair. This third example is for the Roberts–Skinner family. It, too, has a large architectural base but one of a different design than those of the others.

Not surprisingly, Cedar Hill also has mourning-woman-with-wreath statues, ones honoring the Hunt and the Chase families. They were carved in different styles, but the basic poses and symbolism are the same.

Also, there is a male angel remarkably similar to Albany Rural Cemetery's famed *Angel at the Sepulcher*. Created for the Heublein family, the seated male angel at Cedar Hill is mounted atop a large pedestal with flanking exedra benches, which in turn are flanked by large decorative and functional urns. The bench and statue are located just down the slope from the Morgan mausoleum and almost next to the lot is one for the Long family that features a long exedra bench broken by a central pedestal base with a bas-relief of a classical woman.

There are several statues of males, human and otherworldly, at Cedar Hill. Besides those already mentioned, the Waterman and McCorkle memorial has a male with a pen in one hand and a book in the other, and it is perhaps an angel, for, as noted, contemporary images of male angels did not always include readily visible wings. A similar scribe, although one with a scroll instead of a book, marks the burial site of John B. Windsor.

Female statues worth noting, in addition to those already mentioned, include a stunning bronze memorial for the Clark family located on a gentle slope in the historic section. The female figure points upward with one hand while her other hand is extended forward, her face points slightly downward, and her hair is arranged in a classical mourning style complete with a headdress.

Besides the Clark bronze, the Fitzgerald lot has a lovely statue of a woman holding flowers, her eyes downcast, standing on a rectangular architectural base with six ornate, column-style pilasters. In another example, the Brownell memorial features a towering pedestal base upon which stands a woman in classical attire and holding a cross against her chest, her gaze heavenward.

A number of other statues grace the cemetery, male and female, with various symbols included in their figures or added to their bases or pedestals. One final sculpture to note here, however, is different from others at Cedar Hill and is rarely seen anywhere for that matter. The Stone memorial features a work of sculpture emerging from its immense capped architectural base. The sculpture projects too far and is too detailed to be considered a "simple" carving or bas-relief. Instead, the two figures—an angel whose face, figure, and wings could rival those seen on any cemetery angel, and a kneeling woman with her hair shrouded and holding a garland—seem almost independent of the memorial. The angel's upper arm, which points heavenward, does project independently, and she holds the other one protectively behind the woman, touching or almost touching her shoulder.

Other types of markers than the ornate ones are also found at Cedar Hill. These would include Celtic crosses, zinkies (zinc memorials), columns with urns, and so forth.

Such zinc memorials as that for Samuel Colt are worth seeing. The large zinkie is located not far from the Clark bronze memorial. It is one of the more expensive models sold during the era and has numerous embellishments, as well as a corner location. Likewise, the Terry cross is a tremendously large memorial for its type, its face made of rough-hewn stone.

Cedar Hill had military burials besides those already mentioned. An eagle spreads his wings on a globe atop a simple but stately white column near the start of the burial sections. It was erected in honor of the Veteran City Guard of Hartford during 1861–1939. It is inscribed with a simple message: "First in Loyalty and Defense."

One notable memorial for a Civil War soldier is for General Griffin Stedman. Stedman fought at Fredericksburg and in other battles, and his marker is draped with the emblems of his service and closely resembles another such memorial at Swan Point. A stone sword, a flag carved with his battles of service, and a cap top Stedman's marker, and bronze laurel wreaths are fastened to its sides, almost like the handles on a casket.

Weidenman and the cemetery association had envisioned such wonderful markers in the mid-1860s; moreover, they had also wanted a suitable gateway and buildings erected that would further enhance the cemetery. Weidenman had developed plans for an entranceway at Cedar Hill when he designed the cemetery. According to his biographer, his gateway plan was a version of one he had designed for the Concord, New Hampshire State Asylum for the Insane. A complex structure of a Swiss-rustic style, the cemetery board rejected his revised plan, and it would be decades before a gateway would be built for the cemetery. In its own way, that gateway would also be complex in its entirety, but its individual components are simple and ornamental as well as functional. The first component built was not the actual gateway, however.

The cemetery built the Northam Memorial Chapel in 1882–1883. Designed by architect George Keller—who would also design the masterful arch at Bushnell Park—its construction was made possible by a bequest from Colonel Charles H. Northam and a further gift from his wife, Susan. The chapel is of English Gothic design. Constructed of gray Westerly granite, with lighter-colored granite used as dressings, the chapel sits on elevated ground near the entrance to the cemetery, the ground sloping away to the rear, allowing for a more impressive side view of the building and making it a two-story building at the rear entrance. Although there is currently a modern door at the back, the main door faces the street. The chapel has a steep, gabled, slated roof.

Northam's will specified that the building was to be used, "for the purpose of holding funeral services therein by any and all persons of any and all religious denominations or sects, at all proper times, subject to the reasonable rules and regulations" set by the cemetery association. The chapel was consecrated on November 12, 1883, the second anniversary of Northam's death. Although still functional as a chapel in the twenty-first century, it is currently used primarily as office space—the original interior architecture and fittings little impacted by the low cubicle-style partitions used to create workspaces. Its current use may well bring more visitors to chapel than would otherwise be true. Outside the building, above the arched doorway, in the spandrel, is carved the face of a sleeping cherub, meant to convey that the dead are only sleeping.

The woodwork inside the chapel, including the ceiling and pews (since removed), is cherry. A brilliant stained glass window featuring a rose is located above the doorway, and scenes of the Resurrection are depicted in the large stained window at the far or chancel end of the chapel. The word Resurrection is spelled "Resurrrection" in the glass; apparently, no one caught the misspelling with its multiple "r's" before the window was sent to Cedar Hill. The company that made these and the other chapel windows—which feature more subtly shaded glasswork—was Cottier & Co. of London and New York. The floor was subtly yet ornately tiled, and brass details add a finishing touch to the chapel. The chapel was struck by lightning on September 11, 1901, but it was soon repaired.

The chapel was built before the other components, but it was designed with the future additions in mind. The entrance gate itself, known as the Gallup Memorial Gateway, was built soon after, a gift from Julia A. Gallup, according to the cemetery's 1903 history. The chapel and the gateway were built largely of granite, chosen to be in harmony with the natural environment as well as with one another. George Keller also designed the gateway, which is not simply a gate and post or column sort of affair but rather three entranceways, a wall, and three buildings. The gateway was finished in 1889.

The entrance was built with one large—twenty-foot wide—center gate to serve as the entrance for carriages and horses. Two side pedestrian gateways flank it. The gates themselves were made with a hammer and anvil—all handwrought. The supporting gateposts were made of granite, like the buildings.

A waiting room to the south of the gateway was built to serve the needs of cemetery visitors, including those arriving via trolley cars, much like the ornate, circular Webber Waiting Room at Mount Hope or the simpler boulder shelter at Swan Point. Designed by Keller also, the waiting room includes a stained glass window made by Cottier & Co. and designed for Julia Gallup, who died in 1884, featuring "The Ascension." The building's other windows feature leaded white glass. An oak and marble floor set off the room, and a large fireplace was built to warm visitors.

To the right or north of the gateway when one is outside facing into the cemetery is the superintendent's building or office, also a George

Keller design. It kept to the same style as the other newly constructed buildings, and the entranceway itself and the three granite buildings form an impressive complex. None of them is so large as to be overwhelming, but each is impressive. They share not only a granite structure and similar style but also an architect. They were purposely built close to one another to frame the cemetery beyond.

A timber superintendent's house had been constructed earlier, in the late 1800s. The board wanted to see a granite one, in keeping with the others built, however, and in 1903, the corporate history expressed the desire that someone make such a donation as would still make this possible. However, in the twenty-first century, the house remains, and it is now itself an historical building. The entranceway and flanking buildings are each surrounded by flora. Standing in the entranceway center, one can look down the avenue to the ponds and hills beyond.

By 1903, the receiving tomb—located to the rear and side of the chapel—had been in use for almost four decades, and it would remain in use as a tomb for many years more. It would be an important part of the buildings at Cedar Hill, a building people would see as they looked around the entrance area. The tomb held up to sixty caskets in its original form in inclement weather, but before long, those remains would go to the burial area of the cemetery. By the twenty-first century, the receiving tomb was no longer in use. It had been "removed" and its façade used to face a new crematory. Otherwise, the entranceway and foreground are largely unchanged since 1903. The cemetery would, however, build community mausoleums off to the southeastern side of the original historic sections, as well a chapel farther back in the cemetery, to be used for burials in the twenty-first century.

As with other garden cemeteries, Cedar Hill is one to visit more than once and, perhaps, more than twice. It is a large cemetery full of surprises. Some of its memorials may inspire awe, others quiet contemplation, and still others melancholy. Like the other garden cemeteries, Cedar Hill illustrates portions of the history of the Northeast and America as a whole—of changing New England views of death and how to treat the dead—and illuminates an evolving American esthetic in horticulture, landscape design, and memorials that serve the living as well as the dead.

Look for the birds and deer and squirrels, too; Cedar Hill is a haven for many forms of wildlife. Finally, look up to the towering figures of grief and of hope.

Cedar Hill Cemetery has a number of maps and a guide to the cemetery. You may wish to read the cemetery's early history, Cedar Hills Cemetery, 1863–1903, *as well as Jacob Weidenman' two books:* An Essay on the Improvement and Proper Management of Rural Cemeteries, *and* Beautifying Country Homes and American Garden Architecture. *A biography of Weidenman is also available:* Jacob Weidenmann: Pioneer Landscape Architect, *2007, Cedar Hill Cemetery Foundation, Inc., in cooperation with Wesleyan University Press. Many articles and books are also available on the cemetery's many illustrious "residents," and be sure to go look at their fabulous, but sometimes simple, memorials.*

13

The Role of Garden Cemeteries
in New England

Laurel Hill, South Street, Forest Grove, and Hope Cemeteries

CONNECTICUT'S CEDAR HILL WAS ONE OF THE LATER GARDEN OR RURAL cemeteries established, but it was not the only one established in the 1860s or afterward, nor were those garden cemeteries discussed so far by any means the only ones created in New England. Some of the other nineteenth-century garden cemeteries fared quite well over time while others, generally smaller municipal ones, had a harder go of it, such as Forest Glade in Somersworth, New Hampshire.

Moreover, some cemeteries in New England had elements of both the older-style graveyards and the newer rural cemeteries, such as Connecticut's New Haven Burial Grounds, or the lesser-known South Street Cemetery of Portsmouth, New Hampshire. Others, such as Maine's Laurel Hill Cemetery, were hybrids; they had some elements of garden cemeteries, but they incorporated other forms of cemeteries without a preponderance of garden cemetery features and qualities. And then, at the end of the era, Hope Cemetery of Barre, Vermont, would create a garden cemetery blended with a unique twist or two, which puts it in a category of its own.

The trends in rural cemeteries varied over the years, and in many ways, the categories in which we might place them are based as much on the degree of development in each format as anything else. However, after the 1830s, America never returned to the older views of death and burials and graveyards. The art, horticulture, and landscaping of some of the rural cemeteries ushered in something new indeed, something people continue to admire and emulate, even almost 200 years later. Moreover, once one has visited or studied a few of the cemeteries covered thus far, one can more easily ascertain which are truly garden cemeteries at their cores, even if a few other elements have also come into play.

An example of a cemetery much older than New Haven's Grove Street that adapted, in later years, some elements of the garden cemetery movement is South Street Cemetery in Portsmouth, New Hampshire.

South Street Cemetery is something unique. It started differently than did the garden cemeteries discussed herein, and it became something different over time. It, like a few others, would be deemed a haunting—if not haunted—place, and one could almost agree that it was in some ways a tragic place.

South Street Cemetery, or simply South Cemetery, was not created to be a garden cemetery. Rather, it adopted some elements of one as the centuries passed. Located near the ocean in Portsmouth, local and visiting populations would come to increasingly enjoy and utilize the cemetery in the same way that garden or rural cemeteries were used and appreciated. Its history is, in some ways, almost the opposite of Valley Cemetery in nearby Manchester.

After the need for additional burial space became apparent in Manchester even after the creation of Valley Cemetery in 1840, citizens had pushed for another such garden cemetery, the result being Pine Grove Cemetery. In 1851, Pine Grove opened and would try to carry on as a garden cemetery and augment the original, noncontiguous cemetery at the Valley. Other noncontiguous municipal Manchester cemeteries would also be established to try to carry on the rural cemetery tradition, but each would also see modernization in later decades.

In a similar yet reverse manner, South Street Cemetery of Portsmouth, New Hampshire became—in some sections—akin to a garden cemetery over time. It is not one cemetery but rather is composed of a number of small contiguous cemeteries, none of which was designed to be a garden cemetery. Over time, the sum of the five or more burial grounds—most originally private—resulted in a nontraditional cemetery. It eventually became a municipal one, and its popularity continues to increase.

The first components of South Street Cemetery were in place long before the garden cemetery concept was born. Indeed, the first burial grounds that would become part of South Street, or simply South Cemetery, would be established almost as early as the colony.

South Cemetery is located at the intersection of South Street and Sagamore Avenue. The properties included for general purposes in South Cemetery are Cotton's Burying Ground (established circa 1671), Proprietors' Burying Ground (circa 1830), Harmony Grove Cemetery (1847), and a few others.

Little is known about the early history of Cotton's Burying Ground, located in the northeastern section of the combined cemeteries. In 1671, Goodman William Cotton was deeded land for a twenty-year period to be used as a pasture, military training ground, and burying ground. His deed expired, but the basic land uses continued, and in 1721, it was enclosed by a fence and was thereafter known as Cotton's Burying Ground.

The area surrounding the enclosed space was used for military training exercises by Captain John Pickering; then in 1735, a local minister began pasturing his livestock in the fields, other parish ministers followed suit, and the area became known as Minister's Field. Circa 1830, South Parish moved to another location, and the field became a private cemetery known as Proprietor's Burying Ground. It was called so because it was Portland's only private cemetery. This was on the eve of the garden cemetery movement taking root in New England and other parts of America.

Proprietor's Burying Ground is next to Cotton's Burying Ground in the northern section of South Street Cemetery, which is adjacent to South Street. To these two were added Harmony Grove in 1847 and Sagamore in 1871, by which time the garden cemetery movement was well underway, and by the 1870s, some rather notorious individuals had been buried in the combined cemeteries.

In the early 1700s, a "hanging tree" on the grounds claimed the life of more than one person. Sarah Simpson and Penelope Henry were "turned off the back of a cart" and thus left hanging on December 27, 1739. They were hanged for concealing the births of their illegitimate babies.

Better known than these two hangings, however, were those of another young woman and of a convicted male murderer. Both occurred under intense public scrutiny.

In 1768, Ruth Blay, a popular schoolteacher, was executed at the age of twenty-five. She was sentenced to death for concealing the birth of her child. She wrapped the baby in a cloak and hid it under some loose floorboards of her school. A five-year-old girl and her young friends discovered it. Blay's trial was rushed, and she was sentenced to death over the protests of local citizens. Several legal briefs were filed with the British government on her behalf, this still being the colonial era.

While Blay was awaiting word of a possible pardon, the local sheriff, Thomas Packer, decided to move her hanging an hour ahead of its scheduled time—purportedly because he wanted to get home in time for supper. An angry mob gathered at the gallows, and Blay herself protested the hanging. According to a later account by journalist C. W. Brewster, "As Ruth was carried through the streets, her shrieks filled the air. She was dressed in silk, and was driven under the gallows in a cart." The sheriff was not dissuaded, however, and he acted quickly. He looped the noose around her neck and commanded his horses forward, leaving Blay hanging as he rushed home to dinner, supposedly not turning back at all, not even to see the arrival of a horseman bearing her pardon by the royal governor. Blay was dead because of Packer's haste. Moreover, her baby was later determined to have been stillborn.

The crowd went wild. It carried an effigy of Packer through the streets and burned it in front of the unpopular sheriff's house. Blay was the last woman hanged in the colony, and Packer had hanged all three women executed at the South Street site. Blay is said by some to haunt the cemetery and the schoolhouse location, some say with her child. Blay's exact burial spot is unknown but is purportedly at the bottom of the cemetery's hill, about 300 feet north of the "lake."

Then came the Smuttynose murders. As described in detail by the author in *Rogues, Rascals, and Other Villainous Mainers*, Prussian immigrant Louis Wagner was accused, tried, and hanged in Maine for the ax and strangulation murders of two Norwegian women in 1873 on remote Smuttynose Island, located off the coast of Maine and New Hampshire.

The dead women were Karen Christensen and Anethe Christensen, sisters-in-law.

A third woman, Maren Hontvet, was able to escape. She testified and blamed Wagner for the murders. However, Wagner had been in Portsmouth that day and might or might not have been able to row out to the island in the middle of the night alone to commit the murders and then row back. He swore that he had not killed anyone and had not been on the island that night. The men who had lived on the island with the women had also been on the mainland that day.

Convicted of murder, Wagner escaped his jailers. Uproar ensued. He was recaptured, and after a lengthy process and a few delays as Maine examined the legality of the penalty, he and another prisoner were hanged in 1875.

Wagner is buried at the old Maine State Prison where he died, but his two victims are buried at South Street Cemetery, in the Harmony Grove section, their white markers side by side. However, some people continue to doubt Wagner's guilt, and some think it was the third woman alone on the island that night with the other two who killed them, or that she had purposely or mistakenly misled the authorities as to the identity of the murderer.

South Street does, therefore, have a few mysteries and tragedies, and it has a few interesting markers, as well as a couple of tombs or vaults. One is the Proprietor's Burial Ground vault, and a more modern one is the Peter Jenness tomb, built aboveground on a flat area.

Another noted monument is that of Levi Woodbury. His marker features a marble bas-relief portrait on its bases and a towering "stacked" obelisk above. Small markers for four family members are in front of the memorial, showing the move toward family lots that would be a key for garden cemeteries.

Also of interest is the Frank Jones monument, an architectural cathedral-style memorial with four short columns with Corinthian capitals and a soaring spire. Like the Woodbury memorial, the Jones memorial is situated on a family lot and has low decorative stone fencing.

However, although South Street has some interesting memorials, an interesting background, a water view, and is used as a recreation spot by local residents in the twenty-first century, it lacks the lush garden aspect of the rural or garden cemeteries, and for the most part, the grounds were already laid out with the old, too-close spacing of graves squeezed-in-any-old-way burials by the time the garden cemetery movement was underway. Also, hanging trees and the like were simply not part of the newer style cemeteries. This type of situation is true with several older cemeteries in New England, ones that have a few components of garden cemeteries but not enough of them, and their history is simply not sufficient to include them in the category. To find a more apt early or transitional garden cemetery type, one truly does need to look at New Haven, the first private cemetery in America with room for family and other private lots and numerous ornate markers, a powerful entryway, and landscaped grounds, even if Grove Street, in some aspects, was not quite in the style of the garden cemeteries that followed.

There are also a number of garden cemeteries from New York to Maine that are smaller and less "improved" or financially endowed than most of the ones already included. One such cemetery is Forest Glade Cemetery in Somersworth, New Hampshire, not too distant from South Street in Portsmouth, or the previously discussed Valley and Pine Grove Cemeteries in Manchester.

Established in 1851 as the principal public cemetery after the town separated from neighboring Rollinsford, Forest Glade would get off to a good start and include some noteworthy edifices and a number of reinterments. However, it would not reach the degree of development as some other garden cemeteries—in terms of the type and variety of markers, its landscape development, and so forth—but it would still have several interesting features worth visiting. Its first burial occurred in 1852, and the cemetery set aside plots for indigent and Jewish burials.

Forest Glade's Further Chapel, built in 1897 and designed by Henry Vaughn, is a small Gothic building with narrow buttresses and stained glass windows. Its stonework and basic structure resemble those of the chapel at Lakeview in Burlington, Vermont, although the building is smaller and the main entrance is on the "side" of the building.

The cemetery constructed a formal gateway in 1926, the funding provided by Charles Lougee, in honor of his father, Dearborn Lougee. The stone entranceway is rather Egyptian revival in style, and written across the top section are the words, "Until the Day Dawns and the Shadows Flee Away."

The cemetery has shaded avenues and a number of interesting memorials. The grounds lead downward from two entrances, and the slope allowed for the construction of a few tombs to the side below where the chapel was built, including the Hanson tomb. On top of the small ledge are a few mausoleums, the most ornate and tallest being the Burrows mausoleum. The mausoleum has a flight of stairs leading to its front door and decorative curbing that serves in some ways as a low retaining wall.

Forest Glade is one of the smaller rural cemeteries of New England, with just twenty-two acres. The cemetery would have winding avenues and ornamental plantings, however, and in 2017, the cemetery secured inclusion on the National Register of Historic Places, a listing that will aid it in seeking funding for various restoration projects.

Maine's Laurel Hill Cemetery in Saco is an example of the mixed form of cemetery in New England. It has some elements of a garden cemetery, including an advantageous water situation, a few Victorian memorials seen in other garden cemeteries, beautiful trees of various species, and several winding avenues. Additions made in recent decades have a garden-cemetery design aspect to them but use different materials.

The cemetery chapel was constructed in 1890 and offers perhaps the most intriguing architecture at the cemetery. Built in the Queen Anne style, the stone building greets visitors when they enter the cemetery's older section off the roadway.

The garden area of Laurel Hill was essentially added to an older cemetery, one with graves dating to the 1750s. Located off the banks of the Saco River, the newer portion of the cemetery developed as a garden cemetery. Established in 1844, the roughly twenty-five-acre portion was designed by Waldo Higginson, Esq., and developed largely in the cemetery lawn tradition, while a contiguous addition created in 1919, known as Deering Park, took on a more modern cemetery design. Some areas overlap, and in most locations, it is the monuments, fairly simple ones, that draw the eye, not the natural environment, except on the edges bordering the waterway, which include a stunning vista over the river. In the spring, the cemetery is known for its wild daffodils.

The graves at Laurel Hill mark the burial places of some of the most noted members of the locality, as well as of lesser-known people. Indeed, one area holds the remains of eighty-seven children born to paupers, as well as dozens of adults, with the poorer graves set off (although not always visibly) by small stone or metal markers, or concrete plugs inscribed with numbers. These are newer graves or sections than some of the other pauper lots seen in other garden cemeteries, as the dates range from the 1940s to the 1970s.

On the opposite end of the cultural spectrum, Maine governor and US congressman John Fairfield was born in Saco in 1797 and buried at Laurel Hill in 1847. US congressmen John Fairfield Scammon, Moses MacDonald, and Richard Cutts Shannon—who was also a Union Colonel during the Civil War, served as a US minister to a few nations, and has a stone bench marking his grave—were all interred there in the mid-1800s to early 1900s, and Cyrus King was buried in the older section after his 1817 death. Other notable locales were likewise interred at Laurel Hill.

Laurel Hill is known, as are the other garden cemeteries, for some wonderful bits of horticulture as well as opportunities to bird-watch, walk, and simply enjoy nature in an historical setting. Laurel Hill, like the other smaller cemeteries, is worth visiting. And, as are several cemetery chapels elsewhere, although not all, the chapel is available for private use. Laurel Hill is in many ways a hybrid cemetery, one covering most eras of American cemetery history, although some eras are more represented than others.

Garden cemeteries—large or small—are generally noted for their fine stonework as well as their landscaped settings, but the beautiful stonework of the rural cemeteries did take its toll on some people, in particular, the artisans who created it. This was true throughout New England, although it is more evident in some places than others.

Barre, Vermont, witnessed an influx of stonecutters, especially Italian ones, in the late 1800s and early 1900s, as did some other localities where quarries were established to meet the rising demand. Many of the immigrants had worked in their homelands first and undertook further stonework in Vermont, especially working with its famed white granite, so popular in cemeteries by that time. Many would come to be buried at

Barre's Hope Cemetery, and what they created there would be something masterful and truly unique, in a cemetery that would combine some elements of a garden cemetery with something else altogether.

One stonecutter, Louis Brusa, became an activist for workers' health. Breathing fine particles of granite and other stone was not conducive to one's health. Brusa, who created numerous monuments at Hope Cemetery, would make it his life's mission to make ventilation systems a mandatory thing in the granite sheds, according to Alice Levitt in "Death Becomes Them." Brusa himself fell victim to silicosis from years of breathing in stone dust, and seemingly, many of the numerous stonecutters buried at Hope Cemetery died of the same disease. As his death approached, Brusa carved, secretly, his own monument: one portraying his wife holding him as he took his last breath. The statue is a prominent one at Hope Cemetery.

While some stonecutters in the region fell sick, as did stonecutters elsewhere, they created wonderful monuments that appear in rural cemeteries throughout the Northeast and elsewhere. Just down the road from Hope Cemetery, a stonecutter's memorial honors those who made the region a success in rock quarrying and rock carving. Built in 1985, the statue is twenty-five feet tall and towers over the nearby intersection of Route 14 and Main Street. It is dedicated to one sculptor, Carlo Abate, who came to America from Italy at the turn of the twentieth century, as did so many others, and he established the first art school for the stonecutter's trade. Barre is known as the "Granite Capital of the World," although nearby areas and towns, including Montpelier, had their share of quarries and stonecutters also.

It is fitting that Hope Cemetery was established where it was and when it was, in 1895. The cemetery initially contained fifty-three acres, and it was designed by Boston landscape architect Edward P. Adams, born in 1856, a few decades after the garden cemetery movement started. Adams also designed an addition to Maine's Oak Grove Cemetery in Gardiner in 1913, adding curvilinear lines to new sections versus using its older grid pattern. Hope Cemetery would have curvilinear avenues also, and in that respect, it followed the general garden cemetery pattern. Hope Cemetery would eventually reach sixty-five acres.

In the late 1800s, it was estimated that one-third of all grave memorials were being made from Barre granite. Silicosis claimed the lives of many stonecutters, especially when other respiratory-related diseases struck, and in the early 1900s when the Spanish flu struck, several artisans began carving their own memorials. Some had done so earlier, knowing the risks of their trade, influenza or not. Even today, it is estimated that more than 70 percent of the markers at Hope Cemetery were created by those whom they commemorate, while many others had their memorials created by fellow artists and friends.

Some sections of Hope Cemetery are little different from some of the other garden cemeteries covered. The back section of the cemetery contains a row of mausoleums not so different from Albany Rural Cemetery's "Millionaires' Row" or some of those lining one or two of Mount Auburn's ponds. Areas nearby are planted with rows of bushes and hedges—although most of this is recent planting, according to cemetery staff—as are other portions of the grounds planted with hedges and small trees. Moreover, some of the classic forms of garden cemetery statues and funerary art are found here—this is not surprising, as Barre stonecutters were often the carvers of such artwork. In particular in this category is one of the classic angel forms seen elsewhere: a female angel standing in front of a large cross, although the one at Barre does have its unique qualities.

However, while there, look around. One soon senses a difference. Charles Elliot once wrote that Springfield Cemetery had one section that resembled a "stonecutter's yard." Well, in some ways, Hope Cemetery *is* a stonecutter's yard or, rather, the yard of many stonecutters. Numerous stonecutters are buried there, under both simple and ornate markers, and those markers are the dominant feature at the cemetery, not the landscape and nature, as was the goal of most garden cemeteries proper, cemeteries that aimed to balance nature with art. Moreover, at Barre, except for a rare and recent exception, every marker is made of the white Vermont granite, creating a unique effect, and the cemetery almost glows in the dusk and dark.

Still, Hope Cemetery is much different from Grove Street Cemetery in New Haven, which can be seen as a transition cemetery going *into* the garden cemetery movement. Hope Cemetery actually does have a rural setting, with beautiful Vermont hills in the background, but the stone remains the central feature, and not just in the classical markers, or even the unique white granite entranceway, but also in some distinctly non-Victorian, non-Romantic memorials.

Hope Cemetery has not just Brusa's unique sculpture created by himself but it has many other "eccentric" and sometimes humorous memorials. Known as a "museum of art," the art is sometimes a bit eclectic. Such markers as an airplane, a soccer ball, a couple in bed, a double bed without a couple, a racing car, and a "bored, flapper-era" angel all alert one that this is not a Romantic-era cemetery. This is something else.

Hope Cemetery blended the garden cemetery into something new, into a modern lawn cemetery yet a specific type of lawn cemetery. It is both a moving rural cemetery and an amusing art gallery. It is a transitional cemetery. It marks the end of the garden cemetery movement, much like New Haven can be seen to mark its beginning.

The garden or rural cemeteries—also sometimes referred to as pastoral cemeteries—of New England started a movement that spread throughout the nation. They added a richness to the American landscape that had not previously existed and they accompanied new perceptions of how the dead should be treated, ones that would only develop further as the decades progressed.

Although only the wealthy could afford the largest and most ornate memorials and mausoleums such as the Winslow mausoleum at the Albany Rural Cemetery, the Keep mausoleum at Brookside Cemetery, the Hubbard "Black Agnes" memorial at Green Mount, the Howard pyramid at Cedar Hill, or the relatively simple yet diverse lot of the Mallory family at Elm Grove with its ledger table, its baby memorials, its Greek statue, and others, in most instances, at most of the cemeteries, one could go to visit the cemeteries, tour the grounds, and see examples of fine art as well as tree and other plant species that may not have been seen elsewhere, especially during the early to mid-1800s, before the creation of public parks and other green places. Even today, garden cemeteries are often places of wonder, vibrant oases in the midst of concrete streets and crowded housing, quiet places to go for contemplation or to run or walk, and, in some places, to exercise one's pets.

Even though most of the cemeteries have added new markers over the years, except Valley View, which filled up within a few decades of its creation, the old ones are still there. They offer an introduction to artwork from the early 1800s onward, or even earlier, in places like the New Haven's Grove Street Cemetery and the Springfield Cemetery that offer a view of older symbolism and sensibilities on relocated memorials. Some of the artwork is breathtaking; some is heartbreaking. However, it is there, and it is free.

Some of the garden cemeteries were established along major rivers, including Mount Hope Cemetery along Mount Hope's Penobscot River, Swan Point along Rhode Island's Seekonk River, and Elm Grove along Connecticut's Mystic River, while Albany Rural Cemetery has somewhat distant views of the Hudson River and Lakeview enjoys very close views of Lake Champlain. Some cemeteries would take advantage of existing water sources to create brooks or add ponds, like Mount Hope, Mount Auburn, and Brookside, while others like Springfield Cemetery and Valley View would landscape around their natural waters and then force them underground. A few, not discussed in-depth here, would not have a water aspect or would not have space around them to grow or possibly add a water feature, and this seems to have slowed their development.

Several animal species would visit the rural cemeteries, and some would make them their homes. From foxes to deer, and maybe the occasional just-passing-through moose, the allure of green spaces pulled them in, much as they did people. Waterbirds would find many of the cemeteries particularly inviting. Swans still inhabit Swan Point for part of the year, and geese and ducks are pervasive. So, too, do herons inhabit the garden cemeteries for much of the year.

Some of the most visited parts of the garden cemeteries are not necessarily the grandest, however. Many of the garden cemeteries donated lots to the poor, to orphans, to various institutions that aided the poor or the public in general and, especially for the private ones, to veterans of wars, especially to the Civil War, which occurred just when the garden cemetery movement was starting. The Grand Army of the Republic aided immensely in the effort to mark the places of the fallen or to at least mark their passing. At Mount Hope, which had donated land for a memorial while the war was still going on, the GAR would build a miniature fort.

In some places, the poor, orphaned, or unidentified would be given a simple marker, sometimes with just a number to mark their lives, but that was still much more than impoverished people had received for centuries. In times of epidemics, there would still be a few common burials, but at least records—as much as was possible—were kept by the cemeteries. Even in emergency burials, the poor and others were not piled willy-nilly upon each other and then moved out to give another body the space a few years later.

In some places, fraternal organizations established community burial lots for their members, such as the Eternal Order of the Elks or the Grand Order of Masons. Moreover, symbols of various organizations, as well as religious beliefs, are found on markers throughout the garden cemeteries. Symbolism from antiquity is abundant.

The garden cemeteries were open to everyone, regardless of religion, race, gender, or economic status, although the type of lot one could afford, or the marker commissioned, might well be limited by one's finances. In some instances, specific lots were set aside for the poor or people of color, where free burials were available. Again, this might not be the preferred option, but at least it was a possibility. Moreover, that individual's family could visit him or her, visit any other grave they chose, see some marvelous artwork and period architecture, and, in some cases, pass through magnificent gateways.

There is artwork and history available to everyone to experience at the garden cemeteries, and there are trees and flowers and winding paths and peace. Go visit one. Go visit them all, if you can.

You might also want to read Alice Levitt's 2008 article, "Death Becomes Them," published in Seven Days, *regarding silicosis deaths in the Barre, Vermont, area, as well as Ben Meiklejohn's article, "Little Known Resting Area Holds Graves of Babies, the Poor,"* Biddeford Courier Gazette, *May 29, 2014, and the author's* Rogues, Rascals, and Other Villainous Mainers, *Down East Books, 2014. (A new book has also just been published about Laurel Hill.) This section was generally, however, compiled from sources already noted, the author's observations, and from general sources.*

About the Author

Garden Cemeteries of New England is historian and photographer Trudy Irene Scee's fourteenth or fifteenth book, depending on how one counts them, and a long anticipated work. She grew up by one cemetery covered in this work, Brookside Cemetery, and currently lives across the river from another one, Mount Hope Cemetery, about which she previously published a lengthy history. This work includes many other garden cemeteries as well, those beautiful places that preceded the public park movement and filled a need for both burial space and a place where nature and art came together to the benefit of the living. The book is richly illustrated with photographs of stunning memorials, noteworthy gates, and mausoleums.

While Scee writes for the general public, she also holds undergraduate degrees in forestry and history, a masters of arts in history from the University of Montana, and a doctorate of philosophy in history from the University of Maine. She has received a number of academic fellowships and awards and taught history at Mount Allison University in New Brunswick, at the University of Maine, and at Husson University in Bangor. She now works with disadvantaged and other youth part time while working full time as an author.

Scee has published a number of books on Maine history and culture as well as on other subjects. She has held photographic exhibits and worked as a journalist. Books of hers available through Down East Books and Roman & Littlefield include *Dancing in Paradise, Burning in Hell; Women in Maine's Historic Working Class Dance Industry;* and *Public Enemy No. One; The True Story of the Brady Gang.* Additional works are underway. Dr. Scee lives in Maine.